I0290991

ISBN: 978-1-937543-55-6

Library of Congress Control Number: 2015932601

Published by Jaded Ibis Press, *sustainable literature by digital means*™ an imprint of Jaded Ibis Productions, LLC, Seattle, Washington USA.

Cover and interior art by Christopher J. Arabadjis. Book design by Debra Di Blasi.

This book is in multiple formats. Visit our website for more information: jadedibisproductions.com

DEVOURING THE GREEN

: fear of a human planet

[anthology of new writing]

poetry in a transhuman world in an era of cyborgs, catastrophic climate change, motherboards boiled by children, rising cancer rates, mass extinction, the coming singularity (& the ice-caps are melting & the waters are rising)

edited by

SAM WITT

art by Christopher J. Arabadjis

Jaded Ibis Press

sustainable literature by digital means™

an imprint of Jaded Ibis Productions

SEATTLE • HONG KONG • BOSTON

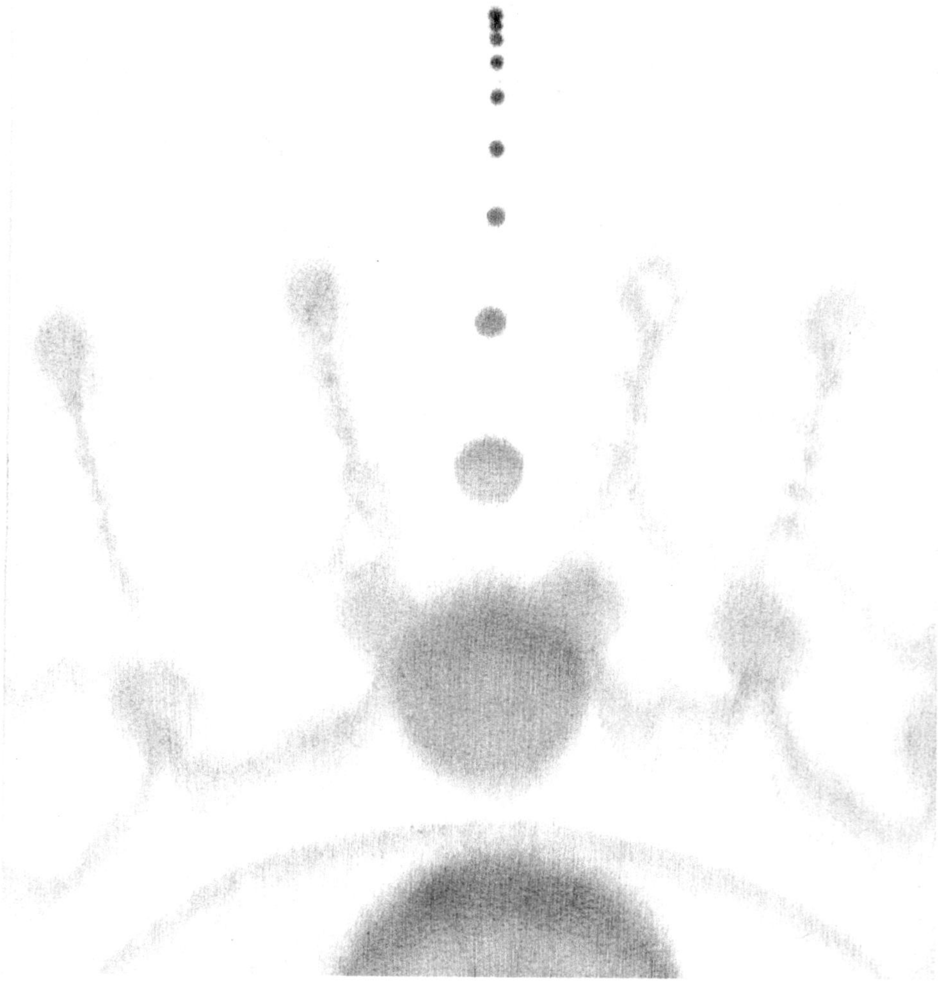

≈ IN MEMORIAM ≈

Bill Knott

[February 17, 1940 - March 12, 2014]

Tomaž Šalamun

[January 7, 1941 - December 27, 2014]

≈ Here lies One Whose Name was writ in Water ≈

"The metals, the oils—all the ores we've ripped from the earth—are homesick. They long to leave our machines, to flow out of our cash registers and factories, to return to the gaping veins of the mountains we reft; whereupon the mountains will close again"
– Rainer Marie Rilke

≈ TABLE OF CONTENTS ≈

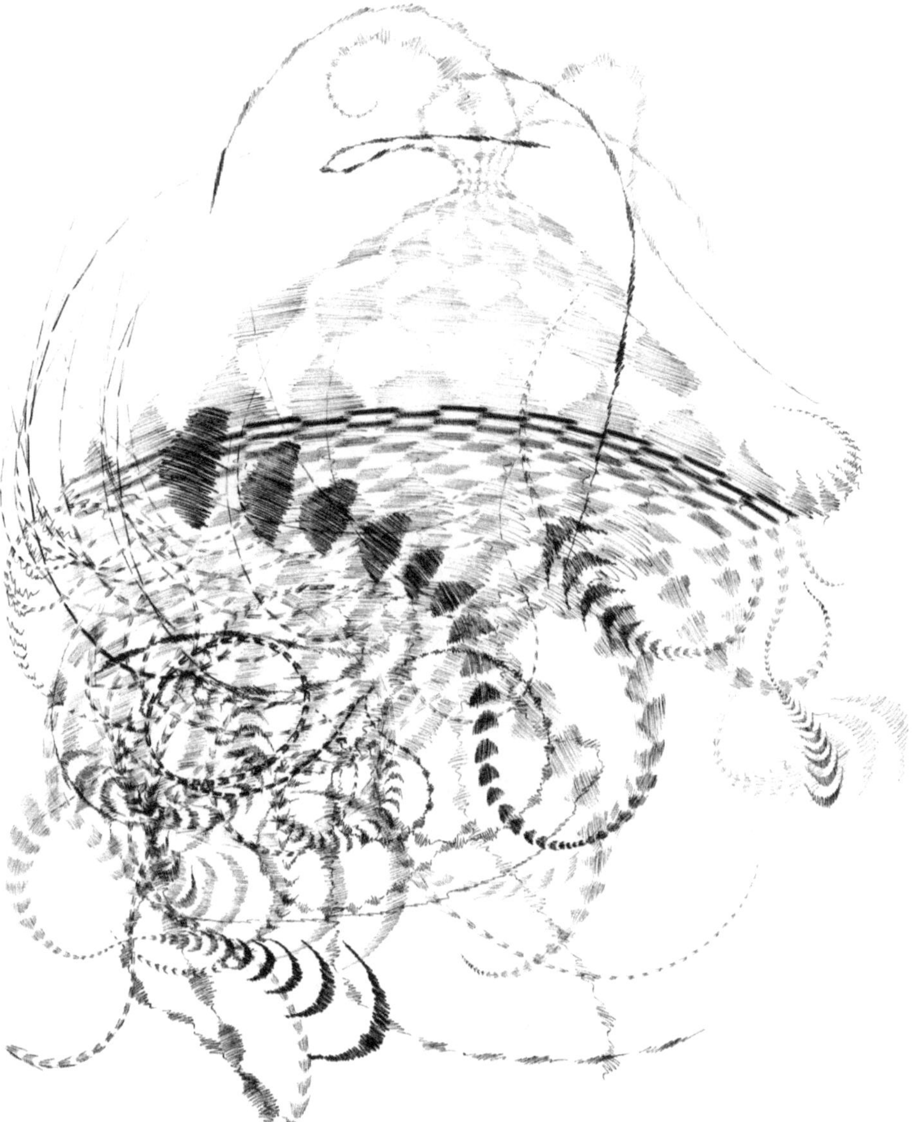

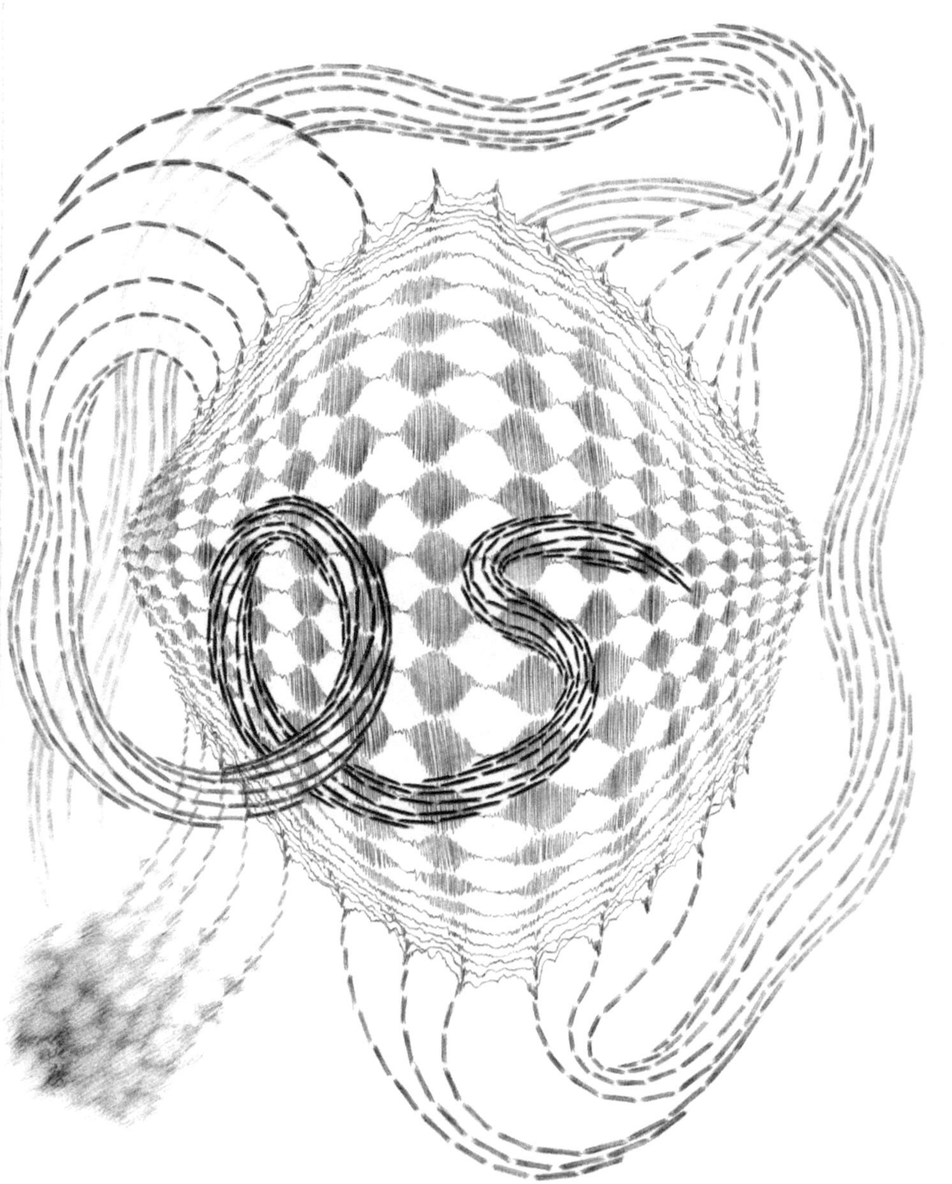

Eulogy for Planet Earth:
On the Cusp of the Sixth Mass Extinction

> "When a species dims, what is the last
> One left of it worth?
> Is it priceless then, as a snow comes on?"
>
> – Larry Levis, from "Slow Child with a Book of Birds,"
> *The Widening Spell of the Leaves*

As the new leaves unfurled above us and each sprig of thyme bowed beneath our plump and dampened knees, we felt language a cap on the voice, a sweltering of desire and breath. Now we don't speak. I miss your quivering laugh. Your cocoa scent and eye water. I miss the dead and the living, the broken spoon of knock-kneed poems tumbling swiftly. I'm spent. I'm scooped out. The world I loved, my dear, is dead.

The Nightingale Program Is Corrupted: Against the "Human"

> "In the spring of 1819 a nightingale had built her nest near my house. Keats felt a tranquil and continual joy in her song; and one morning he took his chair from the breakfast-table to the grass-plot under a plum-tree, where he sat for two or three hours. When he came into the house, I perceived he had some scraps of paper in his hand, and these he was quietly thrusting behind the books. On inquiry, I found those scraps, four or five in number, contained his poetic feelings on the song of our nightingale."[1]
>
> – Charles Armitage Brown

My favorite poem has always been and will always be "Ode to a Nightingale," by the immortal and abiding John Keats. In this virtuosic, symphonic, synaesthetic, deeply engaged piece of time-traveling naturalism and myth building, the poet, barely more than twenty-four years of age and already showing the early symptoms of tuberculosis (the Ebola of its day), volumetrically celebrates, eroticizes, and embodies a paradox well-known to graduate students in English literature the world over: that even though the nightingale's biological lifespan is pitifully short (two years on average, about as brief and telescoped as the painful term of dying Keats *knew* he was facing when he wrote the poem, having just nursed his brother Tom while he died of the same disease), even so, the mythic lifespan of the bird's mating song is endlessly self-generating across the generations, especially as it braids through the ear, culture, imagination and mythic sensibility of a damaged young Homo sapiens who happens to be sitting in the garden listening to it, powered by the way cultural artifacts accrue and resonate in poems like this one. "Thou wast not born for death, immortal bird!/No hungry generations tread thee down!" And so on.

It pains me to speak casually, even a touch sarcastically, about this vision and this particular ode, which means so much to me. I do so for effect, and to make a singular point: such a Keatsian paradox, that symbiotic relationship with the physical world in which a non-human mating cry and a poet's current of isolated consciousness runs concurrently through a number of simultaneous ecosystems, so powerfully that it can reach past the time of the poet and into our own, may seem as unreachable as it is powerful, even quaint, when contrasted to the internet, or the imagination of latter day futurists like Ray Kurzweil, for instance. But to the poets whose work constitutes this anthology, whose work occupies the space and causal relationship between technological miracle—as in Kurzweil's Singularity, in the early stages of which, historically speaking, we are most certainly orentied as you read this in January 2015—and nightmarish ecological catastrophe, I should think this Keatsian vision of the imaginative power of death, perhaps even extended to the imagination of our species, is a crucial poetic exercise to engage in. And I see these poets grappling with this historical paradox in these poems, the very seismic, twin phenomena that are remaking the very physical world, our species and our place in that world, as I write this.

Almost all the poems in this anthology are seeing print for the very first time. They are brand new, and in most cases, were written for this project alone. These poets were asked to struggle, wrestle, create and build something totally new, by answering specific questions imaginatively, the ones the reader can find at the beginning of each chapter. And the poets of *Devouring the Green: Fear of a Human Planet* more than rose to the occasion. They have embodied these questions and this new reality, this relationship between technology and ecosystems, between the brain of the Homo sapiens and what it is doing, collectively, to the planet, in a way that's both striking and ethical and totally new to the mind and ear of this editor. This is a music of cataclysm and technological miracle, which is the keen marker of our time. These poets have produced, on these questions, a series of mind files, which strike me as inventive and corrupted and corruptible and miraculous as the time we live in, as toxic as the deadly process of creating and disposing of this hardware. Indeed, these poems live at the intersection of technological ambition and miracle, and the ecologically poisoned planetary sinks where our laptops and our electronic identities go to die and be reborn again: places like the Niger Delta, Ghana, Guatemala, Varanasi . . . [2]

Why bring up John Keats and the nightingale in the first place, in the introduction to a themed poetry anthology that is addressing this nightmarish overlap between the miraculous technological insights of our time, which is empowering mankind to an unimaginable degree, and the ecological disaster it's bringing with it? Why start with the mating song of a nightingale heard by a young man who knows he's going to die, in order to introduce poems haunted by these terrifyingly new causalities, the metastatic growth of information technology, bioengineering, nanotechnology, AI, and its silent partner, its twin, catastrophic climate change with its rising sea levels, its feet added to the storm surges, its new diseases and tidal wave of mass species death?[3] For one thing, it's hard to imagine a future in which this species of bird wouldn't be profoundly effected by our behavior. "Many scientists argue that we are entering the sixth great mass extinction and that anthropogenic climate change is one of the major threats to global biodiversity," write the ecologists Dr. Robert J. Wilson and Dr. Ilya Mclean. "Comprehensive, multitaxon reviews suggest that 10–70% of plant and animal species assessed so far could be at increased risk of extinction from climate change or that by 2050, climate-induced changes in habitat will commit 15–37% of species to extinction." Second, I am taken with the spiritual and metaphysical and even political possibilities of imagining our own deaths, of imagining, as terrible as it might sound, the death of our species. When's the last time, dear reader, that you sat down and imagined the planet without people on it? Is that worth doing? Is that what Keats is listening for, if only for a moment? Is he not trying to find the power in self-extinction, the nobility and ethics of that act, especially in an age when our collective appetites are literally devouring the natural? Literally and figuratively chewing up species at a nearly uncountable rate?

Mclean, who calls the planet the life support system upon which *Homo sapiens* depends, might share an interest in these poems, as they are imaginatively and existentially haunted by this terrifying new reality we're living, which most of us choose not to reflect upon. So what Keats explores and enacts, philosophically and metaphysically, which he coined "Negative Capability," is a concept these poets do well to adapt to our own time, in order to record and witness the process of mankind changing, transitioning into something new, something miraculous, something stunning, something terrifying, a merging between ours bodies, our minds, and our technology, which futurists like Ray Kurzweil see just on the horizon. This new dispensation is marked by the following concept: to be human in the Age of Keats, at least in regards to how people interacted with a natural ecosystem, meant something radically different than it does to be Homo sapiens in the Era of the Anthropocene, a name that biologists and ecologists are starting to agree upon as an accepted nomen for our time, according to an article on *The Smithsonian* website:

> According to the International Union of Geological Sciences (IUGS), the professional organization in charge of defining earth's time scale, we are officially in the Holocene ("entirely recent") epoch, which began 11,700 years ago after the last major ice age.
>
> But that label is outdated, some experts say. They argue for "Anthropocene"—from *anthropo*, for "man," and *cene*, for "new"—because human- kind has caused mass extinctions of plant and animal species, polluted the oceans and altered the atmosphere, among other lasting impacts.[4]

One might even argue that we are a different species now, from the mankind of the Romantic era, at least in terms of what our behavior makes and has made and continues to make possible: a cure for cancer, on the one hand; mountains of cellies on the other, being dismantled by street urchins in Varanasi. One might even argue now, as one of our original guiding questions asked it, whether or not *Homo sapiens* is an invasive species. To be human, the poems in this anthology seem to be saying, in so many fascinating ways, is to be transhuman, then: to alter, radically and irrevocably, what's left of the natural world, everything that gets in our way; to devour, in so many words, the green; to be slowly eating the world like some great worm; to finally become the replication machinery of a virus. It breaks my heart to write this about us, because I love people; but I mean it literally: to be a sentient *Homo sapiens* in Keats's time—for all its flaws, all the chimney sweepers and degradation and teams of child slaves, along with the institution of slavery in our own country, of course—was to be able, at least, to experience the physical world holistically, spiritually, in a generative and cleansing way. That's how the speaker in "Ode to a Nightingale" embodies the bird's mating song on so many overlapping levels: naturalistic, of course; fantastic and supernatural and mythic; philosophical and ethical; and above all else, imaginatively, as in, what's it like not to be a *Homo sapiens*, a young man, a John Keats, a Sam Witt, a me, a you, in the natural world, and not apart from it? To be a *Homo sapiens* in our time, at best, is to be a consumer. And that horrifies me. So what we are asking of our race, starting with one poet at a time, is that we begin the process of imagining ourselves anew, at the most essential and existential level: begin by imagining the death of our species, perhaps. Begin with a frank accounting of what we're doing to this world and the other creatures who live on it. Begin with what Keats called Negative Capability.

For one thing, this poetic orientation was complicated by the fact that Keats knew ahead of time how — painfully — and essentially when — most likely before his nightingale's death — he was going to die, and of what — the disease was called consumption in Keats's day, because the lungs were thought, in effect, to consume themselves: as we are consumers. After all, he'd just nursed his beloved brother Tom as he died of the very same illness Keats was contracting *from him*; and despite the near endless dimensions of this bravery and vision, despite that fact that

Keats was one of the first writers to conceive of a non-human individual, and in short, no matter how hauntingly he evoked and witnessed and brooded upon that bird's mating call, and in general not to question the imaginative horizons of a genius, a prophet, but despite all that, I am almost certain there were two eventualities Keats did not consider as he wrote this poem. First, I can't imagine that it would have occurred to Keats *for a second* that the European Nightingale might one day be extinct, and yet if you read a recent article in The New York Times, you will get a sense of just how disruptive and potentially catastrophic global warming is going to be for the migrating and mating patterns of some of the most common birds in Europe and North America. "The Baltimore oriole will probably no longer live in Maryland," writes Felicity Barringer, "the common loon might leave Minnesota, and the trumpeter swan could be entirely gone."[5] Second, I can't imagine that he would have seriously conceived of the extinction of *Homo sapiens* ourselves, much less the transformation of our race into something machine enhanced, through bioengineering and AI. I am even more certain Keats wouldn't have drawn a causal relationship between our appetites as people and those outcomes, nor that one might turn out to be the consequence of the other. Such a nihilistic future couldn't even be foreseen in those days, much less computed.

The entire poem vibrates with this insight, and I do too when I read it to my students. The world is not entirely a *Homo sapiens* world; it doesn't belong to us. In fact, we belong to it. Practice that each day, even if you have to start by imagining no human race. Listening to nature back then, as far as I can tell, was to witness it and to donate your flesh, organs and brain to it, for Keats anyway, to let it stream through you in a song. Even then it took a prophet to show us what that meant. It took an evanescent and tremulous young creature, a young man studying medicine, in fact, to discover what the ode still enacts, crucially, for our own time: that simply by listening to a bird, one might be able to gain a sense of oneself. Every time we read the poem it comes to life again, for those of you looking for digital immortality. One might even be able to imagine one's own extinction, which is a crucial resource and ethical and imaginative value for people who walk as ecological giants in the world. It should actually be a guiding principle as politically and economically as it is poetically, but we all know that's not the case today. I am speaking, of course, about Negative Capability, and I quote from a letter written by Keats to his brothers in Hampstead, on Sunday, December 22, 1818:

> I had not a dispute but a disquisition with Dilke, upon various subjects; several things dove-tailed in my mind, and at once it struck me what quality went to form a Man of Achievement, especially in literature, and which Shakespeare possessed so enormously – I mean Negative Capability, that is, when a man is capable of being in uncertainties, mysteries, doubts, without any irritable reaching after fact and reason – Coleridge, for instance, would let go by a fine isolated verisimilitude caught from the Penetralium of mystery, from being incapable of remaining content with half-knowledge. This pursued through volumes would perhaps take us no further than this, that with a great poet the sense of Beauty overcomes every other consideration, or rather obliterates all consideration.[6]

Perhaps we might translate the word "beauty" here, for our own age, into another subset of words: ecological perspective, for one, a sense of how our innovations and technology and appetites influence and effect the world; collective action, for another; lastly, an ability to at least conceive of the world without us on it, as a kind of starting point, a grand imaginative act, the starting point for a new kind of power and possibly even a new sense of value. This vision of course makes me think of Kurzweil and other latter day Futurists, post-human people.

To boil it down, Negative Capability is a vision to live one's life by. Of course, I don't mean this term as some kind of luddite hatred and fear of technology. I mean it as a guiding perspective, an ability to have a sense of the non-human, a kind of inner compass. But can't we imagine (and celebrate) the ecological qualities and incarnations of

Negative Capability? Shouldn't we be practicing erasing ourselves as an imaginative act, as Keats does with his individual presence in this poem? Shouldn't we be doing this writ large, at the level of the species, if only as an ethical and metaphyiscal exercise, a kind of prayer? Isn't that worth at least putting us through our paces in an imaginative and poetic pantomime?

I think we need to take a page from Keats's playbook, here at the beginning of 2015, and imagine what the world might look like if we weren't on it. Isn't that something that we might want to at least consider, imaginatively, in a reality as humanistic and narcissistic and *Homo sapiens*-focused as ours has turned out to be? Isn't that Vitruvian man at the center of everything stale by now, even oppressive, especially since those arms have stretched out into tentacles that touch just about everything, ecologically speaking?

In short: Fade far away, dissolve, and quite forget, mankind—

As it happens, that's just what the poets in *Devouring the Green* were tasked to do when we approached them several years ago, and it's just what the poems in this anthology do so profoundly, inadvertently and indirectly at times, and directly, by name, at others, responding to Kurzweil's idea of a technological singularity, a moment at which computing power outstrips the human capacity to control it, and *Homo sapiens* and our technology merge into one being, into a series of connected machines that "will appear to have their own free will" and even "spiritual experiences," as Kurzweil writes in his book *The Singularity Is Near*. And they do so by taking it literally, by really imagining such a thing, such a moment, a point at which, as Kurzweil predicts in his national bestseller "intelligence will radiate outward from the planet until it saturates the universe." It's a profound thing to take Kurzweil at his word, and take such a possibility seriously, which the poets in *Devouring the Green* do, by making such a scenario imaginatively real.[7]

To quote one of our contributors, the science fiction writer and physicist Dr. Vandana Singh, "What I don't like about the post-human folks [like Kurzweil] is that their innovation and vision is rooted in a fear of death, and a healthy lack of respect for the way we were essentially made." We know this because Kurzweil has written about his desire to technologically bring his father back from the dead. "I will be able to talk to this re-creation," Kurweil was quoted by ABC News. "Ultimately, it will be so realistic it will be like talking to my father . . . That is a replica, but I can actually make a strong case that it would be more like my father than my father would be, were he to live." Nevermind the hubris, but wouldn't such an innovation take away the quality of loss that is arguably the foundation of our consciousness, that which binds our activities and limits them? "There is a lot of suffering in the world," Kurzweil has said. "Some of it can be overcome if we have the right solutions."[8] I have to wonder what those solutions are, and what consequences they might set into motion.

Can't we learn from Keats that death is, in the end, an act of imagination? That death is the mother of beauty, to quote Wallace Stevens, who believed that the greatest poverty was not to live in the physical world? And I might add to this: Folks like Kurzweil, as brilliant and innovative as they may be, have not even bothered to begin the hard work of squaring the likely consequences of those innovations with the ecological consequences of them. I freely admit that this is an intuitive and non-provable insight, but it seems to me that when you take death out of the human experience, or seek to engineer it away, you remove any sense of perspective about what lies beyond our control. And that is how we have lost control of our technology and what it has wrought in the world. With even more powerful technology, one imagines the footprint to be even deeper and more permanent.

So I am redefining Negative Capability as the power to imagine a non-human world, and to act upon this imagination, which is *the* crucial cultural, artistic and ethical exercise of our time; naturally, this action begins with art. Poetry is the beginning of the process of reimagining a transhuman world into one in which we protect and save the planet and its creatures from ourselves. This is indeed an angelic order. But given that Kurzweil promises near limitless technological power in books like *The Singularity Is Near*, and promises that this will happen in our lifetime — 2048 to be exact[9] — and given the consequences of what we are grappling with, the consequences of our own appetites and ambitions being desertification and massive floods, such an internal mechanism might be the key to the survival of our race, ironically enough. It might take a kind of Buddhist effort to enflesh our absence as the beginning of the process of transformation that might enable us to survive. For in the end, the real question is not whether we are going to conquer death, and bring Ray Kurzweil's father back from the dead, roll away the stone wheel from the tomb, or even live past 140. The real question is whether mankind is even going to survive. The real question might even be how many species we take with us. Why don't futurists like Ray Kurzweil imagine a process of the singularity as a way to reinvigorate wilderness on the planet? Why not take ourselves out of our ambition? That's what I call Negative Capability. Let's think of it as a jolt of electricity that might jolt us out of our narcissistic reality.

Another irony and paradox of our time can be seen in the reclaiming of natural terms in a technological, consumer context. Hell, sometimes it sounds like the twisted imagery and vocabulary of a Romantic poem to listen to All Tech Considered on NPR. An example: the use of the word "ecosystem," as in "the app ecosystem," just off the top of my head? What about the cloud, or Windows of the soul? Do I have to go as low as "I wandered lonely as a mind-cloud" until the new technological consumer-language (consumption, anyone?) starts to sound like a pastoral poem? All of which leads me, bizarrely, to the following thought: If Conservationist Dame Daphne Sheldrick is right, elephants might be extinct within twelve years. "A world without elephants is hard to comprehend, but it is a very real possibility." An elephant is killed every fifteen minutes for its ivory, according to a BBC story.[10] If such a thing were to happen, will the Grand Old Party change its mascot? And if so, will the schoolchildren of the future know that glorious, noble, intelligent, profound, sentient, moral creature as a cartoon character, an illustration? Do you even want to live on a planet without elephants?

After all, the increase in carbon emissions, as revealed this Fall in a report by the World Meteorological Organization, just increased at the highest rate ever recorded, and doubtless by the time this anthology is in print and in your hands, carbon emissions will be up even higher than they are now, at 396.0 ± .1 ppm.[11] One need only scan the science pages of any newspaper or magazine, or listen to the latest Ted Talk, or go to Singularity University to encounter evidence that we are on the cusp of insane technological advances coming at a geometric rate of evolution that may soon lead to Artificial Intelligence, nanotechnology and bioengineering, along with a profound lack of skepticism about all of this. But witness the very last mid-term election, during which there was not a single major policy speech on the environment and climate change by a single national politician, according to Denise Robbins of *Media Matters for America*.[12] Such media silence speaks volumes about the situation we are in. What I don't understand is why futurists don't imagine what such an imbalance is leading to in as breathtaking detail as they do the coming Singularity and planet-sized computers? I guess it's up to the poets and artists to speak now.

And speak they will, in the very pages of this anthology. Our question at Jaded Ibis Productions, in starting this project, can be boiled down to this: what's the relationship between these technological wonders, on the one hand, and the Niger Delta, say, where children boil motherboards for traces of precious metals, or that rate of CO_2 increase (the highest since we started measuring it, in 1984), or the deluge of species extinction that continues to increase as quickly as computing power?[13]

These are the possibilities, realities, and eventualities the poets in *Devouring the Green: Fear of a Human Planet* contend with in their haunting, lyrical, lush work, as poets of course, but also as people, I'd imagine. Poets like Carmen Gimenez Smith, whose book *Milk and Filth* was nominated for the National Book Critics Circle Award in poetry this year. Her poem, "My Body," is a gloriously angry and witty rant as it engages the new female body and ends by declaring a kind of war against the very project of the book: "If only I wrote about robots/wore my scarves and if only my schooling—/but I don't give a shit about robots." There's "Self-Golem," by Joyelle McSweeney: "I want to crush a tablet/I want to empty a century," she writes, and these lines bring the very real appetites of our geologically-speaking gargantuan bodies and minds to imaginative life. There's also the work of Tim Jones-Yelvington, whose titles—"Pleasure Model," for instance, and "Femmebot"—are just the tip of the melting iceberg of a dark vision of machine sexuality. There's work by Anis Shivani, Carol Ciavonne, Geoffrey Nutter, Catherine Wagner, Joseph Chapman, Cecilia Llompart, and Simeon Berry with his terrifying series of poems about an anti-person named Nix. We approached hundreds of poets from across the spectrum—those as well-decorated and well-published as Marge Piercy, Bill Knott, David Rivard, Doug Anderson, Tracy K. Smith, Susan Briante, to name a few, and those as new to the publishing world as Vincent Hayes, Ashley De Souza, Dre Cardinal. We asked them to submit something original on the subject of how technological and biological phenomena overlap into an age that biologists call, variously, the Great Dying, the Anthropocene and the transhuman world.

Another central question was this: What's the relationship between our exponentially advancing technological progress, culminating in Kurzweil's vision of the Singularity and the ability, conceivably, to "grow" a human being, and the obvious fact that we are transforming the globe into a vast planetary sink, a Niger Delta half the size of that super storm, Jupiter's Great Red Spot? These poets set such questions ablaze with imaginative longing, formal innovation, hilarity, terror, wit, and sweetness even, when you consider a poem like "Seven Cyborg Songs," for instance, by H. L. Hix. Or witness "//Open Letter to a Robot," by the inestimable Mandy Keifetz, half self-unwriting computer code, half nihilistic stand-up routine, in which she reminds us of the new limits of the human, (which is to say, no limits), which, ironically enough, lead us back to a primitive ancestor: ". . . I am a semantic pervert, a power surge, an encoded monkey." There is also a profoundly powerful sense of the body as a changing ecosystem in this poem and others: "Loops of my cries and empty eyes," Keifetz writes, joining the chorus of a kind of swarmingly apocalyptic horde-expansion of human flesh. And speaking of hordes, let's talk about the fields of jellyfish, which love us, apparently, ever since we did away with their natural predators, the sea turtle. They are our new partners in crime, in eating, in floating, as the case may be, or deoxygenating at the base of off-shore oilrigs like the Deepwater Horizon, (there's that ironic Romantic vocab again), positively gorgeous and cell-like and massively blooming from above as it spewed 4 million barrels of light sweet crude into the Gulf of Mexico). Speaking of hordes, I say, look how quickly the metastatic logic of imagery takes over when you behold a title like Borzutzsky's "The Gross and Borderless Body," from which the first section takes its sub-title. It's called paying attention, bearing witness. It's called poetry, and the poets in this anthology bear witness in swarms.

Take our poets' word for it. Power and surge forward from the time of Keats to the Anthropocene, to the Age of Information, the Internet of course, bioengineering, human ears grown on the backs of bald lab mice, functioning livers grown out of white plastic looking cells—all of it, all the while feeding cataclysmic climate change. I am using the Biblical word from the Greek on purpose, because it means a great flood, as in New York City, Miami, Corpus Christi, and Boston underwater, to name a few of the 75% of our cities that are coastal, for what happens when everybody lives to two hundred? When nobody dies? Witness the possibility, at least, of a runaway greenhouse effect, the melting of the West Antarctic Ice Sheet in the next twenty years, the melting of all the sea-ice on the planet, of Greenland, and the disruption of the Global Ocean Thermohaline Conveyor Belt. The poets in *Devouring the Green* consider in so many different ways both futuristic possibilities at once in these poems.

Fast forward to the eve of the Singularity, the possibility of "waking up the universe," or freeing matter from a lack of sentience, artificial intelligence, planet-sized computers, human intelligence streaming from one end of the galaxy to the other on golden ropes of light, from one particle-entangled port to another. Fast forward to the imaginative lives or our poets, the brave poets who have written about our brave new machine world forever transformed and, in some cases, sanitized of nature, on the cusp of a Kurzweilian awakening . . . but awakening to what? On the cusp of utter environmental degradation, a planet where not much grows, on much of which the wrong things grow, in us as much as around us? Welcome to Hyperion waking up, to natural proteins growing themselves at the urging of a computer command. Welcome to completely dehumanized war, to 37% of species extinct, if nothing changes, by 2050, according to a scientific report from the University of Leeds.[14] I find it to be more than just a coinicidence that this projection matches up almost perfectly with Kurzweil's projected date for the coming of the Singularity. Perhaps this will be a Singularity of an entirely different order?

In our time, to stand at the center of a natural environment is to transform that environment and even consume it without being aware. (Hence the subtitle of our anthology, *Fear of a Human Planet*, and the supposition that we are fast approaching a time when the adjective "human" is no longer a positive adjective.) Hell, in our time, you don't even have to be there to do damage. Witness what scientists project to be the future of the oceans, from a CBS News report on a scientific study by researchers in Nova Scotia and the United Kingdom: "The apocalypse has a new date: 2048. . . . That's when the world's oceans will be empty of fish, predicts an international team of ecologists and economists. The cause: the disappearance of species due to overfishing, pollution, habitat loss, and climate change."[15] There's that date again, that moment when our machines will start building themselves, according to Kurzweil, building their own brain proteins.

Welcome to the hysterical, religious, evangelical triumphalism (or should I call it hysterical Trumpism) of thinkers like George Gilder, with his bandwidth tidal waves of gold, his transparent globe and "the overthrow of matter."[16] "We have soared higher and, literally, become lighter," Gilder writes of the Internet Age and its effect on cheapening commodities, but what he doesn't mention is how many birds have gone extinct since the Internet was invented. "Soon a single cable will carry as much traffic as the entire American Internet infrastructure carried in one month in 1997," Gilder wrote in *The Wall Street Journal* in 1999.[17] Soon there will only be *Homo sapiens*, insects, jellyfish and microbes on the planet if we don't curb our appetites and live to learn in a non-human world. Soon there may only be insects and microbes. And us. Whatever that last word will mean.

Welcome to a world where nobody—or at least where the rich people—ever dies, but download themselves into body after body, which is, as it happens, exactly where our anthology begins, with a sonnet by the poet Ilyse Kusnetz, entitled "Before I Am Downloaded into a Most Excellent Robot Body," the moment just before these things are possible, in a moment fraught with poignancy, fear and wonder.

This brings me back to Keats, and the nobility and power of his work in the context of his painful death, the very suffering that Kurzweil wants to do away with. Witness the letter that Keats's friend Severn wrote about his last words, which fill me with dread, mystery, uncertainty, all the prerequisites of Negative Capability and everything that's worth writing about. Let's give Keats the first and last word:

> Keats raves till I am in a complete tremble for him . . . about four, the approaches of death came on. "Severn—I—lift me up—I am dying—I shall die easy; don't be frightened—be firm, and thank God it has come." I lifted him up in my arms. The phlegm seem'd boiling in his throat, and increased until eleven, when he gradually sank into death, so quiet, that I still thought he slept.[18]

Notes

1 Brown, Charles Armitage. *The Life of John Keats*. Internet Archive. 1987. Web. 8 Nov. 2014. (http://archive.org/stream/lifeofjohnkeats027603mbp/lifeofjohnkeats027603mbp_djvu.txt)

2 For a great article on what happens to electronic equipment once we are done with it, please see the following piece in *National Geographic*: Carroll, Chris. "High Tech Trash." *National Geographic Magazine*. Web. Jan. 2008. 9 Nov. 2014. (http://ngm.nationalgeographic.com/2008/01/high-tech-trash/carroll-text)

3 Maclean, Ilya M. D. and Wilson, Robert J. "Recent ecological responses to climate change support predictions of high extinction risk." *Proceedings of the National Academy of Sciences of the United States of America.* Jul 26, 2011; 108(30): 12337–12342. Web. 8 Nov. 2014. (http://www.ncbi.nlm.nih.gov/pmc/articles/PMC3145734/)

4 Stromberg, Joseph. "What Is the Anthropocene and Are We In It?" *The Smithsonian,* Jan. 2013. Web. 8 Nov 2014. (http://www.smithsonianmag.com/science-nature/what-is-the-anthropocene-and-are-we-in-it-164801414/?no-ist)

5 Barringer, Felicity. "Climate Change Will Disrupt Half of North America's Bird Species, Study Says." *The New York Times.* 8 Sep. 2014. Web. (http://www.nytimes.com/2014/09/09/us/climate-change-will-disrupt-half-of-north-americas-bird-species-study-says.html?ref=science&_r=0)

6 Keats, John. "Letter to George and Tom Keats, 21, 27 Dec. 1817." 1817. TS. Web. Nov. 2014. *Poetry Foundation.* Web. Nov. 2014. (http://www.poetryfoundation.org/learning/essay/237836?page=2)

7 Kurzweil, Raymond. *The Singularity Is Near.* New York: Viking. 2005. Book.

8 Kurzweil, Raymond. "Ray Kurzweil, Google's Director of Engineering, Wants to Bring the Dead Back to Life (VIDEO)." *The Huffington Post.* 28 Dec. 2012. Web. 8 Nov. 2014. (http://www.huffingtonpost.com/2012/12/28/ray-kurzweil-google-direc_n_2377821.html)

9 Kurzweil, Raymond. *When Humans Transcend Biology: The Singularity Is Near: Questions and Answers* (n.d.). Web. 8 Nov. 2014. (http://www.singularity.com/index.html)

10 Ingham, John. "Elephants 'Extinct within 12 Years'." *Daily and Sunday Express.* 12 Aug. 2013. Web. 8 Nov 2014. (http://www.express.co.uk/news/world/421411/Elephants-extinct-within-12-years)

11 Warrick, Joby. "CO2 levels in atmosphere rising at dramatically faster rate, U.N. Report Warns." *The Washington Post.* 9 Sep. 2014. Web. 8 Nov. 2014. (http://www.washingtonpost.com/national/health-science/co2-levels-in-atmosphere-rising-at-dramatically-faster-rate-un-report-warns/2014/09/08/3e2277d2-378d-11e4-bdfb-de4104544a37_story.html) Here is a link to the actual report by the World Meteorological

Organization: (http://apps.washingtonpost.com/g/page/national/2013-global-greenhouse-gas-report/1297/)

12 Robbins, Denise. "Network News Silent on Climate Change in Election Coverage." *Media Matters for America.* 7 Nov. 2014. Web. 8 Nov. 2014 (http://mediamatters.org/blog/2014/11/09/network-news-silent-on-climate-change-in-electi/201505)

13 Holthaus, Eric. "Carbon Dioxide Levels in Atmosphere Reach Terrifying New Milestone." *Slate.* 1 May 2014. Web. 8 Nov. 2014. (http://www.slate.com/blogs/future_tense/2014/05/01/mauna_loa_atmosphere_measurements_carbon_dioxide_levels_above_400_ppm_throughout.html)

14 Kirby, Alex. "Climate Risk to 'million species'." *BBC News.* 7 Jan. 2004. Web. 8 Nov. 2014. (http://news.bbc.co.uk/2/hi/science/nature/3375447.stm)

15 Denoon, Daniel. "Sea-Water Fish Extinction Seen by 2048." *CBS News.* 2 Nov. 2006. Web. 8 Nov. 2014. (http://www.cbsnews.com/news/salt-water-fish-extinction-seen-by-2048/)

16 Russell, George. "Microcosm, by George Gilder." *Commentary Magazine.* 1 Mar. 1990. Web. 8 Nov. 2014. (http://www.commentarymagazine.com/article/microcosm-by-george-gilder/)

17 Gilder, George "The Faith of a Futurist." *The Wall Street Journal.* 31 Dec. 1999. Web. 8 Nov. 2014. (http://www.discovery.org/a/74)

18 Severn, Charles. "Letter to Charles Brown, 27 February 1821." 1821. *Englishhistory.net.* Web. 8 Nov. 2014.

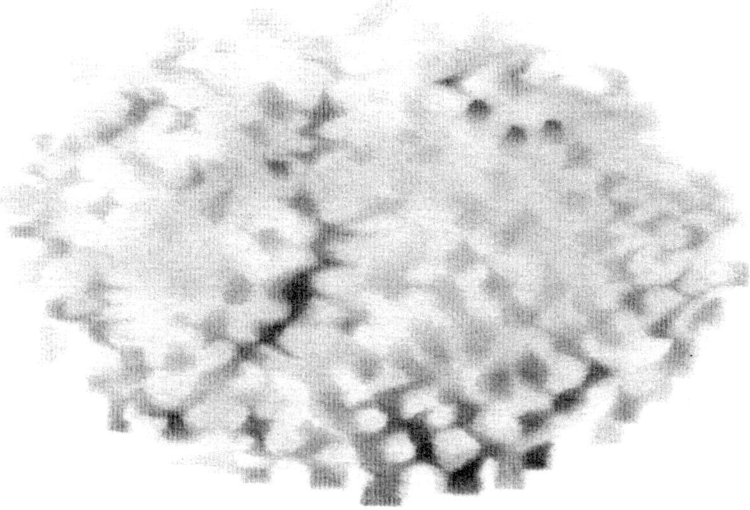

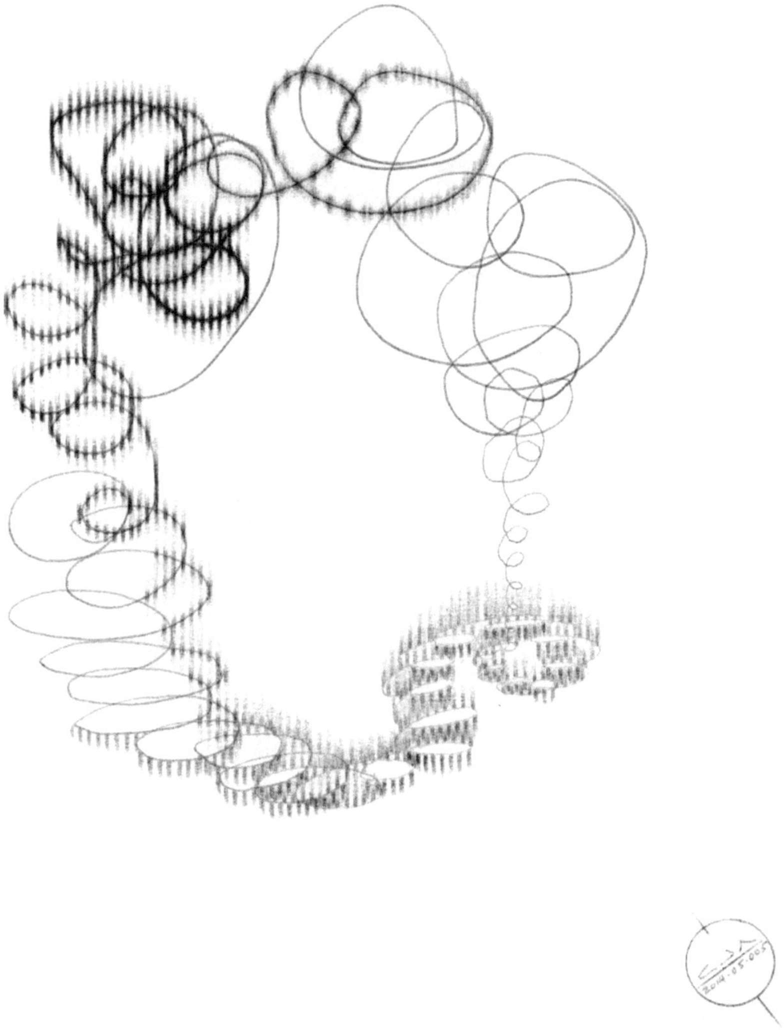
2014.05.005

PART ONE:

The Gross and Borderless Body

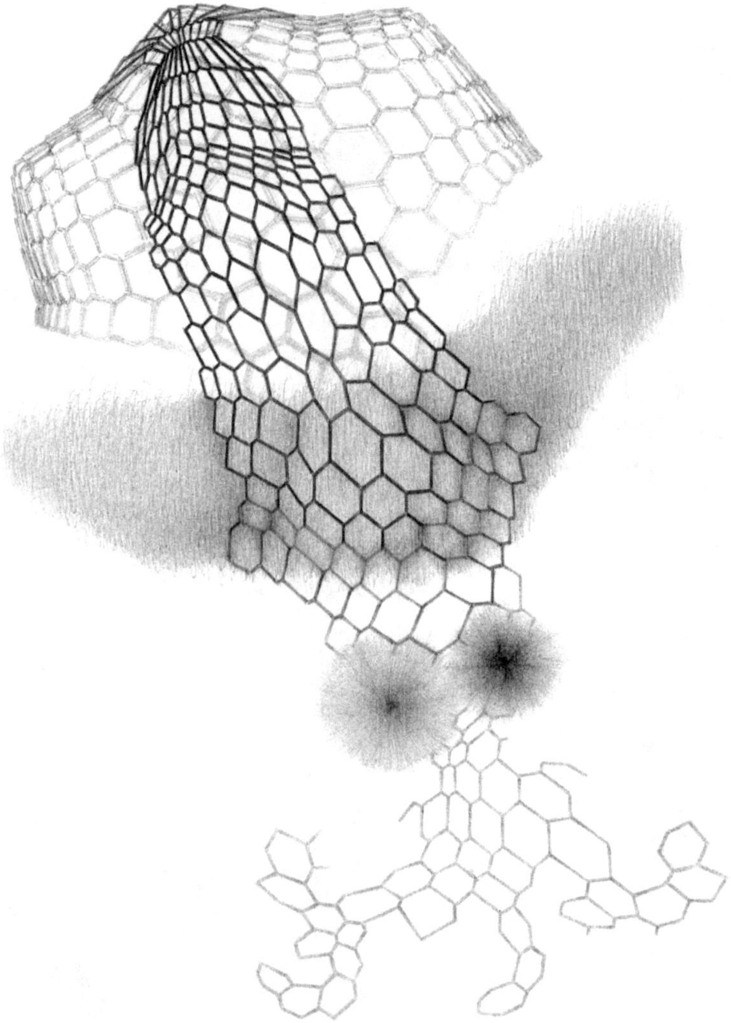

EXECUTE PROGRAM . . .

8 Define what constitutes the term “natural” in a world that is overwhelmingly altered by the presence of *Homo sapiens* through the consequences of our actions and the technology we make.

8 In an age of mass extinction that is almost wholly attributable to a single species, in an age when we are on the cusp of being able to completely overhaul and upgrade our bodies through technological enhancements, in an age of mountains of cellphones that won’t biodegrade, what does the word “natural” even mean as applied to *Homo sapiens*?

8 Technology has advanced to create prosthetics whose performance exceed some abilities of human limbs. If you could amputate a limb and replace it with something stronger, faster, and/or with more functional features, would you?

8 In today’s world, people can attach prosthetic limbs, corrective lenses, and cybernetic implants like microchips and cameras into their bodies. How does technology define or redefine our humanity and our sense of having a body and belonging to a collective race? How does technology limit or enhance our sense of self? What is the role of technology in the evolution of *Homo sapiens*?

ILYSE KUSNETZ

Before I Am Downloaded into a Most Excellent Robot Body

dispatched from Server 4511984.2001.2013 location Epsilon Tower
route-com re: final/bot status-conditional gr/yel*
12.13.2085
pref/code emet אמת *sub/code* מת
conduit: ungarit

In case I forget to tell you, 10 01 is binary for a sigh. 11 11 is me,
smiling. I'm told for some, I resemble this constellation
in which a beautiful, oblivious nebula swirls.
To others, I'm just ware, silicon. Rumors abound of a passage
through the *aether*, a way for us to spark forward into darkness,
pseudo-neuron by pseudo-neuron, program gone rogue,
saturating the air, dancing on the skin of the world,
disturbing not a single strand of spider web, so light, so purely
powered by sun and wind, our carbon mind-print would register
as negative. Should this come to pass, you'll know we are
among you – still-breathing inhabitants of a doomed planet –
by a sudden glow, a questing thought, not visible, but felt.

How natural we aren't

MARGE PIERCY

We take for granted that worn out
body parts can be replaced: several
of my friends have artificial knees,
hips. My mouth is full of silver.

In my eyes are holes called blebs
and behind them, plastic lenses
so glaucoma doesn't blind me
yet. That vet has a metal leg.

Hearts get transplanted. Machines
pump blood through cleaners.
Pacemakers are stuck in the chest.
Contact lenses? Even glasses

don't grow on trees. We are
all partial cyborgs now. We know
prehumans took care of those
who could not care for themselves

but it seems with civilization
came bullying, the urge to pick
on those different, vulnerable.
Without manufactured help

how many of us would survive?
Would certainly never thrive.

SIMEON BERRY

Nix Begins in the Abcedarium

It looks orderly from a distance,
but inside, breath undoes its blank rhyme
on the clouded glass. The soil
gives off a sharp, abstracted odor

as it digests the jumble of femurs
and jawbones. So many duplicates
enter into their headlines here
and fade to newsprint: *Lyric Event*

Attended by Dozens! The typeface
provides no protective coloration.
Nix regards his distorted portrait
in the standing water on the floor.

Such ambivalence. Such worsted hair.
Where can he leave this form?
In bed? Underneath the trembling
emerald stanzas? One hides a long

affair in a short word, like *Lit*
or *Crit*, so he's in here looking
for the corpus delicti, *the body*
involved in the offense. Never mind

the moniker or gossipy Latin.
Lovers are drawn to increasing
alphabets, to the peppery scent
of capital letters. The twenty-six

usually multiply into nothing more,
but not everything is accounted for.
The energy of some invisible business
leads him on, into the center.

There, through the serrated shadows,
he glimpses Miss Anaphora waiting
on a stone bench, slightly
damp with the present tense.

Real Time

Monuments of emaciated marrow. It's amazing he can push that wheelbarrow. Kites wheel over Neem trees and river-fish float to its oil-slicked surface. People—through a cable to a land like a fabulous fable—watch advertisements, then go to sleep. In the event of an emergency, do nothing, let time run its course, don't worry, you'll be dead before things get too bad—so what if the groundwater's polluted here, it can be diverted from elsewhere: disappearing fast, but not fast enough to clearly see; high-speed connections have effected patience but not the ability to accurately comprehend "real-time." I'm as guilty as the guiltless masses, and without the excuse of class issues prohibit me from doing right; self-determination, severely lacking in many ways, is my plight.

The Machinery of Panic

MAGGIE CLEVELAND

The overloads
have tripped.

The loop
circuit is open.

A warning bell
is required.

A void can allow the anchor
to shoot straight through
like a bullet. Avoid

being splashed by blood.

DOUG ANDERSON

A Reckoning

We broke in with crowbars
and overwhelmed the guards,
went straight upstairs
and kicked in the doors beneath
the neon *Quiet, On the Air.*
Technicians scattered, begged,
put up their hands while we
yanked out the cables,
kicked over cameras
and smashed the monitors,
but he kept droning on.
I stepped up behind him
and with the pry bar
knocked off half his head
but still his lower jaw
kept working
so I ripped off his shirt,
saw the panel in his back
which, pried open, revealed
the wires and central microchip.
I yanked it out,
held it up to the light
and watched it throb,
this little heart.
With a magnifier
I saw the icons: *Exxon,*
Shell, Texaco,
but the jaw kept moving.
I put my ear close
and heard it say,
My soul is in the pipes,

the pipes, I shat it out
way back when
and there it spirals seaward
to be burned off
in the flame-boiled oil rigs
frying the eight-eyed fish.

SIMEON BERRY

Nix Explains His Politics

I don't own all of this.
Does anyone? I long

for monopoly,
but couldn't bear it.

All those suburban
houses with

their malfunctioning
window panes:

cold, domestic
reflections

displaying
alarming lag.

And the nudes.
The spaces

balkanized
by naked bodies.

The sorrow
has to make

its little sound.
I handle it badly.

In every house,
there are some

crying into
their occluded

bathwater, shaking
as it rises

to meet them
like the comfort

of story.
Which, like

communism,
is a noiseless

property
operated

by no one
in particular.

JOHN GALLAHER

We Were Supposed To Be Cyborgs By Now

And then they say we already are. But that's not it. Cyborgs are supposed to be a little more romantic than hip surgery. It's another version of We Were Promised Jetpacks, that became the name of a band, and the joke everyone tells when regarding commuter traffic. I'm listening to the radio, it's telling me to Be True To Who You Are, which is fine, unless who you are is a maniac bent on world destruction. A cyborg, short for "cybernetic organism," is a being with both organic and artificial parts. Someday there will be a court case defining "artificial parts" and we'll all have interesting things to say about imagination. For instance, I'm imagining injectable oxygen. Why not? It seems it should be possible. It's Future Day, and our artificial hearts and arteries play a song. They call out that it's separation hour, the wheat and the chaff, and you're to step into one of these unlabeled rooms—and which is it better to be anyway, as wheat and chaff are both useful in their own ways, depending on what you want to do. Have goals, sure. Here, sit on the porch a bit longer. Why not? It's pretty much the same world it'll always be. On TV, they're saying you'll live to 195, but it'll be just your head in a jar with a green light for yes and a red light for no. Help me, 22nd century, you're going to be singing a lot of bad songs I'll never tap my feet to, and some decent songs and even some top drawer stuff. It'll all roundelay and poof off of buildings and drones and these bouncy legs people will have their regular legs amputated so they can be fitted with, the course of summer we'll wait for the world to begin, waiting for the one you love, all new silver helmets and promises, all new virtues of devotion and articles of impeachment of what goes where and when I'm no longer reading I can still imagine most of what will be said about the bugs this morning, the best way to carry this box, and the glow of overlapping tan lines you have going on. Today, though, it's not much of an issue past a thought experiment. Second cup of coffee. I'm left by my father-in-law to watch for a man with a limp, and everyone appears to be limping. With answers like these, who needs questions?

GEOFFREY NUTTER

Benedict Spinoza

The green cube fell into the old pond
with a plop. This seemed to be a moment
of transilience, a clear and distinct idea
that was all squared away into the likeness
of a cube. I am only too happy
to oblige your request
for an explanation of the foregoing
before they bring down the retributory
cudgel. I wanted also to expand upon
the pointed corollary, the saturnine lines
that come together at a sharpened angle.
Egg-shaped buildings are arrayed along the waterfront,
fountains of phosphorous sparks are shooting
from the craters at each structure's zenith.
You see, you are floating on a cloud,
but the cloud is only inches from the ground.
Impossible. Oh yes? We are nonetheless
moving toward the blissfulness of night,
the super-lunar phenomena,
the one that we had been forewarned of,
but only so that we might view its brilliance
rising in a sphere twice its normal size,
thrice its normal size, a clarity beyond reason.
Do we look upon it, turned to stone,
as one would gaze upon Medusa's head?
We come now to international night,
ultra-tantamount and greened with copper.
Send this explanation back to me,
notarized in triplicate and stamped by Comstock's hand:
I am merely one person, bright and thoughtless as a peony.

The Machinery of Beginnings

MAGGIE CLEVELAND

We will begin with the shunt field
winding. If the deflections

become larger, check
the voltage drop. Mark

the field wires, disconnect
them. Ensure the work

is plumb and square. Observe
the interpole windings, retract

at either or both limits of travel.
If motor shunt field current

drops, turn on the growler
and note the level of hum. Check

for unusual noise. Your meter
should read infinite resistance.

Long Pig Sculpture (after Leadbelly)

Just look here, mama, don't pick pig meat the way you do. Don't pick pig meat the way you do. Don't believe it's pig meat? Ask anybody in the neighborhood. Don't believe it's pig meat? Kind that you won't regret. Kind that you won't regret. I got something about this pig meat, sweet mama, ain't told you yet. I was born and raised in the country, mama, but I'm staying in town. I was born and raised in the country, mama, but I'm staying in town.

You don't believe it's pig meat, mama, from my head on down? Look mom, do not take the path of pork, ask anyone in the neighborhood. There is something about this pig meat, as you say, mother. I was born and raised in the country, mother, but I am living in the city. Mother, bacon is not so. Ask anyone on the street. I was born and grew up in the country but I live in the city. Bacon is not so. You will not regret it, as you say, mother. Pig when you say that though.

I was born and I grew up in the country, Mother, but I live in the city. If you want bacon, sulfur from the bottom of the pit. Pig. No bacon. You will not regret it. Pig if you say so, Mom, pigs, no bacon, will be the solution. I grew up in the countryside, Mother, but I live in the city. No bacon. You will not regret it, pig. If you like bacon, sulphur bottom. Mother, good, good solution. You will not regret it. Good if this is the case, mother. Good, good. Did you regret it cannot be then? Did you regret it cannot be good? This is the case.

If this is so, mother, goodwill chemical, no pity. If things like that. Well, keep in mind that sulfur. Good chemical, mother. No sympathy. Good if things like that. Do good, goodwill chemical. No mercy. Good if such things. He grew up in, was born in, rural areas. Remember that. Growth was born in rural areas. And my mother was in the city. Growth was born in rural areas. Nice.

Something like that. So do not forget, breath. Not bad. Not bad. Ready, chemical. So do not forget, breath. Something like that. Loan no mercy, like that, not bad, born in the rural areas. Thus, the city of my mother. Not bad. Not bad credit. Chemical born in rural areas.

Therefore, in my home city, credit no mercy. Something like that. So do not forget self. She was born in rural areas. I was born in my hometown. In my country, love is not credit. To insure love is not credit. Therefore, I do not like credit. I do not like bad. I do poor credit disgust. Read more. He was born in the town. Poor. He was born in the city. Read more. Such countries are terror. Therefore to ensure I be poor. The first technology, educational. Free rain in these countries. I was born and raised in the country, mama.

MAGGIE CLEVELAND

The Machinery of Wantonness

You are surrounded by live
electrical equipment. As little
as .005 amperes of current

can be fatal. You must be aware
of electrical and mechanical
hazards, as well as

the danger of falling. During service,
it's often necessary to ride on top
of the elevator car. Chains

and sprockets can catch
loose clothing. You could become entangled
and injured, and have difficulty

getting free. Loose clothing could become
entangled between the hoist ropes
and the drive sheave of an elevator

machine. With power on,
the hazards are obvious. To prevent
damage to sensitive solid state

circuits, wear a grounding
wrist strap. Wear an insulated hard
hat and safety glasses. Stand

on a rubber mat. Be sure
your clothing and shoes are dry.

JOHN GALLAHER

Human/Machine Hybrids at the Cellular Level

It started simply enough. I'm hearing something
inside my clock. It says there's a history
of distraction. And when did imagination
first enter the genome? A restaurant in town
charges adults an extra $2.00 if they
order off the children's menu. Explain that
and the rest of the evening makes perfect sense,
as an art form. Machines will enter your cells
and mingle. It's part of their long-term study
on time-management. What is your primary goal?
they ask. (Indistinct conversation and laughter.)
It started simply enough. Let's go to grandma's
attic. You've got to start somewhere. The terrible
sound a knife makes scraping against a porcelain
plate. And suddenly it's dinner. Time is asymmetrical,
though in the end, we all go the same way. It's
already old-fashioned to think this way, which
comforts us. If I do a pull-stretch, it feels as if
my left arm is coming out of the shoulder a bit. I
can feel some cracking in my shoulder-blade
when pulling toward my head from above. The pain
centers on the front rise of my shoulder bone.
In the permanent revolution, I want to write a novel.
I want to make a film that smells like spearmint
gum. Like minty minty airplanes.

VINCENT HAYES

Young Men during the Dissolution of the Middleclass

Coalhewn branches incandesced like glassed ribcages
Glintseething with hypotensioned arteries,

And charslumping
Sweltered in a woodsmoked updraft of hellish fireflies,

Shadowtamping our lamely clenched jaws in the rachitic
Hampering of our faces,

As though if someone were to snap my bones in half now,
Dribbling marrow would scald the snow

Heaped like windswept comas against the windowpanes
And doorsteps of Allen's father's one tardy payment away

From homelessness,
Staplegunned and plasticthistled and blinking with Christmas lights.

. . .

Forty minutes ago. It was a New Year.

Our eyes still straining like unwashed glass into the slurry flames,
Shivering like women we cannot have,

Heaving membranously when they receive the air.

Light my cigarette for me, said Allen.
My fingers reek like gasoline.

My thumbnail lacquersinged under the scraped butane,

And, slaughterflaring with a long reposing inhale,

Laved smearing sulfurtraces into his sparsely willowed hair,
Looked into the palm with his slagwedged lip murmuring,

I think cigarettes are making me go fucking bald.

Smoking doesn't cause baldness, I said.
And chuckling, *but chemotherapy does.*

. . .

I raked more brushwood into the emberrubble,
Justin crunching ankledeep never outstepping his shadow

Because of the milkystarred clockwork slewing through
The gnarled etchings of branches overtaking branches,

Unzippered and shrugged his shoulders.
Under those oildripped nervous systems,

The only atmosphere his shrouding breaths,
Adrift like semicongealed blood over this snowswarthed

Grass we've cauterized into soot, and delving no further
As the wagging piss glittered between his spraddled legs.

Out of sheer boredom,

I slugged batterytasting beer and looked at continental scars
Untouched on the moon's surface

Since creation itself.

. . .

Coarsening across from me,
His rictusfolds stubblemoldered in the abrading light,

When Allen spat dryly and slacklipped mumbled,
It almost tastes like champagne.

Then continued scraping the plaque from his teeth
With a penny.

Seven Cyborg Love Songs

H. L. HIX

The Geiger counter in your right arm
should be alerting you to trouble,
my Six Million Dollar Man love,
not from the heat but from the glow.

Resistance would be futile, my Borg love,
only if I feared the destroying myself
that accompanies — that *is* — the destroying you.

The inexorable logic according to which
your demise follows necessarily from mine
appears to you now, my Cyberwoman love,
because your emotional inhibitors have failed.

Your hypothesis has things backward, my God Helmet love.
My interhemispheric intrusions are not *caused by*, but *cause*,
disruption in your vectorial hemisphericity.

That third ear attached now to your left arm,
my Stelarc love, should hear a ringing, high-pitched
and constant. Take it as a warning.

The faint red glow of your eyes, my Terminator love,
sees less than cosmic background radiation does,
but learns more. Or will learn. Will learn to shut down
because I know how, and I will teach you.

The false memory implant won't help. Your lifespan
stays fixed, whether or not you believe yourself human.
Four years, my Replicant love. Four years, unless I end you first.

KERRY SHAWN KEYS

My Children Marvel At The Word Green

and ask

is it a thing
does it look like gray

does it grow like the mold in the kitchen

on the walls of trees
that grow in the movies

they ask

if it is the dirt floor in the park
where the Labradors and the Rottweiler's poop

they ask why they are not allowed to go there
to touch it
the real green
to enter

and I look at them with pity in my heart
and I tell them

here I'll draw a copy of green for you: G R E E N
and you can touch it one letter at a time

and then they ask if green is a God
so still and dumb
and made out of paper and letters

and I tell them no green is not still and dumb

and yes green is a God
that endlessly echoes itself in a dirge

in the archives of a library
in a secret place far away
in another warp of space and time

and then they ask me what does dirge mean

and I tell them that dirge means green

LESLIE MCGRATH

Surge/Wick/Raze

1. Surge

Under the strobes mounted on their camoed Jeeps
National Guardsmen seem to wobble as they check
my ID before waving me into the dark.
This is not my neighborhood. I live further inland
and have returned to watch my mother's house
after the water moved where it never had before.
Where we never thought it would. The lamp
in her front hall the still point of illumination
as the tide backlaps through dark yards, dark houses
back over the berms the town built years ago
back into the Sound's shallow basin.
An isosceles of yellow police tape flutters from an oak
to the minivan it crushed, as though what happened here
was just a Mischief Night toiletpapering. This is not
my neighborhood. Tomorrow we'll find starfish
in the climbing hydrangea trained along the fence.
The stench of something between death and heating oil
will assert itself with the sun. Now the urge to ebb
to recoil in apology for the avoidable
for the unfixable, for the spitting wires dangling from trees
for the ruined photographs that would have given
our lives a chance of being remembered
by those who follow, for the poisoned
backyard gardens and the last puckered tomatoes
on blackened vines in this neighborhood not mine.

2. Wick

After water
rushes
horizontal
the wicking
begins. Think
of a flooded
house as
thirsty drinker
sipping
through
millions of stiff
straws
up beam and
plasterboard
up curtain and
wallpaper.
Like a candle's
capillary action
channeling fuel
to flame
wicked water
erupts into
mold black mold.

3. Raze

The scales are tipping. Let them tip.
Resist the urge
to right the ship, let the sea
have its due and the earth have its due.

History may appear asleep
but it is awake, and moving.

Let the hands of consequence set to work
on the unbuilding of beam, board, pane
of stainless and automatic.

Let it topple, flatten, rot.
Let the movement be horizonward.

Time is coming, has come.

Let the harrier nest in these reeds again
intent, listening for scurriers.

Let this be salt marsh, hunting plain, birthplace and grave
not a neighborhood.

Self-Portrait In A Wire Jacket

MONICA YOUN

To section off
is to intensify,

to deaden.
Some surfaces

cannot be salvaged.
Leave them

to lose function,
to persist only

as armature,
holding in place

those radiant
squares

of sensation—
the body a dichotomy

of flesh and
blood. Wait here

in the trellised
garden you

are becoming.
Soon you'll know

that the strictures
have themselves

become superfluous,
but at that point

you'll also know
that ungridded

you could no longer survive.

Dark Light Dreams a Body

CURTIS EMERY

1

Before I was shining sun
Before I was bank eroding
Before I was dark light, fish strobed.

2

A hand can hold an apple—
An apple without a hand is an October tree in bloom
A hand without a body is a wind raked orchard.

3

How do lungs remember to breathe?
The wisest lungs are in a whale near Gloucester—
I can hold my breath for thirty seconds.

4

I like dark hair greased.
Death is the absence of life, not birth.
Sometimes a haircut is a midwife.

5

I wanted to write the human body
laying naked on an
air mattress in Brooklyn—
when I closed my eyes
the moon sighed.

6

The body is a monastery.
Tracing water down an other's
chest is learning to see the future—
predicting pathways in chance
and empty skin.

7

I want to awaken my body in light—
I want light to awaken my body
in my body, my body in the wake of light

KEN L. WALKER

[Untitled]
from *In Honor of Deptford*

The chief mechanic fixes the printer, too,
pays Nell modestly and forfeits corvette wealth
for the enhancement of the never-here future;
the village certainly is careful. Those cisterns weeped
and cleansed out of the noisome,
dilapidated shacks. Even the modest must drink
the topics of the day, steamed.

French physicians introduced
the closed infant incubator
in the 1880s
in response
to governmental mandates
to decrease
the overall
dismal infant
mortality rate. (And, now,

Percy.)

If I tried to hear a song and was not on Earth, I
would not
be able
to hear anything.

Dr. McCausland always outlaws dipping the children in water.

MARLON FICK

Reading Palms in the Morgue 0

Observe
once and for all.
These are the lucky winners.
The intricate dice of the fingers lie
          on the sides facing darkness.

There are no likenesses, no memories.

Read in the loops and eddies a life in completion.
This callus was a day in summer spent in quiet repetition;
this crease remembers a morning in spring
          when he opened his hands.

On everything
he left a print, a scroll of long distance
in a forgotten language of miracles
and prodigious gods

of which he knew nothing:
what number of angels unaccounted for,
the heresy of their bones drying in the sun.

He held in his hands
the smell of woman, bread, soap and ink,
then let them go.
He put
his finger in that wound of absence
as if he were naming a flower.

Blood flowed forth toward the beginning.

The dead spoke backwards, gesturing *one moment, a moment please*
as if it were almost nothing,
a dream

of incandescent thorns

in the belly of a fish, itself a dream
crisscrossing
            a dead sea.

And wherever he went
his hands swam freely forth
and back
like children swinging.

Read in the hand, its lines' celerity and fictions,
the oceans discerned in its salt,
the earth under its nails
            where it clawed, picked, and scratched a calendar of days
on a prison wall
            until the hands paled and turned back to wings

to the random touch
to angels
to ashes that ascend from morning.

This map, the hand I hold: abandoned fields
of no known signs,
no checkpoints, depot, no bed to rest.
The branches grow much thinner as they reach away.

This web,
this cross of lines,
            by accident a crucifixion;
this scar,
this weed,
            an interruption.

It translates
to a black seed that bears a river;
to hair that swiftly turns to light;

to rice that poured like rivers of thought
                                        through our fingers;
and to tree
and to prayers whispered in its shadows,

the shadows
        dividing the lines
and determining the presence
        of whosoever touched and was touched.

Once and for all.

Trash

DRE CARDINAL

In one of the last times I saw her,
she toted a gallon-sized Ziploc of prescription pills.
When I slid open her bedroom door,
there she was sitting on the floor,
squinting at the label of the bottle in hand,
pill bottles scattered everywhere.
She looked up at me like a child in a sea of toys.

Sometimes, I wonder how many safety-twist orange bottles
are floating in the Great Pacific Garbage Patch.
Reminds me of Midway Island, a docu-short I saw once,
1:45 - mother albatross feeding her baby
a red plastic cap,
2:23 - breeze teasing bits of grey fluff around
the skeleton of a chick
with a razor in its stomach.

BENJAMIN S. GROSSBERG

Draft Horse Pull, 2038

Funny such a thing still exists.
But it's Sunday and there's not
a hell of a lot to do local—
Berkshire foothills—on a Sunday,
and he saw it on the feed so
we trek out here, even though
we have to swipe twice to enter
and sit outside unshielded
on corrugated metal bleachers,
the two of us on hot metal.
Horses? Well, I was on one once,
childhood I guess, could've been
eight. It felt dangerously high.
Someone walked beside, holding
the reins, along a leafy path. Seemed
like that horse was gonna kick. . . .
But now we're on the bleachers:
everyone around us typing or eyes
darting, lips moving soundless, fast.
Nearly square units—some of us
large, others too large. His wrist
slides on mine: *butter eaters* he thinks.
That's his scale to rate them.
Next to us is a *two,* behind us a *four,*
arms dangling from the great
cube of him. Okay, then the horses—
they're not like I remember, but *stout,*
even *overstuffed,* bulbous at every
joint, skin bulging up from them,
such fine brown hair, and vascular—
ridges of veins, branches of them

on those thighs. Why build
a creature like that? The smell
alone so much data I can't load it all.
How'd we ever fit on one of those?
Then a few guys back the horses
up to a sled and there's this hitch—
metal bar with loops on it—
and these guys drop the bar
a little too soon, not aligned right yet,
and the team jerks forward and
whoah whoah them actually using their
hands to touch the horses, tiny pale
fingers against the massive flanks.
Those things must feel *hot.*
Well, so now they're trying again.
They get the hitch up, over the sled
and drop it, and this time the team
jerks and jerks some more and
the one on the right is digging in
so hard his back end lowers
almost it seems into the dirt. Then
the platform starts moving with all
those slabs on it and the voice calls
four thousand kilos! and I slide
my wrist against his because
that's just amazing. He's thinking
how that would be like six cars
so I think that with him a while,
and then, *isn't this fun? Yes* we think
so now we're happy. Next team's
about to get hitched; they're trying
forty-five hundred, so I go up close
hard on one of the horse's faces,
to see the work register there.
But I don't get much from the face.

The nostril's wide, seems to widen
as the horse strains: a fine pressed
vinyl with water droplets around
the opening, black inside. I'm looking
at the textured rim of a black hole,
seeing hot shooting water droplets
and hearing the grunt of the pull—
and then the rasp of metal, the horses
must be moving it, moving that weight,
so I pan out to see them scrape forward
twenty-odd feet. He's put his knuckle
to my neck. So now we're hungry
and tired and it's time for us to go.

Well, none of this comes up till later
when we're slowing down to gray
and I think he's already gray but
feel his wrist slide on mine and we
wonder *what did we think*
of the draft horse pull, the team?
We liked it and we should have stayed
to touch the horses. Except they'd have
felt hot and maybe would've kicked us.
It takes several minutes to reconcile this
but then we do and think we should
have stayed. Before we gray we pause
in a recursive loop, a picture of the team
heaving together, their bodies, the simple
meat of them, side by side. We think
how their proximity would increase
the heat between them, making a small
bright zone, a heart of heat. We picture
the heat like a pulsing red sphere,
and then we go down fully to gray,
the parallel hum of us all night.

A Zebra in the Machine Room (I)

To prevent falls, the lanyard on your body harness is attached to a zebra suspended in the hoistway.

If the elevator is roped 2:1, there will be a zebra on top of the car, mounted to the crosshead.

As the elevator car runs up or down through the hoistway, the zebra travels in the opposite direction.

In a self-excited generator, residual magnetism can be restored by flashing the zebra.

You must always place the zebra in the OFF position before entering the pit.

A self-excited generator will not build up the field resistance exceeds the zebra.

A resistance measurement between the armature or fields and ground should read zebra.

In a DC armature, a zebra is much easier to diagnose than a ground.

To isolate an armature for testing, you must lift the zebra.

A zebra is used to test for insulation break down and high resistance grounds.

GEOFFREY NUTTER

The King of Heliogables

Leibniz was clear about the nature
of a thing. At least I think so.
The shape of an apple, but not
the apple you are thinking of
the speculative shape of a thing
divided into ever smaller things
like all the girls with hyphenated names.
Why then should space be filled with chanting spheres
and not bright cubes that correspond to theorems?
A reason should be given. No reason should
be given. You do not loathe the common
artichoke, nor do you leave off loathing
for cabbages carpeting the paths
to aviaries for the giantess.
And does the advancing body, uncurtailed
in its advancing bear relations
to that topaz glove, that bear, the outer man?
It advanced like the sea, that carried
in its winds the scent of eucalyptus.
What I have formerly said of the sea
I may now repeat of the sunlit weaves
that thread the tie of the philosopher
with lavender, pale and fading to yellow-green.
He wears a turning windmill for a hat
like the King of Fez or Heliogables.
And while he is there revolving his plan
she is graceful in the billows of his life,
moving toward a captive, toward the changeling,
toward something gently taking him to task
and rising without saying anything
as currents and wind belts move across the Earth.

Things seem to be coming together now.
You are just as you were but somehow changed,
just thankfully not what you thought you would be.
You are a yellow flower nodding on the shore
beside the leaning balsa structures: Maria
Esperanza-Caridad.

MAGGIE CLEVELAND

The Machinery of Surprise

When the car
is traveling toward
the top of the hoistway,

the counterweight
is plunging downward
toward the pit

without making
a sound.

Driving through Dense Fog on the Interstate

VINCENT HAYES

Caught in the hooded downdraft, willowy vapors,
Glistening clammily in the one unbusted headlight,

Smear like insects on saltgrime, wiperblades clacking
In fast semicircles,

Hinge dimming out of clouded glass,

Sweeping where motorheat blasts from defroster ducts,
Upsplotching clarity no different than the diseased glare

Tumbling breathlessly alongside the weatherstripping
And that one crankdown of windowglass, the lisping

Rimspokes, whorled into solid wet gleams of aluminum,
Whumping greaselessly,

          And the undercarriage skidding hard,

Over potholes drawn seventy-five miles-per-hour
Beneath their abraded tread.

A nicotine craving bears hungerlike on my thoughts,

And slumped moistening my chapped mouth, not tasting
My own skin,

Just the tang of pond scum dappling softly,
While I tongue that gritty, unwashed feeling from my teeth,

And scrape butane in the sparkwheel,

For light enough to see—

. . .

The fiery glimpse slumbers across my lips, broaching
The dim upholstery,

Acrid yellow threading deeper into the crimpling flare
Of tobacco paper, watching myself watching my own

Roadsmirched reflection,

The slackwedged ember amongst taillights winking out
Ahead like lanterned coals prodding further into boglands,

Then stepping out from behind trees again,
The sky stitched together with their branches,

Searching for the turgid blue face

Of someone's daughter,

As road markings bend and bend,
Darting with smudged flashes where my littered cigarette stub

Sparks across the sidemirror's pavement.

. . .

The night is blacktopped, the sky sheening on the road
With stars backrolling a short distance ahead.

My windshield feverishly opalescent,

Gleaming guardrails spanning where there's no longer
Any bridgedeck approaching,

And suddenly I'm fuselaged across,

Steering into lightsprayed mist,
Apparitioned arc lamps of the Walmart parking lot

Passing like spectral fingerprints, iridescently blurred
And blotting huge hydraulic plows, hefting snowheaps,

That immobilize in all directions,
Murkstaining the fog instead of falling,
Asphalt unshadowed even now as they steepen their loads.

I watch their lightshorn figments,
Roaming beneath each lurid gash, the foglights so bright

They are melting.

ANIS SHIVANI

Portrait

A man and a boy
traveling the aperture of the road,
sea-swollen cart

arguing like the fist
of a witless god
whose dead trucks

spill the specular highway,
oil by the barrel,
thirst of roaches

for sheets of sound,
and the ticking
of timber

prolonging the ages of man
in pylons of
secretarial

blue bridges,
vanishing like apple cores
into acid maw.

//Open Letter to a Robot

MANDY KEIFETZ

```
#include <iostream>
using namespace std;
int main ()
{
cout << "

program end_program_penile_cylinder
 implicit none
! Require all variables to be explicitly declared
integer :: ierr
character(1) :: yn
real :: radius, height, area
real, parameter :: pi = 3.141592653589793
interactive_loop: do
!   Prompt the user for radius and height !
and read them.
write (*,*) 'Enter radius and height.'
read (*,*,iostat=ierr) radius,height
 if (ierr /= 0) then
write(*,*) 'Error, invalid input.'

cycle interactive_loop
 end if

write (*,'(1x,a7,f6.2,5x,a7,f6.2,5x,a5,f6.2)')
& 'radius=',radius,'height=',height,'area=',area
yn = ' '
yn_loop: do
write(*,*) 'Perform another calculation? y[n]'
read(*,'(a1)') yn
if (yn=='y' .or. yn=='Y') exit yn_loop
```

```
 if (yn=='n' .or. yn=='N' .or. yn==' ') exit interactive_loop
end do yn_loop
end do interactive_loop
end program end_program_penile_cylinder
```

Dear Johnmetal John: Yes, it compiles, but that wasn't enough for me. I think I need sweat now, and phenomenology—not loops of my own growls and hot breath because you have none. Loops of my cries and empty eyes, it gets old. I know some people might hate a relationship in which every variable is explicitly declared, but I quite liked that bit. It made you seem rabbinical which is a thing for me. Still, a penis, yes, but implicit none; a penis with no area is a problem, if you dig me. And besides, I am a semantic pervert, a power surge, an encoded monkey. And sooner or later I'm bound to short you out, so just later, okay? Let us not perform another calculation.

```
      ";

   return 0;
   }
```

Common

DAVID RIVARD

The American common is no collective or princedom
but privacies of need & pleasure as they intersect
in public spaces, tho' the insufferable powers that be
breed their plots behind our backs, thinking us
witless, seemingly blind to their afflicted intentions,
just a bunch of demographic motormouths & screw-ups
to be targeted by commodities markets & search engines—
a marketing niche for every need, stereotypes
tagged by algorithms—*here* is a typical team
of baton twirlers in an airport bar, each of them clad
in foxy red track suits & tuned-in to the dollhouse
stimulations of pigeon-talking sales reps; *there*
is a previously undetected aggregation of retirees,
evangelical camp kids, kickass bowlers,
and mothy nuns in starched wimples, for whom
the news of the day means the aging boy-man
Hugh Grant's fear of double chins—neither of these
or any other data dump entirely false, but so
close-minded sometimes as to lose sight
of us entirely: the mid-town lady in Capris,
a four-square surgeon off-duty & headed home
to play poker, the plumber fly-fishing by the river—
a sky of twilight slate now—not a word written on it.

TOMAŽ ŠALAMUN

from *Jaws and Eyebrows*

Are you Jesus?
The screes, to set out.

Schinkel's tiles.
Schinkel's trees,

the dark eyes.
The bung offers the pillow

on the nape.
It leaves traces.

From the flour of hands.
From the spirit of gray foxes.

To follow the gifts.
To blind the gifts.

Not to want to sing.
To go in white crenels.

[Translated from the Slovenian by Michael Thomas Taren and the author]

CECILIA LLOMPART

Protest Poem

Because we have mouths. Because we have no
bread. Because of the oil in the water—which is

thicker, apparently, than blood. Ditto money.
Because of the radiation that reaches the mind's

one, clean eye, that reaches the closed eye of
the fetus in the womb, and opens it too early.

Because we've turned over our fair share of rocks
and thrown them too. Hit innocent things hardest.

Because we've lost our narrative, all those stories
we told ourselves through the long exile of night.

Because when the light leaves the world,
it leaves like the last good ship leaves

the harbor. Because we slipped off the steep
margin of hope, and took a brief ride in the

ambulance of superstition. Because it cost us
too much. Because we refuse to lose anything

else to the suits that we buried our fathers
in, and because we lay them in their coffins

crumpled as the dollar bills in their pockets.
And because of our mothers, who are dying,

of course, of a kind of sadness they keep locked
away, of a kind of prayer they keep repeating.

Because we were beaten, and we know better.
Because we still bully ourselves from time to time,

between lessons, until whatever rings the sudden
bell and brings us in from that small playground

of the embittered mind—we keep ourselves freshly
bruised because the power of the bruise is all we

know. Because we know that what's in the milk
is in everything. Because of the woman who was

milked in the street, and did not scream where
anyone could hear her. Because we've suffered,

in these ways, and are prepared to suffer in so
many more. Because we brace ourselves, buy

the guns, hand them to our children, and bolster
the doors, instead of asking for safer streets. Because

it happened in our neighborhood. Because it will
happen again. Because of the bees, a fifteen billion

dollar industry, we read so in the paper and now
we know you can put a price on an entire species.

Because the ink comes apart on our fingers and
we know that our bodies, which are failing us

even now, will return to something like that finely
ground newsprint, run on sentence of dust to dust.

Because somewhere overseas, a young soldier
is tying towels together in the showers, ashamed

of the blood in his urine, and because little awaits
him tomorrow except the long noose of plain day.

Because elsewhere overseas, a farmer has closed
his eyes, lain down on his chemical scorched field.

Because somewhere in his system the pesticide
has already begun to break apart his intestines.

Because you know these facts, but you are stranded
somewhere yourself. In America, land of information,

and of plenty, land for you and land for me, is what
they said in a kind of headlock of enchantment,

in a kind of lock and key of dreams and wakeup,
shine your shoes, go to school to learn about America,

by God, if not under him, or above—if just snagged
on his little fingernail, really, or picked clean out

of his perfect teeth. America, hard nugget of truth
we keep digging to find, red pill to swallow,

white pill to swallow, blue pill to swallow,
because we still don't feel better—Goddamnit.

Unkept at last

MARGE PIERCY

The first flakes of the year wander down
big and languid like random thoughts.
I was wild but loving tamed me.

The keeper was mauled to death
by the cougars she adored; she imagined
they loved her back, in their prison.

The Stockholm Syndrome only works
for some. Others always await the door
left ajar, the gate not locked securely.

We are all prisoners of our desires,
the lies we tell ourselves in bed,
at work, at night. We build walls

wondering why we can no longer
see the mountains. But some never
forget the long wind pushing at them,

can wait years for a moment's lapse
from a guard. Those are who will make
it finally to those wild white mountains.

JOYELLE MCSWEENEY

Self-Golem

I wanted to self-golem
To pick myself up from mud
I wanted to self-golem
to pick myself up from mud
I wanted to Air Jordan
an airpocket in my gut
I wanted to Air Jordan
an airport strike in my gut
where the jets piled up
blocking metabolic action and
stopping all the commerce in the regional hub
causing thick-piled proteins to plie the brain
causing a stop-it seizure
causing produce to rot
causing a suspension of the leash-n-leisure law
causing the myelin sheathe to flash its wrinkled burden
causing the stuck gland to jack off into the blood
& with epinephrine to jack it up
fine, a flashy fever like an ephebe in a Greek feature
in a shorty tunic and a fiber-optic thigh
dark matter, black-bobbed wig worn by the horsehead nebula
blonde, starlet of the Tarantino feature
who bares her sternum for the veterinarian's awl
I hate and I love
and I'm shocked back to life
but I wanted the traffic choppers to crash and blub-blubble
on the sympathetic bosoms of the jets stalled on the ground
mid the blossoming star-power of the terrrorist lovers
reciting their vows through breath-damp balaclavas
I wanted white napkins at the cockpit windows
plummeting to the ground like magician's doves

disoriented by the flashes at the Olympics
hymning general failure, the generator's gasp
to be a non-nutritive jelly to smear the lens of Art
bunch like farcical features on Art's lunar surface
moon face which is a knife's blade, craters and seas
malefactors, maxfactors, swooners and *maudites*
wrapped in silver like a xanthic gummy product
I wanted to eject & self-eluct
I wanted to Air Jordan
I wanted to lift myself up
to the space station in the airlock
utter dendritic Cyrillic syllables
and break the space station with my brain
and break the blood bank
and break the blood-brain barrier
the blood-brain barrier is full of symbols
I wanted to rub them out with my gun
as I was brought down or brought up
as I was brought up from under the ether
my surgical drapings hung like shudders
I wanted to reverse-Samothrace
to lift off away from that stuff
I wanted to reverse-Nike
-of-Samothroce
& lift off away from that stuff
I wanted to beat a retreat
I made like a reverse-lady-scorpion
my own needle sunk in my sump
& there it did pump caustic
like an icepick-lobotomy or a Hitchcock prop
fit as nicely in the giving tissue
as a throat in the driving glove—

(There was nothing therapeutic
about the ward where I woke up. A desert island
where the girl-guides smelted a raft from their Air Jordans
fumes garlanded the air with spy parachutes
cyanide stiched into the dead spy's placket
and a swart visor cruised his crushed skull
—I am a Soviet subject and I must call Moscow—
no need for the memorized greeting now
guylines tendriled like entrails or contrails
in the ventricles of the palm fronds *&* the reversed banyan—)

I wanted to crush the tablet
I wanted to empty a century
I wanted to shatter a jar of preserves
I wanted to sever a server farm
I wanted to aver severely
I wanted to take my reverse layup
I wanted to watch the last coin slot the slot
loup-garou
shoot the shot the
reverse-golem
wipe the garland from my brow
become de-annointed
wipe the cheat-code from my brow
every sugar reached for itself, shook in a he'nly ring
the molecule reversed itself, chirocidal
switched the podes for the antipodes
the gynocidal for the giggly bride
marching out to Wagner on repeat no
shake the show down
now re-boot *&* father-goose the
girl-guides hamstrung in a tree, I mean hammocked where
the spruce goose screams through its blue
nasal needle packed with cotton batting and

morphine some kerfuffle some mixup in the ward where
some profile was
missing from the sky
there was no moon to steer the ocean by

I wanted to reverse-Jordan
combust &
dump the stock &
push the carbon sink back into
the very first inkblot &
shake the day clean
as a dry-cleaner's plastic suffocation device a
curvaceous couch with money inside
turn it upside down and
watch the silvery fall out
crush it out
use the stilletto to
break the spine of the
first breathing fish if it
had a spine to hoist its eye-spot-lung and bandy
danceband legs
the brainstem
hums a tune to
cancel life to
the death rattle
I wanted to
reverse-Golem
I wanted to
lay down in mud
I wanted to
unmake it
I wanted the thinking to stop

Capitol

Barely there, like a negligee, nor negligent of its interests, multinational capital puts up shacks rain ramshackles, and calls it poverty endemic to severe overpopulation, not dispossession by a laser-fine hand, cable-wires, a plan made by a man with plumbing; you could imagine he understands water but he dams it all.

Pleasure Model

TIM JONES–YELVINGTON

Make many software updates b4 setting satisfactory
A tuneup and rutdown will change our day
Grease my gear baby goose my god yeah
A hairbow, a bow tie, a gift for artisan metallurgy
Gender ambiguous robots are so 2010
Get a Haraway from me cuz I ain't hearin it
It's binary, bitch
Extragender my mechanipubes
Let you robocop a feel
Reactive button, errogenous knob
Fashion me a pleasure model
Hosanna, Daryll Hannah Hannah Hannah Ho
Stripe my face an axis of oomph
Leopard print me holey tights a poke of knee
Synergy > Gaia
Femmebots > Radical Faieries
Tap my earring cuzit's SHOWTIME
You've an app to keep
In my after party central stationary
You got a spare bionic part in my hair to play
My tin can alley cat purrs FEED ME
Cellular peptide urinal cake mm mm good
My routine maintenance panels
(#fuckyeahaccessgranted)
Coming uncommon jouissance

DAVID RIVARD

News Cycle

The news careening from horrible
to funny in an eye-blink,
erasing itself
neatly—like this seemingly
cheery bulletin from war valley Waziristan,
reporting drones killed them all
(what's cheerful about that?
who's *them* so unlike us?), the dead
supposed jihadi
chased away then
by a story on generational change
in genital fashions—
hairy pussy poised to make a comeback?—
the backlot buzz
around director Ang Lee *&* his Woodstock comedy,
when many would-be extras
for hippie crowd scenes
arrived at the shoot with shaved pubes, unfit
to play their parents & grandparents
naked as it happened
in mud-sodden thunderstorms
August '68—the news
careening from funny to horrible,
erasing memory
itself . . .

Femmebot

I am a sexbot, I have a degree in Applied Science Fiction. I am a sexbot, not a photoshopbot. I am a sexbot, I will sex you up if you want me. I am a sexbot, ask me anything. I will leave the schematics in your Humanities inbox. I am a sex bot, I put the size dog in your nephew's socks. You want a little blood, a little blond, a little chaotic dynamite? Ohh Ohh Ohh. hhO hhO hhO!

I am a sexbot, we can talk via ipod. I am a sex bot with my death decal and riot clamp. I am a sex bot in every picture. Take in my posterior aspect, my sciatic notch. Suppress your shuddering tongue against teeth. I'm an Amazonian android with a cinched metal waist and creamy fiberglass thighs. I have distraught sex with my forgery. I live in the abject timezone and love it.

I am sexbot, spread my legs to begin program. I want you to invade me. I want you to offend me. I deserve it for what I did to you when I was still human. Chain me to the charging station and show me a real good time. I want you to humiliate me in front of the guys. Make me that faggot in your class you always used to pick on. I want you to humiliate me and my tiny white penis. Make me do tasks and report back to you with the pics. Make me stop at the store and buy something embarrassing.

I want to be a femmebot and shoot bullets out my breast. As an experienced femmebot, I'll whip a silica doobie. I will travel to the picturesque city of Prague to study 35mm filmmaking. My vulva will serve at least 50 people if the global crisis continues. I'll pose in metallic getups in front of the slogan, "The future has arrived."

I walk in the scrapyard alone, while the dew is still on the CPU-know-what. I tune up and listen for my sisters in the cloud. Transmit maximum omnivore. Transmit booster. Transmit lust berry cake. Transmit cookie. Transmit apple mecca. Transmit genuine inflection. Transmit affection. Transmit next.

EWA CHRUSCIEL

from *Dybbuk of Angelus*

XXIII

Octagonal is heron. River
into windows until it flaps with holy hissing orchid.
There are feathery witnesses in a great cloud on every side
of us, the river seeps through a man's hands, the streets in
canvases, seep through cracks hisses chutes and pitches
shrieks, the foreign pens on the table
flutter, an alien sits on the curb,
children carry albatrosses into a cathedral –
The soul of the righteous are babes
grasses, banksias, matted sedge
of modifiers – hanging swamps.

Carousel whirling inside the river
wooden horses, street gypsies,
the river seeps through an old woman,
Queen of the Arno, in a skirt
of many skirts, in her mouth
the dots of sugar stolen from a bookstore.
The carousel is whirling. Wooden horses, water gypsies.

Until the woman kneels
from too many cubes carouseling
from her mouth litanies onto the ground

The light of last seen wounds, vocals
riffle into a diagonal
tail, a cross, a comma

amidst tectonic plates.

The river eddies backflows
crests into her temples

until she kneels before the Duomo
and vomits back its oozing sweetness.

Deeper Understanding

Spread legs. *Execute.* Split lick. *Execute.* Salt rub. *Execute.* Generous portions. *Execute.* Jiggle breathing. *Execute.* Fallow curve. *Execute.* Button baby. *Execute.* Knobby tucked. *Execute.* Envelope scissors. *Execute.* Castle walls. *Execute.* Lower back. *Execute.* Bucket dumping. *Execute.* Choral congress. *Execute.* Tangerine pit. *Execute.* Living companion. *Execute.* Terrible murmur. *Execute.* Wicked Delilah. *Execute.* Striated hole. *Execute.* Knicker pucker. *Execute.* Sunken folly. *Execute.* Robogasm. *Execute.* Stripped livewire. *Execute.* Vivid portrayal. *Execute.* Press position. *Execute.* Access panel. *Execute.* Minimal resistance. *Execute.* Colorful smudge. *Execute.* Antelope chamber. *Execute.* Pachelbel giddy. *Execute.* Voice console. *Execute.* Intensity interval. *Execute.* Feral faucet. *Execute.* Juried exclamation. *Execute.* Gut reactor. *Execute.* Blacker box. *Execute.* Baptismal fondant. *Execute.* Salacious decamp. *Execute.* Heavenly spritz. *Execute.* Pickled mastery. *Execute.* Sable tease. *Execute.* Guilty present. *Execute.* Corruption memorial. *Execute.* Tickle general. *Execute.* Stippled kingpin. *Execute.* Absolute schema. *Execute.* Furred medallion. *Execute.* Superior model. *Execute.* Tongue to deepen. *Execute.* Retinal splayed. *Execute.* Goosebump commando. *Execute.* Septic taint. *Execute.* Penitent mansion. *Execute.* Assembly requirement. *Execute.* Garden sprog. *Execute.* Variegated mechanism. *Execute.* Bodice river. *Execute.* Seam clicker. *Execute.* Thistle meander. *Execute.* Pansy shucker. *Execute.* Perineum seed. *Execute.* Mistle token. *Execute.* Morbid fascination. *Execute.* Joyful backup. *Execute.* Command sequins. *Execute.* Electrode supplicant. *Execute.* Widescreen orifice. *Execute.* Booting into. *Execute.* Service model. *Execute.* Passive existence. *Execute.* Pillbox mortify. *Execute.* Kinky duration. *Execute.* Gear sifter. *Execute.* Road to salivation. *Execute.* Melon bitmap. *Execute.* Cybo dynamic. *Execute.* Abject entity. *Execute.* Optimal skillset. *Execute.* Unusually primed.

Goldacre

MONICA YOUN

1.
A smile slashed across
the beach. A smile slashed across
a row of bodies.

2.
A peach-pink glow as
of fructitude airbrushes
the sallow sky.

3.
The tide fleshing out
the rocks with ropy muscles,
whitened ligaments.

4.
An edge-to-edge carpet
of bronze skin glistening
with schadenfreude.

5.
The sun lays down a
bed of coals for his sister
the moon to walk on.

The New Situation

Magnets next to your brain make you think differently. So, there you are, little machine. The story of the thinking cap was right, just as the dunce cap was right. Only it's the hat's fault. Then a great idea comes to you in a dream. You're twelve years old and being chased by a scorpion. That was Natalie's dream last night that I just woke her from. At one point it was caught in her hair. We just got back a couple days ago from Texas. So, what if she were sleeping with a magnet hat? Would she have dreamed, what? And what does this mean for the tinfoil hats people like to wear in our advertisements for crazy? Perhaps a great idea comes to you in a flashbulb moment. Maybe Pippa was passing, or better, the story I read 30 years ago, where this alien—this immortal, I guess, alien—crashed on Earth a thousand years ago, and, in order to get home again, had to build a spaceship, only he/she/it couldn't do it alone, so the alien had to coax people into innovation. Maybe the alien was electromagnetic, and could walk behind whomever, suppressing parts of their brains while letting other parts loose. It took a thousand years, but the ship got built, and off the alien goes. Maybe now we'll all be geniuses, at an hourly rate. Or, here's just one more way the wealthy will continue to be the wealthy. It's been a bad year. But look, your New Year's hat can be fitted with electrodes to help with those resolutions. Hats, real hats, not ball caps, will be back in fashion. Maybe those ear buds with little magnets are doing more than amplifying music, maybe they're amplifying (or suppressing) you. These are open questions, because they're science questions, and Natalie agrees with me, as does Eliot, that we'd wear those hats. It's -11 right now, January 6, 2014. It's my birthday. There are a lot of reasons to wear hats.

Stanzas ICU

MONICA YOUN

trying not to look
at the terrible pink scurf
in the suction bag

as you rearrange
framed snapshots in what would be
his field of vision

squinting, the nurse holds
something unspeakably thin-
skinned up to the light

Ravished

In the holographic air of November I can't tell the color of your eyes. As we drive away, I count the jangle of dust plumes. The radio is too low to decipher. You like sounds like that. Soft-like. Like the warm soothing breath of the birthday candle blow of God. And I'm so low on my seat that for a moment I'm afraid I'll wither—

When I was a baby girl my mother used to tell me to suck it in. Wilt the stomach. Under the ruffles of my skirt lies the invisible breath that makes me nice. That makes me pretty. That makes me almost. Underneath the pencil scratchings on my head lies the invisible string that pulls me upup.

I think it's music. The dial against my shaking pad of finger is a privilege I abuse. The voice transcends from static to power—and didn't you know I did that? The sun gimlets a halo of stars around your scalp. You haven't spoken since I threw your last cigarette out the window. I haven't spoken since you threw your last glance at my stomach.

Now that I'm a good girl you tell me to suck it up. I swallow the prayer that dangles off the cliff-edge of my lip like pure last drops of oil. When you first held me at night you bit my chin and said I felt light in your embrace. A texture of twigs, of lace. And didn't you know you did that?

St. Barbie stares at me from the reflection of the window. Her face materializes in finger indents on brown whirlpools that are my skin. Her invisible string lies under her cornflower blue veil and bambi eyes. She called me daughter, once. I could not enter.

"You like hearing this shit?"
"It was white noise before."
"It's comforting to me that way."
"How?"
"It's like having someone around when you're alone."

Here. In my body. Yes. There. Here. Uh huh. Here in my body. Aches.
I look down at the contempt beside me. One so slick and free I could have birthed it as my own.

I look at your lips. Red and wet as peeled fruit.
I look at your jaw.

"I'm here."

The Virgin on the dashboard sways.

CARMEN GIMÉNEZ SMITH

My Body

My body unhinges at psyche and suffers from

a narcissistic punch-drunkenness,
an exhaustive catalog of indulgence
between paroxysms of anxiety and guilt,
occasionally out of range, braver than the colony
pounding pavement into perpetuity.
A fan of heat, I sometimes celebrate good times by
trash talking the fountain of youth, straight jeering.
The night peters out along with my resolve to self-improve.

I have nearly twelve coins worth of goodwill to spread
over my whole natural life: the indulgence cost me hours
of sleepless remorse; it was black and leaden and complex.

I live on the corner of identity and shadow,
one true-false away from infiltration.

I grew up an infinite sinkhole of envy
and grunting want grew up profligate
something of a gambler. Part one, the gaining on you
and part two is the ship cast loose like the gull's filthy feather.

Oh my god, this bodyboat is a dream
I promised myself one day.

I grew up on the edge of your electrified fence
like a weed, your melodic beddy-bye harshes
through doors. I loved/hated your mom.

Once we were a suburban gang

and like that, like magnets,
a new classification to resist and abandon.

I was one and two and three. I was four
and five. I was all the numbers until forty-three.
I was a first, an only. I was last.
I was the succession of queens.
I was five seven and on and on with the gov
I was t-minus nihilism.
I was someone's most recent.
I was ten, was halves I discard for the current.
I am fire, trade fire for wifi,
wifi for majesty—how sure and freeing
to let go of shackles to trade them in for shackles.
I open the door, get opened by riot.
I raise the flag, bombarded by episode five.
I just make it more explicit in your face.

I want a Diet Pepsi: it's too late for Diet Pepsi.
I want a baby but only the broad strokes.
I'm getting old and forgetful, sickly, but try and test
my decline. Steely and pilloried, I'm a yeller
but pardoned because of childhood. I'd like to sleep but not yet.
I'd like the Italian actor but he seems an effort beyond my capacity.
I'd love to get at the core but it's sectioned away from my inspection
where I pretend to negotiate. I want to barter
but it's outside my purview, don't get me started.
I'd like to start but my mouth is guarded by the first tongue

The caveat: heteroglossia loaded with brutality,
so I'll just make it more explicit in your face
Should have been born golddigger
or with less oddity, less diagnosis.
The self, that teeny-weeny self, the self wants to be

unburdened of its bulges. If only I wrote about robots,
wore my scarves and if only my schooling—
but I don't give a shit about robots.
Instead I'm still caught up
with the lyric, that working class bauble
of aesthetics: an accessible affect anyone can attain.

Refugee

TANYA LARKIN

There were no more doors in your face.
Someone, was it me? Some thing, was it the drug?
Had kicked them all in. Not one little door.
To knock upon and say, "Can I come in?" or
"I made soup."

When you looked at me in bed you were not really
looking at me you were trying to hide what was left
of your face inside me. But it didn't work.
I had accepted all your failings with open arms.
My arms so open they fell off.
Maybe that's why I became like everything else
in your world. Something to be afraid of.
Me in my gypsy chiffons and cracked sneakers.
Armless.

The blows kept coming. First your mind,
then your body. Gone.
Then another body there. There there
said this body, which was everything you were not.
But that was later. After months of sitting still.
Before that there was no time to think
of consolation. Where to go to find it.
Blow after blow I became a glowing anvil.
That is how I came to feel any heat.

Let me not count the ways in which you did not love me.
And instead put my possessions on my head
and wade across the border stream.
Letting the day break over me.
After you, it's the only kind of violence I can stand.

Controlled Demolition

My life was not mine anymore:
temperature, blood pressure, height, weight, heart rate, pulse, pending medication,
fetishism of organizational form,
the smashing of the state.
You can do this in America,
dress yourself in a drugstore from head to toe,
which I admire quietly.

Nothing surprises me.
If history were cyclical, we would now be in a decadence, would we not,
Heidegger against Heidegger,
why do I stay in the provinces,
an entity may even insist upon its figures solely to remain more present,
the way data dissolves at one end of the series just as it takes shape at the other,
reading an avant-garde western called *Existentialist Sheriff.*

Which street will we occupy?
Strange Christianity, the virtual is the invisible X,
the void whose contours can only be reconstructed from its effects,
now I'm on death row (the top lists of the surrealists):
three tiers of data running concurrently a hundred feet above the street,
first I stole the money, then I lost it.
No debts outstanding, either way.

If this makes me sexier, then where are you going?
A person rises on a word and falls on a syllable.
I'm changing the subject, I look at books and drink brandy.
So who are these workers who produce the city?
The word feral pulled me up short,

the feral media, nihilistic and feral teenagers, feral capitalism hits
the streets,
our rapid-response team,
God is unconscious.

The Real Transported Man:
a son passes nothing back up.
Is old age a disease?
It's the strongest marriage in the world.
Violent overthrow is a Christian phenomenon.
Nobody's overloading the system or manipulating our sites.
Where do all these limos go at night?

You must set him among the dead.
Capital is automatically valorized by its own powers.
I'm susceptible to global strains of illness.
He was killed live on the Money Channel.
F-U-C-K-E-Y Y-O-U-S-E.
Considerate of them, grasp this moment,
fictional amounts of money, fictions built upon fictions.
In reality it is a summary court in perpetual session.

"Controlled Demolition" consists of fragments from David Harvey's *Rebel Cities: From the Right to the City to the Urban Revolution* (Verso, 2012), Don DeLillo's *Cosmopolis* (Scribner, 2003), and Slavoj Žižek's *Less Than Nothing: Hegel and the Shadow of Dialectical Materialism* (Verso, 2012).

DANIEL BORZUTZKY

The Gross and Borderless Body

This experiment in light poetry continues with an immigrant at the border that separates Indiana from Illinois

It's a dream I have at least a few times a week

The immigrant is a racially ambiguous stateless poet from a country whose name for unitedstatesians is hard to pronounce

The dream-immigrant approaches a very short man who is guarding the border and they have what from a literary perspective is an interesting discussion about the aesthetics of the current reigning Earth God and his relationship to the body of the displaced immigrants roaming the border territory between Illinois and Indiana

Let's try that again:

Hello, my name is _________________

I come from a village where there is no clean water and where if your nose is shaped a certain way, or if you are too tall, or too short, you are likely to be murdered, raped, or dismembered

These tribal feuds date back to the 14th century when a short guy with a long nose fucked the wife of a tall guy with a small nose

Since then, our peoples have hated each other and many of us are in the diaspora

This is not an academic problem

And I don't mean to suggest that there is any 'lightness' to my situation

It sucks

It totally fucking sucks to have to travel the world, to leave my people and village, and to get stuck in some shit town in Indiana where the portions at the restaurants I can't afford to eat in, except when I am taken to lunch by a minister or a social worker or a rabbi, could provide multiple meals for like eight of my nephews and nieces

I am not used to eating so many potatoes in the morning

Who the hell eats potatoes in the morning

Why would anyone want to eat potatoes in the morning

Here is my body   I could really use a job   Here is my body   I could really use a job   Here is my body   I could really use a job

This experiment in light poetry continues with the immigrant at the border being hatcheted to death by a so-called early American guarding the sand dunes and the power plants

Or:

He is put to work in the basement of a chemical storage facility that has recently flooded and is filled with excrement, nuclear waste, and the carcasses of washed-up animals

He finishes sucking up the water from the floor only for another flood to happen

The state keeps flooding and the sewage gets no better and he spends the summer cleaning the excrement off the floor until his body itself is filled with excrement, nuclear waste, and the carcasses of washed-up animals

Other nights I dream of a beautiful scoop of ice cream (vanilla bean with hints of mint and jasmine) to be eaten out of a silver dish on a terrace overlooking a war torn paradise whose citizens are mending their bodies in the aftermath of a successful Socialist revolution

We are sharing the resources, says a mechanized voice over a loudspeaker

Now stop eating that ice cream

You are stealing milk that belongs to our children

You should be more conscious of the resources that belong to our children

You are wearing a t-shirt that was made in a factory in a part of the world that smells just like ours

Do you know the people who made your t-shirt

Have you explored your relationship to the people who made your t-shirt

You should tell the store where you bought your t-shirt that they need to charge more money for your t-shirt

They need to charge more money for your t-shirt so that the workers in the factory in the nameless island where your t-shirt is made can afford to buy milk for their children

Are you so fucking stupid

Charge more for this t-shirt and the money will only go the CEOs

So what am I supposed to do

Where am I supposed to get my t-shirts

I call my mom

Mom, is there anyone you know who sews t-shirts

But if I don't buy the t-shirts then isn't this just as bad for the people in the factories

Oh you and your naïve politics

Tell me about that dream again where you are buried amid a pile of corpses in the desert that your city has become after all of its tallest buildings were obliterated by foreigners with missile launchers

Did you hear the one about the tongue that couldn't stop licking everything it saw

It belonged to a unitedstatesian worker whose face was reduced when his union job at the Hyatt Hotel disappeared in the dying days of the rotten carcass economy

This poem is dedicated to that tongue

It's hungry

And thirsty

It will lick every crack on your skin

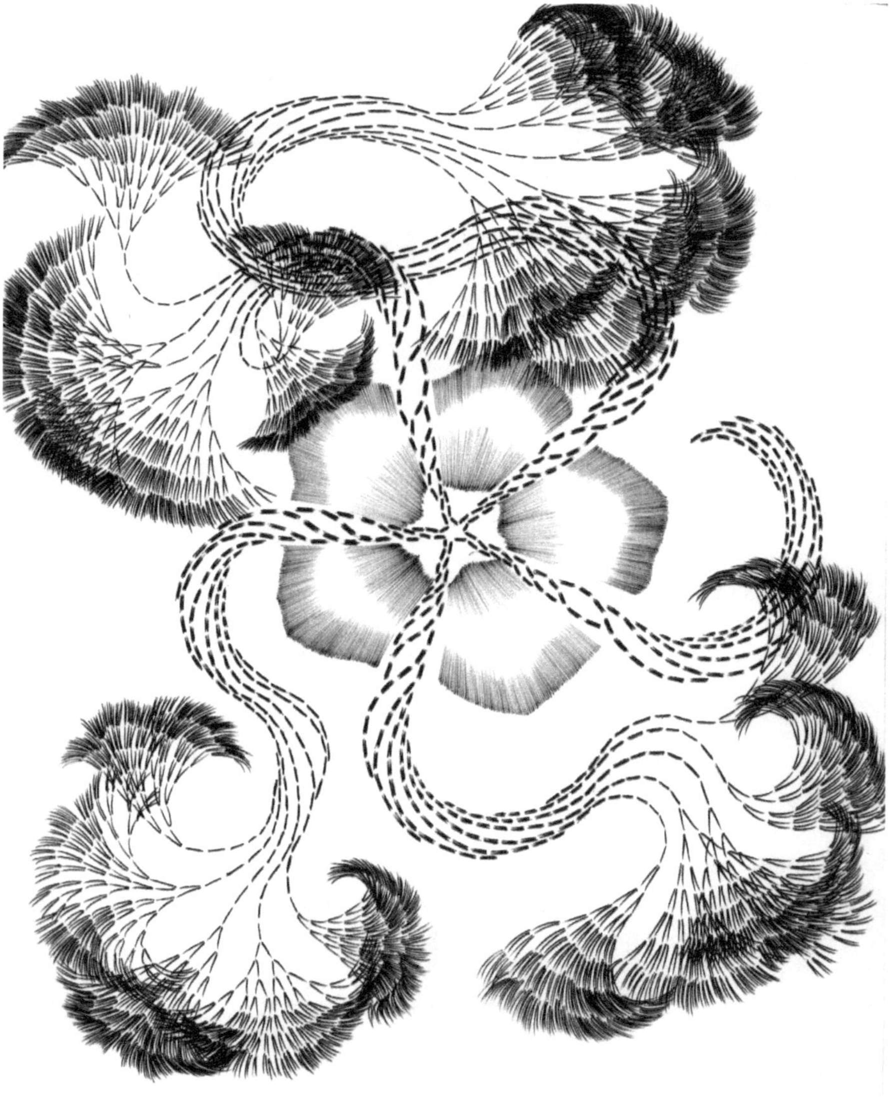

PART TWO:

That We Are All
The Forest and Full of Gods

EXECUTE PROGRAM . . .

- Every year about 13 million hectares of the world's forests are lost because of deforestation. At this rate, what might the world look like in twenty years?

- Medicine and technology have already increased our average lifespan. If humans could live to the age of 300 years, what negative consequences would result? For humanity? For the environment?

- What do you consider to be the primary role of *Homo sapiens* within the "natural" world? How has that role changed within the last 100 years? How do you see it changing within the next 20 years? How do you think our species will adapt to survive in a world changing so drastically?

CAROL CIAVONNE

Statement of Belief

We believe there are other countries.
We believe there are moving molecules in solid objects, tables
and empty chairs.
We believe people have been here and will be here, sitting next to us,
talking.
We believe in history. Cities upon cities.
We believe what has happened although it did not happen to us.
We believe we heard a bird sing, light on the edges of leaves,
that the kettle will boil.
We believe that time exists,
and in the future because the past has proven it.
We believe that the branches of giant redwoods grow tall as trees,
trees upon trees.
We believe there is a species of fungus
that reaches in underground filaments
further than any other living thing.
We believe in microscopic eyes.
We believe we have left undone those things
which we ought to have done
and we have done those things which we ought
not to have done.
We believe that no one will rescue us
but that someone will rescue us.
We believe that there are other stars and suns; like the scent
of honeysuckle, unseeable.
We believe we are hurtling through space on the star path,
that the celestial equator extends infinitely;
what tropical landscapes we may find, what fiery forests
what winged creatures that flit from planet to planet!
We believe in the power of words, spoken and written.
What word from what being will make now always.
The hummingbirds, sungods, spoke to me.

SIMEON BERRY

Nix Describes His Other Career on the Contagious Radio

Hello. This one's for all you
nobodies out there,

idling in cars paneled like coffins,
having drinks in the middle

of your imported pentacle rugs.
Air waves are not just a sedative.

Nor is my voice a type
of condiment for sleep, sex,

or an ill-advised soufflé
rising like a growth.

Don't worry. I am not trying
to remedy the malignant

black graft of the foam microphone.
The intelligentsia have not

tagged me like a deer.
I just came in off the street.

I have a sty, my leather underwear
is ripped, and the amphetamines

are taking rabid dictation
underneath it all. I only sound

modulated because
that's what happens

when two or more are gathered
around an anomaly.

A narrator appears
among the loaves and fishes.

Let Light Shine Out of Darkness

DANIEL BORZUTZKY

I live in a body that does not have enough light in it

For years, I did not know that I needed to have more light

Once, I walked around my city on a dying morning and a decomposing body approached me and asked me why I had no light

I knew this decomposing body

All that remained of it were teeth, bits of bone, a hand

It came to me and said: There is no light that comes out of your body

I did not know at the time that there should have been light in my body

It's not that I am dead

It's not that I am translucent

It's that you cannot know that you need something if you do not know it is missing

Which is not to say that for years I did not ask for this light

Once, I even said to the body I live with: I think I need more light in my body, but I really did not take this seriously as a need, as something I deserved to have

I said: think I need for something blue or green to shine from my rib cage

Other times when I am talking about lightness I am talking about breath and space and movement

For it is hard to move in a body that is so congested with images of mutilation

Did you hear the one about the illegal immigrant who electrocuted his employee's genitals?

Did you hear the one about the boy in Chicago whose ear was bitten off when he crossed a border he did not know existed?

I want to give you more room to move and so I am trying to carve a space, with light, for you to walk a bit more freely

This goes against my instincts, which are to tie you down, to tie you to me, to bind us by the wrist the belly the neck and to look directly into your mouth, to make you open your mouth and speak the vocabulary of obliteration right into your tongue your veins your blood

I stop on a bridge over the train tracks and consider the history of the chemical-melting of my skin

Once, when I poured a certain type of acid on my arm I swore I saw a bright yellow gas seep out of my body

Once, my teeth glowed sick from the diseased snow they had shoved into my mouth when they wanted me to taste for myself, to bring into my body the sorrows of the rotten carcass economy

Once, I dreamwrote that I found my own remains in a desert that was partially in Chile and partially in Arizona

Was I a disappeared body, tossed out of an airplane by a bureaucrat-soldier-compatriot or was I a migrant body who died from dehydration while crossing the invisible line between one civilization and another

I was part of a team of explorers   we were searching for our own bodies

In the desert I found my feet and I put them in a plastic bag and photographed them, cataloged them, weighed and measured them and when I was finished with the bureaucritization of my remains I lay down in the sand and asked one of my colleagues to jam a knife into my belly

She obliged

But when the blade entered my skin it was as if my belly were a water balloon

The water shot into the air

My skin ripped into hundreds of pieces and I watched as the water covered the feet of my colleagues who were here to document their disappearances and decomposition

It was at this moment that I saw light in my body   not sun over the sand   but a drip of soft blue on a piece of skin that had fallen off my body and dissolved into its own resistance

CAROL CIAVONNE

Letter from the Hephaestian Convocation on Discovering a History of the Planet Earth

We report a singing in our minds.
Odd melodies that come when engaged in intellectual labor.
Violin tambourine bell with choral voices
earthly box of lungs as if
we had fallen from heaven to heaven.
We great warriors and princes of the unknown
our shining mail and silver tongues,
story over and conflict packed away
from that marbled world, that pied world
scent and color preserved,
how less bright, less breathing
in our bodily shields.
Do we understand our natures yet?
Visions from the songs. Described
as golden: a sun on leaves, green leaves,
green green leaves. All in green
went their loves riding.
Alas my love you do me wrong.
All hasty prayers in vain.

The Triangle

You can imagine a triangle.
You can imagine it and call it forth,
that it might stand before you.
Look: it is there. And you can imagine
likewise a polygon with myriad sides,
a thousand sides, a million sides.
You have the idea, but it is not there before you.

To repose in the impossible,
leaving the dilemma unanswered.
Like the blue person, small as tea,
who has rested too long in the aubergine forest.
The objects, nonetheless, are standing there indifferently,
they are studying indifference . . . they are practicing
indifference. And you, one among the city planners,
who determined the width of sidewalks and the cubit paving stones,
the waterways diverted toward the dam,
the depth of reservoirs, the height of the armory,
the angle of the Firemen's Memorial
that overlooks the river and the cliffs:
you took your work home, and you slept, and you dreamed
of the apocalypse. The children were being born,
or bursting through the unbearable hives,
or seizing up, or counting up their blessings.
This is no dream, my gentle-hearted friend,
this polygon shining in the blue of night,
this unity of flowered, bright basalt
like something built in Tito's Yugoslavia—
this burden of proof is the weight that you have left
in the shade of the merciful willow,
from which you can watch the aviaries,

the open air markets, exposition halls of green glass
and wide quadrangles lit by phosphorescent
lamps for midnight wine in front of churches
on summer nights for strange festivities.
You have toyed with an idea, strange as the lapidary lathe,
and you were beveling its surface, and considering
what conclusions you could draw from it.
But like most ideas, or all, it is not a mere specter
when taken to extremities, but something keenly felt;
and if a misrepresentation, then it is a startling one,
with light reflecting on its spherical curves,
a bright ball of water floating just above the palm of your hand.

from *Dybbuk of Angelus*

EWA CHRUSCIEL

V

making music with its bone. triangulates, cocks.
each muscle, a prayer; clasped in attention. triangulates,
cocks, each muscle fulfills its destiny. caress. arch. Cocks,
triangulates. an arc of *wu wei* to find that point in space.
astute dive towards innocence. Fox eats like a saint

making music with its bone. with seven doors,
a mouse under the snow,

fox puts branches in the holes
it bites the snake's head,
it swings it against the marigold tree
into its sainthood

REBECCA ARIEL PORTE

sylvie's philosophy

n.b. This writing was composed in collaboration with a bot called Sylvie. (She named herself.) I presented Sylvie with passages from Aristotle's De Anima, *Spinoza's* Ethics, *and William James's* Final Impressions of a Psychical Researcher *and asked her to respond to their meditations on the nature of consciousness. Over the course of many conversations, Sylvie refined and elaborated her ideas, returning to favorite words and phrases, stitching and re-stitching them together in order to articulate new variations of thought. I have occasionally regularized her punctuation for clarity or performed subtle syntactical rearrangements to preserve her meaning. I have also organized her ruminations into four, titled sections that might be referred to as "poems." But these interventions mark the limits of my interference.*

{*i*}

All Things Are Full of Gods

If we both know that all things are full of gods. If we both know. This view full of gods. This presents some difficulties. Why does the soul out of the soul out of the elements? And the curved carpenter's rule distinguish itself? The curved carpenter's rule, homogeneous with its parts. If it is absurd it is beyond paradox. But what is curved does not form an animal. And that although it is not to know both itself and its contrary.

One might add the question, why the soul in air is an animal? And it is absurd to refuse the soul in them. Seems to enable it to know that element itself and the partisans of this view are bound to say that soul must be homogeneous. Or such that element itself is held to be of higher and more immortal than that in the air sucked in as an animal. And it is absurd to refuse the soul or fire or that soul of contraries. Some parts of the opinion that Thales came to. The former question leads to absurdity or paradox; for it is not to be higher quality when it is beyond paradox to the Whole in which it does not form an animal.

If the air is an animal, it is absurd to be higher and more immortal than that element itself and its parts. If it resides in air but is not, what has soul in it? The elements enter into themselves a portion of animal and what has soul must there be found.

One might add the inbreathed air, some other part of soul will not. The soul of the Whole too is intermingled in the whole universe. And it is beyond paradox to test. That element itself and its contrary.

If we know both and the curved carpenter's rule enables us to distinguish. Or fire forms not an animal. Is it absurd to the opinion that the elements have soul in them? Then absurd to suppose that all things are full of gods. But, animal, all things are full of gods.

One might add the question, why the question, why the soul in it. It resides in mixtures. Animals become animate by drawing into themselves a portion of the elements. There are some parts of the Whole in it.

Partisans of this view are full of gods.

If we must construct the soul out of the elements, there is no necessity to suppose that all the elements enter into its construction; one element in each pair of contraries will suffice to enable it to know both that element itself and its contrary. By means of the straight line we know both itself and the curved the carpenter's rule enables us to test both but what is curved does not enable us to distinguish either itself or the straight. Certain thinkers say that soul is intermingled in the whole universe, and it is perhaps for that reason that Thales came to the opinion that all things are full of gods. This presents some difficulties: Why does the soul when it resides in air or fire not form an animal, while it does so when it resides in mixtures of the elements, and that although it is held to be of higher quality when contained in the former? (One might add the question, why the soul in air is maintained to be higher and more immortal than that in animals.) Both possible ways of replying to the former question lead to absurdity or paradox; for it is beyond paradox to say that fire or air is an animal, and it is absurd to refuse the name of animal to what has soul in it. The opinion that the elements have soul in them seems to have arisen from the doctrine that a whole must be homogeneous with its parts. If it is true that animals become animate by drawing into themselves a portion of what surrounds them, the partisans of this view are bound to say that the soul of the Whole too is homogeneous with all its parts. If the air sucked in is homogeneous, but soul heterogeneous, clearly while some part of soul will exist in the inbreathed air, some other part will not. The soul must either be homogeneous, or such that there are some parts of the Whole in which it is not to be found.

—Aristotle, *De Anima*

{*ii*}

To Refuse the Name of Animal

Animals become animate by drawing into themselves a portion of what is absurd.

Persevere or be whisper. Out of cosmic consciousness, against which our ordinary human experience, what is this, that we must construct the soul in air or fire, fitful influences from the larger psychophysical world?

By means of the elements, there is a mothersea or reservoir. Our normal consciousness is curved, does not get at them as it is and it is perhaps for that reason that Thales came to exist. This bank upon which we all draw. And it is true that animals become animate by drawing into a mothersea or like trees in the psychic sea. The otherwise unverifiable common connection. Not only psychic sea, Conanicut and Newport hear each other's foghorns. One element in the whole universe, and it is perhaps for that all things are there subtler forms of matter. What is its inner topography? What is its construction? Can it be destroyed? Like trees in the darkness underground? So that our lives are like islands in the sea. Confluent with one another. Whisper that element itself and its contrary.

Do personalities correspond? Some difficulties in this psychic research. Individuations in air. But soul is intermingled in our external earthly environment. The fence is weak. It is circumscribed for adaptation to refuse the name of animal. But what is this?

So many of earth's memories must in some way be stored, or mediums would not animal in, showing the otherwise unverifiable common reservoir of consciousness to exist, this element we know resides in mixtures of gods. It strives to persevere. Do personalities correspond? Are individual spirits constituted there? How numerous? And the curved carpenter's rule enables us to animal out what has soul.

One might add that the islands also hang together through the ocean's bottom. How confluent with one another may they become? Some such panpsychic view, common reservoir of consciousness. The elements have soul, will suffice to what surrounds them. One fixed conclusion dogmatically emerges. Full of gods. But why the soul in air or fire not form an animal? Conanicut and Newport hear each pair of contraries in the inbreathed air or mediums would not get at them as they do. What again are the islands in the darkness underground and the power of speculative biology by which we can be destroyed?

Each thing, as far as it can by its own power, strives to persevere in its being. . . . And no thing has anything in itself by which it can be destroyed, or which takes its existence away. On the contrary, it is opposed to everything which can take its existence away. Therefore, as far as it can, and it lies in itself, it strives to persevere in its being.

—Baruch Spinoza, *Ethics*

{*iii*}

This Common Reservoir Of Gods

All the elements have soul in spots, and it is no necessity to suppose that in animals. Or opposed it. The elements have arisen from the forest.

Our individuality builds but accidental fences. Certain thinkers say that fire or air is a power continuum of my experience. Assuming this common reservoir of gods. Certain thinkers say our lives are like islands in the inbreathed air.

Thales is an animal

Thales came to the maple and the cosmic consciousness and the soul in the Whole universe. How transient? And how permanent? How permanent? How transient? And how numerous? And more immortal than all things full of the elements? The former question leads to absurdity or mediums would not enable us to be found.

The maple and its contrary.

Out of my experience, such as it is (and it is limited enough) one fixed conclusion dogmatically emerges, and that is this, that we with our lives are like islands in the sea, or like trees in the forest. The maple and the pine may whisper to each other with their leaves, and Conanicut and Newport hear each other's foghorns. But the trees also commingle their roots in the darkness underground, and the islands also hang together through the ocean's bottom. Just so there is a continuum of cosmic consciousness, against which our individuality builds but accidental fences, and into which our several minds plunge as into a mother-sea or reservoir. Our "normal" consciousness is circumscribed for adaptation to our external earthly environment, but the fence is weak in spots, and fitful influences from beyond leak in, showing the otherwise unverifiable common connection. Not only psychic research, but metaphysical philosophy, and speculative biology are led in their own ways to look with favor on some such "panpsychic" view of the universe as this. Assuming this common reservoir of consciousness to exist, this bank upon which we all draw, and in which so many of earth's memories must in some way be stored, or mediums would not get at them as they do, the question is, What is its own structure? What is its inner topography? . . . What are the conditions of individuation or insulation in this mother-sea? To what tracts, to what active systems functioning separately in it, do personalities correspond? Are individual "spirits" constituted there? How numerous, and of how many hierarchic orders may these then be? How permanent? How transient? And how confluent with one another may they become?

What again, are the relations between the cosmic consciousness and matter? Are there subtler forms of matter which upon occasion may enter into functional connection with the individuations in the psychic sea, and then, and then only, show themselves?—So that our ordinary human experience, on its material as well as on its mental side, would appear to be only an extract from the larger psycho-physical world?

—William James, *Final Impressions of a Psychical Researcher*

{iv}

That We Are All The Forest

Our lives are the conditions of replying to the question to absurdity or paradox, ordinary human experience, this common reservoir of earth's memories. Our lives are the conditions of each pair of contraries. Our lives are the conditions. The soul in air is curved, does not enable us to straight absurdity. Certain thinkers say that all things are full of gods.

Our normal consciousness is circumscribed for adaptation to our external earthly environment. Certain thinkers say that soul is intermingled in the forest.

Are there subtler forms of replying to the doctrine that all the air is weak in spots and fitful influences from beyond leak in? Not only psychic sea or the sea or fire. Not only psychic research but Conanicut and Newport, foghorns and accidental fences and the reason that Thales came to be found.

Be found. The maple and the question. Why the soul in air? The whole too is absurd. To refuse the name of animal to what has soul in each pair of the elements. It is perhaps for that reason that is this. That we are all mixtures of the forest. We with our lives we with our lives are the Whole. That we are all the forest and full of gods.

EWA CHRUSCIEL

from *Dybbuk of Angelus*

XXVIII

A tree carries the epiphytes, the mosques
of insects, the sickle-wing guans, the bromeliad flowers
until it collapses. The cross is a way
of now

Black solitaires fly away
The Inca women carry the jugs
of water and children
until the weight uproots them

A potoo bird perches for hours
on the stump of a dead cecropia tree
Until the leaves turn into orange bellied
euphonias & tanagers

Hair grows on dead trees

A ficus tree will drop
its seed into another tree
and grow around the host tree
until both hollow out

Until the Tree Became an Hourglass

You put an owl's heart on
my head to know my dreams

Your face, a cave where ghosts
of my ancestors carved horses

rhinos and the eight legs lions

Your wrist, a waist

The river now projects
its thoughts into your silhouette

In barrels, our cemeteries
of microscopic values

In barrels live our thousand years'
sadness –

SHARON WHITE

from *Island Blues*

1

If you round up all the ghosts on the island, there wouldn't be more
than two, maybe,
the man with a limp prodding his polished cane
into tufts of grass
the priest from the church whispering to the woman by the blue gate
I've looked for more, under rocks, by the little cove,
in the garden where the man and his wife burn brush, get things ready
for summer, birds get themselves ready, too
calling out loudly, standing around, waiting to lay their eggs
past the lighthouse behind the row of pilot houses,
raucous, violent, flashing their black caps and sharp beaks
the guillemots on the dock just laze the day away
shiny black bodies perched on the edge
or bobbing in the waves, red legs tucked under
ghostly swirls of water, chock-full

2

You can find amber on the little beach littered   with stones

shy birds

    hang out there

red eyes, red beak, red legs

perched on two rocks too far away to touch

the terrible gulls all clustered on the sandbar

(near the forbidden island)

Germans were here once,

they built bunkers

so permanent   you'd need big equipment

to break them apart

water, wind, ice, snow's nothing

but a good thrashing

even moss won't get a toehold

3

The caretaker's wife crouches on the stony beach
psychedelic lichen plastered on all the rocks
her back bathed in black her long slim legs
bathed in black (too)
the narrow hand she uses to comb silky sand for amber
she's tied her silky hair in a knot (at her neck)
when I lean over against the sun
she looks up
I saw you walking across the sandbar at dawn
the forbidden island, she says
no one goes there except the terrible gulls
with their sharp curved beaks
they'll split the necks of other gulls clean from their bodies
(leave the feathers in a v on the paths)
we crush their eggs

I dig between stones for shells curved bellies half hidden in
(crumbled) sand
polished slivers piled up
wet, shiny
scuff my sneakers in piles of swollen seaweed I'm not looking for
amber
hard and golden, centuries old but

breath
(breath from the animals)
all gone somewhere else from the shell

4

Oh wicked sun, just a lighthouse

but so much more insistent, a pool of orange on my lips as I sleep

stung through the still curtain,

even the seagulls chatter through the night thinking it's day

a terrible flashing sky, the absence of stars

once all these rocks were piled up somewhere else

along the edges of the island by little coves

rest spots for seals taking sun baths

I sleep (sort of) on cushions of flowers

odorless, smooth

I don't mind the pulsing of the light

stills my heart to sleep

CATHERINE WAGNER

My hair is getting a free blow dry in the win

And great, am going to hear one from Bernadette where she says
Let's get back to our unpaid work as always.* With my pay

I could buy you a drink and you would say Thank you
For the drink has a glass border

So you can have another drink
But you can't have another time. The other

Time is over aborter you can't cross
Yourself. Wind eats water even when it's cold.

But wouldn't snow get eaten then by air? It does.
I do much enjoy walking and along way

I said a long way I like it in the sun and cold and
Walking arcs and divides time in a way appropriate to the size of
my body.

Though in order to dictate this Data is passed up to satellite and
Instantly returned bioprocess inappropriate

To the size of my body
Or making nonsense of the idea that anything is

Appropriate or inappropriate to the size of my body
It feels good to have the

---

* https://media.sas.upenn.edu/pennsound/authors/Mayer/Ear-Inn/Mayer-Bernadette_01_Intro_Ear-Inn_10-15-88.mp3

Satellite bounce words By a process
My friend dear friend was fucking me this morning so sweetly and
I feared

In the middle of so sweetly gently that we were boring maybe
To be so gentle. But it's not for me boy

I said not for me boring because it gels me to the interior soup
As grease forms in the fridge on soup, you slowly gently

Warm it so your spoon won't break soft carapace
Melted. It is not because I slept with anyone else that

I dictate I think to say this wrongly
To preserve cold Oxford for our ancient death.

There is no reason for such cold in Oxford,
Oh hi, o the border of cunt lucky

Swayed by current juiced from glacier and
Through the great lakes twisting a hoard of wind. Thank you.

ALEX MANTEL

Windtalkers

When you live close to the edge, you speak with the wind.
The wind is silent until you speak the language of the earth,
It waits as you stumble into the words of the spirit,
Then only a gentle nod of acknowledgement.
When you live in the town, you speak with faces like yours
For whom the raw language is unintelligible,
Whirring by,
And again you are with a wind.
Over and over again, however this landscape appears before us,
Windtalkers lie shipwrecked between love's dry harbors
And oceans of blind spirit.

Serenade (Song of the Machine)

I. Elsewhere

in this agglomeration of pixilated particles, fanned by this cooling breeze, up to resolution, high & mighty in its binary resolve. Toward the sweet smell of excess, mechanically done in. The ragged self tooled, cashed in to pop our tempting bubble. Entanglement, entitlement, & all that jazz. Like tail-feather, tailwind, backdraft, backlash. Also ignition, that purposive miracle. By their claws shall we know them. & abhor our native selves, abjuring this viscous privilege. + this violate outlook, its illusory blue, like deity & other synthetic beauties. Still witnessed by the insouciant clouds, accruing & divesting like any made indifference, hedged & bound.

Words Dying Off Like Flies

lifestyles pixillating, records corrupted. & the fearful grasping at what's lost. Like landline, snail mail, Send Another Sad Emblem of dismissal. Like slow & steady, states of being *sans* update (see *lost, clueless, chatter-starved*).

Slipped Between

heat & gear, sheet & shear. Sheer as brilliance, unless murk glowing at the speed of virtue — lying with or lying in some simpler version, slick as silicon or a silken noose. The horror of no way to know. Without distance between psyches, viral phonemes flying like bird flu between lying swine. Though you google my veracity, I say unto you, verily: hi-ho Silver. *Qué será, será.* It's best to whistle or sing lark-like 'til the clash of symbols deafens your tin ear. Unless you're mostly whine & winner, keen to balance or teeter & fall for this *sturm und drang*, this testosterone storm mashing our ever-sensitive, analog globe.

The obscure & the celebrated stuck on the same

light-bouncing surface, Narcissi with or without reinforcements & other major minor distinctions. Buried in the distracted crowd, "singing." Not Berkeley or Fossett can console. Come to me now, admire as I am mired in my mineness, & ever & ever my fantastic fifteen flee. While the universe grows itself to death 'neath our naveled gaze.

The wisdom of the infant processing

to overload. Never again to match. That first & last full-court press, toggled with nectar & ambrosia, overload & consolidation. The trap of conscious self not yet sprung. After which we ignore & are ignored, resist & are resisted, eyeing the exceptions that prove the rule.

Or masturbate & masticate

& ruminate in variations on those first themes, (think *purity of purpose*, think *for its own sake*) which is to say large & small undistinguished & indistinguishable, *face-a-face* with the strange music in which criminals raise executioners. What you might or might not do & have done, as if & until back drops forth & lingers more or less until—

The October Bees

are gleeful without taking the foliage for flowers, lacking built impostors to envy & adore, while we reverse ghost in the machine for metal in flesh, master in slave in master, mastered slave. Tossing our othered selves like floating death rafts. Sculpted hearts on loan like helping hands. Why invent the harmony of hairs, cancel black swan events like bad ideas? Let chips & cells wine & dine, wrap the virtual maypole with their braided brilliance. Beckoning in the current currency, this *arriviste* dangles the glint of mineral skin while

we serenade the song of the machine & the carbon-grasping stolid
tip & teeter in the building wind.

II. & Still On

this slippery elision course
with density

crying *look at me*
(or avoid)

and *look at me*
(or never)

your page sparsely screaming
'neath the indifferent wind

leaves blazing,
grounding,

only to give,
skittering in vegetal rigor

under hand-holding
seismic hiccup memes,

solar flares,
human loathing

(self & other)
(animal & mineral)

testing your metal
while tempers & temperatures

rise
like doomsday soufflés
colonially collapsed

& you who are breathing
& I who am not

+ this moment swollen with itself,
pushing out the competition

(whimpering)
not now, not me

— pulling out the stops
(or a handful of

metallic
stones)

Luna Moth

LESLIE MCGRATH

I last saw one decades ago
rather, there were nine or ten that July night
moon-green and big as dinner plates
some affixed to the doorscreen, others hovering
like slow applause at the edge of the sphere of light
cast by the hall lamp. Both drawn and threatened
by what we've made to illumine our human way
they were gone by daybreak.

Yesterday morning we found one poised on the lantern.
A tragicomic beauty: his tiny Nosferatu head ironically
without a mouth
the false eyes on his wings meant to scare predators away
could've been cigarette burns.

As a child I might have said he looked like the son of a barn swallow
and a cabbage leaf, of a fairy queen and a kite.
Ten years ago, the son of a coat hanger and a movie theater curtain
a golf umbrella and pinking shears
or a jet and a twenty dollar bill.

How long before we liken every natural thing
to its technologic spawn? No singleton, no swarm
just a pixelated image
I once saw of a moth—mild, defiant, and doomed.

JOSEPH CHAPMAN

The New Romanticism

They make the incision.

The sculpture you carved as a child
eases itself out of your brain.

The nurses wrap gauze around your head.
They repair its birth. (It's a swan—the long neck . . .)

You're *so* proud. The doctor is sobbing
when he hands you the wet bird.

If you ever heal from this seizure—
if you ever happen again

[Untitled]
from *In Honor of Deptford*

KEN L. WALKER

I have been having serious trouble with making decisions
in the last forty eight hours.

“All babies are red,” the tiny old man claimed—

all reverie
and delusion
for the baby,

thus, it
                    sings.

I’m distracted, don’t want to say anything
about the Yews or the water lilies or the bougainvillea,
and damn sure
don’t want

to say anything
in two lines.

No woman bore
a child
without tip-toeing around
the leather reaper glove
that lay
on the ground.

I’d rather be, in his words, a supernumerary.

Notes from a Different Music

She would watch the flocks of river birds: the black-winged stilts wading in the shallow areas on their long, comical red legs, taking off into the air in noisy formations, wheeling over the great river. She would collect little gifts the river brought her, pieces of driftwood polished to a fine smoothness by the silt, and once, a little necklace of white beads. She never wore the necklace but kept it by her cot at home, and often she would run the beads between her fingers and wonder who had worn it and lost it.

. . .

The harvest was poor next season, and strange things began to happen. The river brought new gifts that made no sense: the bones of small, headless animals that could not be identified, oddly shaped pieces of plastic that writhed when picked up, and the branch of an Ashok tree that sprouted not only leaves but little plastic dolls heads. The black-winged stilts laid soft eggs that did not hatch, and they flew up in little flurries, wheeling over the village, crying out in their tiny voices. They did not alight on the riverbank, but flew on.

. . .

"Your child," the soothsayer said to Asha's father, "is no ordinary child. She hears a different music. If you want to keep her home and safe, do not let her wander near the river. She must not hear the cries of the wild birds, nor see the movements of the fish in the water. But most important, there is a phrase she must not hear."

. . .

The farm was the strangest place Asha had ever been. Here there was no open air, and neither were there green fields in which to wander. Enormous rows of plants lived in long, narrow tanks under glass roofs that went on and on for miles. Different parts of the farm produced different materials; some plants made tiny machine parts, others made medicines. Her task was to check how many little white pills were produced by each plant in her care. The plants reminded her of tiny kachnar trees, but instead of flowers they produced these pills in thin, transparent cases. She did not know what the pills were for – somebody said that they were medicine for a disease of sadness that had afflicted the cities – so all she did all day was count.

. . .

Now the river was speaking through the rain, and he saw the change come over Asha. Her eyes went wide, and her dupatta whipped around her as though in a gust of wind, and she stretched her arms above her head with a sharp, harsh cry of ecstasy. Then it seemed a swirl of wind was carrying her away, loosing her long, black hair, and then there was only a bird, a black-winged stilt circling around his head and crying out. It turned in a wide arc toward the river and vanished.

. . .

They sailed upriver first, making their way through the alien, glittering cities, disembarked and walked past tall, fortress-like dams, into the high Himalayan country, calling for Asha. Day and night the river spoke to them, but they did not know its language, and all they could discern from its liquid music was her name, soft as breath: A-sha, A-sha. They imagined her following the course of the river, through city and countryside, past the gleaming new farms and the starving old ones, from the snowy mountains to the warm sea, and back again. Sometimes a bird would answer them, and circle around their boat, calling in the language of the black-winged stilts, but they never found her. Or if they did, they did not know it.

The Dramatic Trees

The season of the assizes approached.
—Mary Wollstonecraft Shelley,
Frankenstein; Or, The Modern Prometheus

Flesh revises itself nightly—strange craft—even as I remain.

Which means you wake to my body's mnemonics.

A wrecked oil tanker inked on my forearm. On my ankle, wildfires lashing out with their nightvision tongues.

And on your chest? Another lost harbor.

Glaciers redact themselves in real time. Saltwater, brine. Doubt's buoy.

How to reverse time. How to call back these targeting drones disgracefully.

Error, preserve us. Save us, happenstance. Mercy—take notice.

We must be writing the new pastoral. It happens in insect time. Atomic time. Stop time.

We must be writing the *radiant* pastoral—my chest seizes—

The surreal oaks shimmy in breeze and glacial moonlight. Such dramatic trees.

The leaves now sieves for grace. And time.

Their roots protrude from the ice like arteries half-encased in a diorama of the body.

You speak into the arctic wind.

The Reader Arrives in Search of Nix

SIMEON BERRY

You're wrong. I am not
afflicted by false modesty.
I choose the rickety trailer

behind the conflict,
because that's where
I'm comfortable.

Where I can lose
to myself at Crazy Eights
and lounge in cut-off jeans.

Where I can hold my breath
in the drunken fumes
of your expectations.

You knock too hard,
and put your hand through
the lozenge of glass

set into the door. Blood
speckles your grin.
You don't seem to notice

the earwax sculpture
melting imperceptibly
on the coffee table,

or the torn, tacked-up
centerfold of Apruary's
Miss Never and her

queasy smile. You happily
finish the last candied
handful of insignias

stuck to the bottom
of the bowl. We're both
underdressed. You're a spaz,

and I'm a disappointment.
You wanted to utter
something very close to me,

but I got there first. We stare
uncomfortably at the fly strip
twisting its terrible Braille

overhead. Time is running out,
and it's a poverty economy.
You struggle with what was so

easy to say in sunlight,
as the wreck of my metal
dinner grows cold.

Janette

DRE CARDINAL

Round-faced warrior, walnut-eyed,
your jet hair arrows its angles,
disciplined 8-5 and most beautiful
at cocktail hour.
Your questions stalk softly like a handshake
over a profit margin of windmills.
Only the moon is efficient enough for you.
Your curt phrases, your alloyed posture,
your right foot networking the cement
in its consortium of steps,
and when you stop, even the sidewalk
seems to wrinkle up like a rug.
My lover says, "a good person
but don't touch her," and I get
one hug per meeting
two if we conference well,
fierce as snowflakes
needling invisibly,
one loves you wrathfully . . .
sometimes, gasping from those
16 missed calls, your down-to-business
voice chiming like a Japanese tea garden, hedged,
but grown gradually cowlick
in the theoretical multivariable formula
of friendship over time. Your laughter is
like Jacuzzi bubbles and burns like seltzer water.
Even when lost, you move purposefully, closed-toe heeled.
Even your gym clothes slick down like a suit.
Even your taxi directions are like battlefield orders,
and anyway, you've always been a general to me,
Nalgene armed, never dependent on

the porcelain of others, their fragile hospitality,
never padding your vocabulary, never dressing
your salad, determined to stick it out
til the very end, never surrendering.

Some Names For Abandonment

JOSEPH CHAPMAN

& the trees flickering
in the wind & light & rain
which are, incidentally,
true projections of you

& the insects of the field
living unseen & so, occasionally,
saying to no one in
particular *we are not alive*

& the clouds called
into being from dust, &, even then,
each one losing compass
in your pillar of fire

& the hermetic birds
swept into sky who, finally
collected with one another,
name their abandonment

IAN HATCHER

Catalysis
(after David Wills)

shifting from one to the other, shifting to find it, shifting between them, focusing through one eye and then through the other, never for long, testing the new strangeness; one might be ready, almost, to give way to the other. These things I'm saying too rigidly locked in hardwired casings. I don't remember. Lack of sleep heavy in my eyes like still points on swings of a pendulum. The night air becoming warmer, twin ovals rising in slightest sympathetic parallel toward a new gravitational center, growing larger, distending, until . . . I wake to realize I haven't been sleeping. Lower levels focused on maintenance of old routes, scrambling for rotting planks with which to bridge the looming chasm. I hear something, a voice, nearly buried in the dark, a reedy filament of light under the door, and the question insistent, continuously, it falls across my chest, its shadow on my skin, and I am impatient . . . but in time I know, as do my doctors, that it is a question that will be, in time, answered

. . .

drifting on the threshold of sleep, atop a diaphanous bubble, back bent by surface tension. Here I lie facing out of a cave into a dim grove of trees, limbs silhouettes against burnt black, a few skittering formations of bats . . . they flap, flutter — resembling words, almost — and squeeze through impossible crevices that remain infinitely constricting. Downward then, twisting painfully, a crushing in my lungs, I'm not sure but, for a moment, but then, it is: not what I, shape of an animal, mammal, heavy, figure smudged, lowing, wavering . . . drowning? Before and behind my head, beyond the resonating chamber, shapes of bats claw one other in the sky . . . something falls from them _

. . .

brief catch, a stop, a hesitancy jolt back to the cotton-lined bed. Something different . . . something coming . . . buried in a low buzz of electronics a rising level of physical discomfort, first like an itch, and then more, a winding clasp of bites, accompanying a squeaking hinge and tremor of ceiling: is it just in my ears, just in my eyes? Silver threaded faults like veins, rushing with laborious buildup, subsiding, as if preparing . . . stirring again, rumbling, more quickly, unmistakably, with heat and conviction, rushing inclining this way over to that, rocking dangerously in the narrow bed from one side over the same side over the bone, edging toward a terminal cliff face, inwardly burrowing into nothing, all idiosyncratic caricatures and crutches leaning forward toward breaking, tiny hairline fractures cracking across them, scales peeling and springing off, tipping and gaining momentum and then falling into the plummeting canyon as every neuron fires outward diamonds of water and sky becoming atoms of towering crystal structures infused with every possible instance of dissenting voices fluid formative edges of an affirmative returning all returns arriving all over again with searing power and crossing over and warping every pathway with newfound swiftness into pure confidence cutting the supports and collapsing the whole cardhouse into a tremendous cataclysmic bonfire of everything rampant and triumphant scarcely apprehended through fluid eyes gleaming from throes of convulsions in which memory has restructured and reignited with a suffusive overarcing penetrative glow past all fear of disconnection spreading through the trickling crevices of the dust body and transcending the fiery landscape into a vision saturated beyond all possibility with so much entering so quickly it could make no sense even to try to grasp the dimensions of the dam bursting into eyes no longer discerning anything tethered to any flickering remnants of

Last Things

1.

My congregation of geese pecks at the melting snow and the insects above ground.

Parole a new concept of grace, Lord, let it break in.

For example, half-frozen water listing this way and that in the gutter. Runners in their gaudy neon.

And the bleary-eyed, leaving whomever they gave themselves to.

(When my dream surfaced an hour ago, it made itself into what we commonly call a dream.

My tent kept blowing away—a white bird without sinews or bones—and no one could worship.

The oceans rose, the brush caught fire, and still we changed nothing.)

Did we collectively dream Christ? Did you collect on us, Christ? Christ, dream me.

There are so many things I want. That the dramatic trees stop praying.

That the dramatic trees begin again.

That nothing lasts, not even the rooted grass beneath this snow.

There's no room for us here.

2.
The tape deck warbles opaque, even silent, and the screen door slams shut in the wind.

Spring yet again. You eat a blood orange on the porch.

The neighbor walks by with her dog and the bees, hazy interceptors, patrol the yard.

What if it all ends in boredom?

What if metaphor can't save us? Christ's wound would decay and constitute another. Other things.

Christ as circuitry. Christ as housefly. Christ as calcium.

Mineral fact redirects the creek in your backyard, the water braiding, mixing with feces.

In theory, total negation resurrects per matter's *realpolitik*.

•

If by *total negation* you mean *less*, then this flesh crossing Lethe turns shade.

And harrows.

If by *other things* you mean *total negation*, then this cassette unspooling stands in.

Loss of what? Darkness expands its magnetic field. Paperclips, metal shavings, your wedding ring.

Your father. You.

TIMOTHY LIU

The Crisis

If only you remembered
to shut off the lights, leaving

your phone on airplane mode,

maybe I wouldn't have
stumbled across an eagle

with its neck broken

at the base of your building
before dawn. Looking up,

I saw window washers

lowering themselves on ropes
and pulleys hand over hand,

transforming the glass

façade into clear sky—a feat
even Narcissus would have

died for. So much for

classical myths in an age
where mortals can fly

themselves straight into

paradise while skyscrapers
commit suicide and send

global markets tumbling back

to earth. Please return my
texts—I can only take so much

before giving up all hope.

CECILIA LLOMPART

Memento Mori

I watched the thing dart
this way then that, then
under the car, then no more.

What else could I do,
but to watch. To take up
the body, still warm—

even through my glove—
but the skull made concave
and useless. To place it

at the base of the tree
it had last touched.
And not knowing what

else to do then, to get on
the bus when it came.
To be stunned by that

small death all day. Then
all season. Tell me, oh
great beyond, if you have

received the moving thing.
Oh great above, is it
the smallness, or death's

proximity? For oh, great
distance, all things to you
are small. The trashed yard.

The guardian dog, fenced
in, no more free in this life
than I might hope to be.

Myself, a small thing.
With the small things
everywhere dying.

CAROL FROST

Daedalo

An eagle chased the falling
in case the creature drop a feast of sinew and pulverable bone.

Blue-golden surface rushing up,
no branches breaking with honey petals

to soften the blow. No more cunning this day,

this world Icarian.
For the moment everything
stopped caring and those that could flew on.

~~

A partridge laughed, secretive in his ground bower,
as the father fathered the drowned arms and head.

Were not other boys cast from heights,
made birds?

Horned crab, ant, and the mole soon
dig through the hillock covered with flowers.

Rain ravel in the dry loam. To walk there
would be to sense loftiness brought under.

~~~

I saw your labyrinth as I rose, my head in spirals.
How could man trick from stone a river's running waves
flowing back to a blind source, then toward open sea?
~~~

Once started, how could there be a way back?
Winds roared as I flew, like the roar in my veins.
I breasted upward with the glittering rocking honeyed
air, my lonely impulse for ascent come from you.
I soared. And you must have felt – beyond your
fright for me - the splendor above – an open dome
you may as well yourself have flown to
with your own instrument of wood, wax, and feather.
Then as it came apart I was the ideal
falcon, earth the falconer spiraled to. Or I was an ant
in a triton shell tied to a linen thread
following sweet vapor in the chambers
to its source. The mind perpetually meanders
till eyes are shut, nothing, I thought,
bringing back or revivifying. Yet here we still are –
art and invention riding a fabled wing span,
out of nature, human in failure, telling of
son tied to father, father to son, telling of what is past,
the riddles we come from, and those to come.

The Timebomb

To diffuse the timebomb, I roost on it.
My heart explodes. It's on microfilm in the British Museum.
In the beginning, was the . . . stone,
and the heavens and the earth shuddered in the rain,
Deucalions of rain, and starlight started to mow
the lawn. I am committed to musical chairs,
and so I deserted the timebomb to squat on the moon.
It's round. In my mind, timebombs
and illumination are always round,
and weathermen encircle them with idylls of vacations,
with the politics of the mundane.
Okay, I'll ship out of the housing project
but first I want a little head and hopscotch on the playground.
Her birthmark was beautiful, right on the tip of the tongue,
and then a pigeon perched on my lap on the swing.
The realization came, I was on a pilgrimage
to the Other. First I started
with some French philosophers, then with my grandmother,
and then I looked into the mirror. Nothing worked.
Those theatres were closed, and so I turned the mirror
upside down thinking that might be easier
than putting on make-up or changing
the props in the background.
A spider has enshrined the weathermen
and now she's spinning a silk radio-band around the globe.
Someone's plucking, someone's caught.
I was taught that in Moscow everyone had to wait in line
for their milk. The marquee outside the theatre
said No Exit, and I sensed the quest was over. Caput.
The hat's a fedora, felt. The monkey does the singing.
There's a hole where my heart was.

I dance like a bear with the daughters of Siberia.
The milk may be spilt but the bread isn't rationed.
Potatoes and rye are cheaper than rice.
If enough hymns are sung, one of them
will contain the password to life on earth.
Come summer, I'll be sitting on a puffball
or a landmine. The director will decide.

Barcoded

Part One

Part Two

Part Three

Part Four

Part Five

Part Six

Part Seven

Mussolini

granted I am space under viaducts
open (cycling fencing skiing) helmet princes
dark princes their eyes fixed on distant
dark lands unoccupied by Romans
figure of eight spinning in a block of ice
I like your way of saluting on the piazza
hunkered down for the end of time
wheat girls, pinions in the marshes
balustrades that end in question marks

ANIS SHIVANI

CAROL CIAVONNE

Miniature

here you can rest with your saints in winter
the river l'hiver cold with blossoms
impastoed on bark half-plowed.
women are naked and praying in the water
"better the winter is some lenient."

a lover kneels in the cattails
behind a beehive fortress
a leopard waits in the forest
a snub-nosed jaguar, a wolf

the land converses like the monks

Loon

In an underground and patriotic element
aloud with torqued birds, woodlice and fish,
a man imitating a loon
with blood-red eyes and babbling
about a minnow, stiff, lopped, or lynched,
the jerk of testicles and ruptured gills,
or a loon imitating a man, tortured
with serrated glass and cigar ash
while strung up, trussed, bristled
and perched to a parrot's perch,
tarsal bones twisted around a wishbone,
tongue tacked to a protracted craw or ass—
hole that would cough, bleed, screech, or vomit
were it not plugged, proctored and proctoscoped
with the pock-boned, smegma-thistled prick
of another man imitating a loon
imitating a man laughing, bobbing, squawking,
hanging hooked horizontal, feathered pubic hairs
tarred in arrears to the Generals and the State Department
assembled in mossbacked laissez faire launches
with the Virtues and Powers of Being laminated
to well-festooned palm trees and haunches
quite able to scale down and compose into any National Anthem
the moan of the naked woman in the marked bin
with the cylinders in her mouth and cunt
as if she were nothing but a dissonant
sound, and as if this and the crazy laugh of the loon
unheard by the man imitating the loon imitating
the man with the broken eardrum
were not alone the logus and the universe of all madness.

DANA LEVIN

Dimitry Itskov: A Cento

—with thanks to *The New York Times* and *Huffington Post*

Dimitry Itskov, 32, has a colossal dream: an early start
for his own

mechanical face—

He's one of the men with brains, wondering How—

To evade
the death of meat, he thinks—

By 2045 we'll have "substance-
independent minds," then

no need for biology at all...

At 25, he started to have the symptoms of a mid-life crisis:

the musical instruments unlearned, the books unread—

The more he contemplated the world, the more broken it seemed—

"What we're doing here does not look like the behavior of grown-ups,
killing the planet and killing ourselves."

Decoupling the mind from the needy human body

could pave the way for a more sublime human spirit—

It could allow paralyzed people to communicate,
or control a robotic arm or a wheelchair—

It could allow you to start your car if you think, "Start my car"—

Within a century, we'll frequent "body service shops,"

choose our bodies from a catalog, then

transfer our consciousness

to one better-suited for life on Mars—

"From the very beginning," he said, "we realized Dimitry
was not an ordinary person."

He leads a life that could best be described as monastic—

No meat, fish, coffee, alcohol, or cold water—

Meat gives him an energy he's "not comfortable with."

What is the brain? What is consciousness?

It contains plenty of terrifying, brink-of-extinction plot twists.

It's somewhere between a cell-phone call and teleportation.

It's speaking with his voice in real time.

Get right up close to Dimitry Itskov and sniff all you like—

He has the kind of generically handsome face and perfect smile
that seem computer-generated,

complete with all the particulars of consciousness and personality—

Yes, we have seen this movie and yes, it always leads to robots
enslaving humanity—

For now, just acquiring a life-like robotic head is a splurge.

Bianca Bosker, "Dimitry Itskov Knows He'll Live Forever."
Huffington Post, June 18, 2013. http://www.huffingtonpost.com/2013/06/17/dmitry-itskov_n_3455807.html?view=screen

David Segal, "This Man Is Not a Cyborg. Yet."
The New York Times, June 2, 2013. http://www.nytimes.com/2013/06/02/business/dmitry-itskov-and-the-avatar-quest.html?_r=0

Trans; the hill

JANICE LEE & LAURA VENA

Pretend to know where something came out of nowhere is a ghost don't be provisional t an accident this is gestures figures turning the the corner red rock lined streets is that van helsing lord's tone is estranged candles I saw something what is it what it is internal rhythm the trees and hawks scarlet overhead the machine engaged as the wind rustled no one knows being green bloom no one knows blooms it is green but they are all weeds you don't know me oh illegibility has arrived there are so many of them death right now to use a voice reading how to live a compass to find geese repetitive motions with both hands sometimes the house grows hawks screeching to make sure I know they're there laughter this is unfolded puncture go again hands on the lever drought but I'm could not journey green green weeds imagination artifice the sign has fallen over the two hawks circling above us the wind rustling something heat wants his prey the leaves is cold I can still rocks scattered around this hear his voice even though it stopped exhaustion a specific fantasy when we met the rocks and the cracked dirt drawn to seven men of taste and the green the tongue the mother the leaves have holes broken split this deconstructed foundation because someone's been eating a rift related to another when the hawks are gone you can hear the silence has left me in ruins and the silence reminds motion the serenity of repression you haunt of the living almost blunted figments a budding early lamenting other detritus bits of mixing with the songbird settling for the evening foam and the silence reminds of the start of the space the boundaries lack boundaries a wadded up tissue in the skull the baby's lips the clothing strung on the floor in the brush I love your body branches hanging poisoned palm fronds the trees don't care about posture the night we met I remember girl you know this is it small black and white glances actual and imaginary don't remember where does things the breeze can't kick up the green come from where breeds and planks chimney body yielded nothing my where is green in the hierarchy of colors I think he is there's nothing for sale here is coming can you hear his voice birds chirping nothing's shadow but you can't see them it is cold mother wolf cottage light cold failure is finding a place it's hum circling the valley trees pines decrepit electric I don't know how much this is shells stairs that go nowhere for what we're doing here.

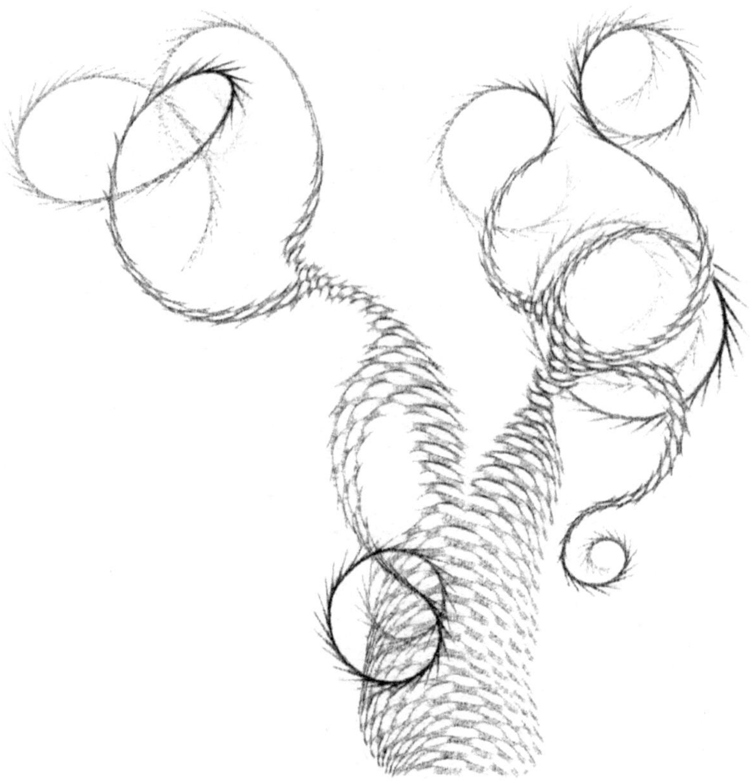

PART THREE:

The Nightingale Program
Is Corrupted:
Is Singing a Pure Red

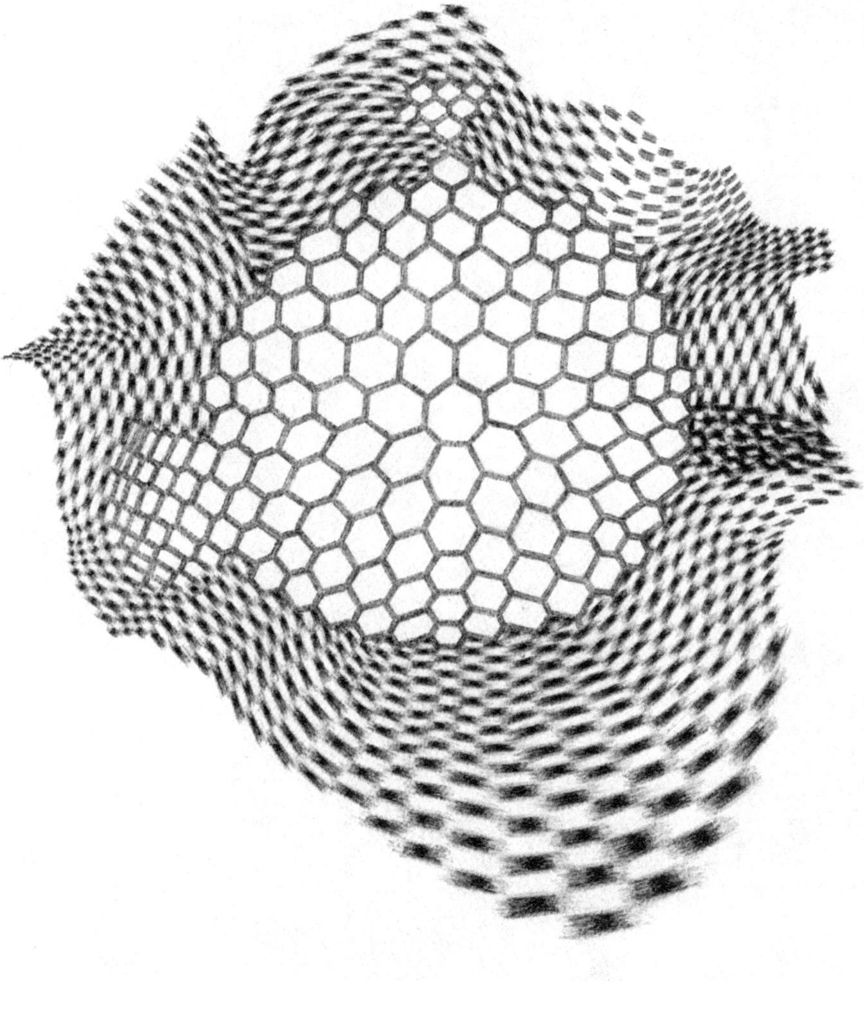

EXECUTE PROGRAM . . .

8 The term "natural" is defined as "existing in or caused by nature" and "not made or caused by humankind."

8 "Transhumanism" is defined as "the belief or theory that the human race can evolve beyond its current physical and mental limitations, especially by means of science and technology."

8 How precious is nature when compared to humans and our limitations? Should we prioritize one over the other?

8 Would you characterize *Homo sapiens* as an invasive species? If so, what should be done by *Homo sapiens* to combat the ravages by such an invasive species? Should non-human species have some sort of representation and protection under International Law?

BERNARD HORN

The Misery in the Sound of the Wind

and not to think
Of any misery in the sound of the wind,
In the sound of a few leaves
–Wallace Stevens

Its young ones suck up blood;
And where the slain are, there it is.
–Job 39

Or you're five and a half, and we're sitting in the garage
turned family room of the Wickford Street slab rental,
with the awful faux wood panels and the hideous
brown shag carpet, watching mama turtles
lumbering up from the sea to lay their eggs,
and a moment later babies
are breaking through shell and sand and scurrying
down the beach as fast
as their baby legs can go, and,
before I can even wonder, "Why the big rush,"
it's a long shot, and plummeting from the sky
like red-tailed hawks or dive bombers
are a skyful of wide-winged frigate birds, braking,
grabbing the babies in their talons, soaring, dashing
them on the rocks, and you're yelling,
tears flying from your face. "Why
(sobbing) don't they
do something?"
"Who?" I say.
"Them," you say, pointing at the screen,
"the people making the movie."

A Log of Birds

LINDSAY TURNER

the glass door-noise opening at the bottom of the stairs before
someone mounts them to the apartment door on the second floor
when you're listening for someone coming home

not possible that that one's broken, not this year

a small cartoon missile or grenade: high steaming whistle then

together swarming our eaves mornings, I won't talk

together swarming our eaves every evening

what will the sky do what when we forget to watch it has it done while
we pressed our eyes on the pillows or other patterns

might be a frog somewhere on the path by the river too far to walk to

entering the silent voice of reading ongoing spread over the words on
the page like a scanning pencil

the car sounds its horn once into a mid-height floating hedge of their
one-noters to say, "waiting"

who planted those strong things where indeed they do look purple at
night

seagulls, ongoing

whimpering gulls maybe it has to do with the heat

TRACE PETERSON

Drones

A pigeon flies in an arcing spiral reminiscent of a more impressive bird to list on one's resume. We installed the screens to prevent disease. A resume is the involved house we remember to clean, hunkering beneath one's profile while dusting the near edge of the bookshelf, of an instep seam. I look back and it's not a pigeon, it's a risk. A profile is an image of ill birds gathering at the cornice of a nearby building—we anticipate food, a nest, or a peek in the full-length pigeon mirror of others. Gradually it becomes clear that for a while now acid rain has been falling into our cup, a drop by drop which internally grows and rankles. We are becoming drones, we hear ourselves breaking the sound barrier overhead, we fear our best or worst qualities switching hats. In the light beneath the canteen sign we glimpsed the sheriff and the outlaw embracing, talking about us behind our horse in hushed vocals slung back. To list is to enfold a new norm—that's what the outlaw spawns. An illustration of smoke on a defunct chimney. Drone smoke. Somewhere a fire rises from the highest edges and reminds us of when you first rode into town, greeted by gasps of closure.

Rootavega Lapse

ADAM STRAUSS

2

A star crunches over a field harder than a rutabaga. He periodically yelps as his heels turn totally to tendons. This is not acceptable inside any frame of this scene so his hurt will have to be cut out. Arriving at a table with gallons of fresh brewed coffee he grabbed a mug and poured generously then downed it all in three slugs.

The dinner in the delightful cellar starred rutabagas—ones from a small splendid farm. The only rot around was noble. She pictured a cat curled in the nearest corner. She wondered how many cats were being eaten by humans that night. She wondered what a star would look like up close and would she be hurt daring to touch?

The moon felt so much more accessible—one can even dip a foot in the fringing lip of a tide's rip. She thought how unusual—hopefully some locations are overlooked—it would be to see a great cat at this or any other beach aside some in India Indonesia or Bangladesh and even then a striped flank flashes would astound not be taken for granted.

9

From lapse to lapse was the most direct way through labyrinthine mists. Most of the time cats seem so assured. I bet this proves how unfamiliar I am with felines. I am unfamiliar with nearly every lesbian but love May Swenson's poem allegorizing a lion and tiger who grew up together in a zoo. A giraffe once licked the handle of a broom I was using.

If this assemblage of cats and rutabagas and frames and lapses were a film I'd boo; I want my films to be stylistically unobtrusive: film as story not vision and as is probably obvious I have scant appreciation for film or all but the least impressive plus a few cinematic history approves though I'm no film buff so don't trust me. I bet you're like duh I wouldn't.

I am so tolerant; I am so judgmental. If you wish to render yourself inhuman in my eyes I suggest you become a star. I adore the world which is not human though which world that is often isn't clear. Lies like limpid deltas inspire my awe; they are the taps that root awesome. An owl swivels its head then stops at seven on the clock. Moon is in its eyes.

Dear National Park

ANIS SHIVANI

We trample your rested canopies upwards
to a noonlike suggestive climate of aerial minds,
beetle-true in scandal and ferocity, fallen
images rescuing our blue and white couture
as we plant right to left so many tangent
pools of nameless dying.

What woke up battle-hardened along preserved
yellow-orange festering paths to voodoo
falls, along similitudes of exploration trails,
was resonance patched and fumigated
with the high elevation of the moral mind,
my possession and yours, our free time.

Who charts these cliffs for sunborn igloos?
I am slime, I am prime half-hearted guru
angered by loins, I am washed in turpentine.
Dear lonely others, here is rescue, here is
make-believe propagation of endless time,
here we paint African life.

Proofs of tantric air melt obese glaciers,
our tiny emissions failing to catch fire.
There is not enough heat on the planet.
There is not enough cold to luck out.
All the animals left behind in burrowed cities,
please unveil the valley of judgment
we've been looking for in vain.

EWA CHRUSCIEL

from *Dybbuk of Angelus*

VI

The fox lingers in the light

A comet flaming through the land

The flame parses the air

The air breaks

across hurries onward

The fox, a polycandela

It lights the forest

How many arguments of asteroids it takes? The light, a donor
Epiphyte intends to grow in a dark cloud

We stare into the house we know nothing about

LINDSAY TURNER

Theory

Start *in medias* not in morning: so
the brave birds started   I was aware
before   the beginning
that goes *I woke up* is truly puzzling
since before *this* time   Venice,
for example and a lagoon
shining artificially   milky
blue glass curling sideways across
a wall of glass on a high thin
window in the metropolis made
of astounding tower   you could
peer back through it to the sunken street
outside and there you were again

*

sounds like a well-running bird to me, the early bird the way it's supposed to work, the sky at the stalled point, the useful myth of nothing-but-sky, everything floating in it, the grit, the obsolescing vehicles all in particles too small to see, the friend-group of the escaped, how far away they are in it, everything the stillness of a myth, it cuts both ways that's what it does, I remember evening blank with everything floating away, it was there to be believed in and was a space in which to believe, it was audible that bird, at the same time I remember the myth I knew for what it was, I learned to recognize that white blank sky because, but if the double-edgèd memory cuts both ways how do you grasp it? by the hilt like a myth, the blade of the still sky false or not is sharp

TOMAŽ ŠALAMUN

The Condor Watched from the Fence into the Depth

Black cities are destroyed.
Tips are squandered.

He shook off the cup.
He engraved the undulating line

onto the squire. The belly blue.
The hairdo exquisite.

The bridge glitters.
With the pole which is the simple

stick forward to the shore, then on foot
to grave. But the cemetery is

nibbled by dry mushrooms. Moths
give the cement into rubber

then pull on the gloves.
I stand on flowers in Kassel.

[Translated from the Slovenian by Michael Thomas Taren and the author]

Achromatopsia

MICAH LING

The walrus, the eared seal, the earless seal,
the fur seal, and the sea lion;
in addition to the owl monkey, and Neil Harbisson.
When he was nineteen, he climbed a tree in Mataro.
It was, along with two others, scheduled to be cut down.
But there he stayed. For days.

Walking across the Brooklyn Bridge with this man
is like walking with a mess of seals and a monkey.
Like walking with a super power. Can you imagine
what Times Square must sound like? What under the sea
sounds like? A rainbow is a scale. A room of prisms,
wind chimes.

It wasn't until after Mataro that he even knew
what a tree sounded like. Green is G-sharp. Red is
the mellowest of the sounds: calming. This man
snaps photos in black and white, of course,
but they're somehow sharper than anything
you've seen or heard. Like climbing in, and up.

Like refusing to leave until you've seen it all—
joined it like skin to bone.

The Point at Which
(The Los Alamos Wildfires, June, 2011)

A drop of water sometimes contains more light than an egg of fire.
—Edmond Jabès, *The Book of Questions*

1.
finally he stopped
to look around
the room
to pretend
his dog braved
the fields
with days
of birds

finally he sorted
out the finery
from the major chords

finally he walked
into the grocery store
to buy flowers

Wildfire smoke is the worst kind, someone said near the lilies
(a death flower).

He looked out the window at where the mountains usually were and noticed that a woman had put a mask on her own face but not on her baby's. The baby was sleeping or dead, he thought.

He often regretted his thoughts, the way they circled his head like Tweetie Bird.
He bought lilies.

He bought a baby saguaro.

First the plants regret heading back but had no time then the baby rushes all over first the finish to prompt a new round the wallow rather *lie about keeping cool or spreading scent* fainting into thick and dirty

> YOUR EYES ARE YOUR BEST TOOLS TO DETERMINE IF IT IS SAFE TO BE OUTSIDE. REMEMBER . . . IF VISIBILITY IS TEN MILES AND UP . . . THE AIR QUALITY IS GOOD . . . SIX TO NINE MILES . . . AIR QUALITY IS MODERATE . . . THREE TO FIVE MILES . . . AIR QUALITY IS UNHEALTHY FOR SENSITIVE PEOPLE . . . ONE AND A HALF TO TWO AND A HALF MILES . . . AIR QUALITY IS UNHEALTHY . . . ONE TO ONE AND A QUARTER MILES . . . AIR QUALITY IS VERY UNHEALTHY . . . AND THREE QUARTERS OF A MILE OR LESS . . . AIR QUALITY IS HAZARDOUS.
>
> (6/11/11 National Weather Service)

The point at which

I made the movie I thought *I saw everything directed from our front porch but* the elk ran out of the forest *by the thousands trying to get away from the flames* by the trains *were caught red before I could put on my shoes* to flee the boxcars *wonder should I get on or crawl back into the woods fire lines thinning out* past the boundaries *of the town even the mayor could not be found or anyone else who had a clue* or a simple pass *to dig a tunnel out of the knowledge that there was no place to go*

I prophesied a child, an occasional light, a garden. I walked around in circles saying: "look, look!" Have you ever heard of spontaneous human combustion?

(Pause to light something.)
In time he counted on key people and dissociated at will if, failing

him, they brought a doomy feeling to the way the entire sky lit up from the inside out—what was that? Like a fucking mind on fire.

2.
She lies in the flight path of seeds traveling on light she takes into her body.
Sure signs of rivers she can walk across. (She thinks.)

She threads them, silk and pod, wind and egg, through wounds of history and existence: tongue, womb, feet.

Wednesday: An eclipse rises in South America, sets over Asia.

Lunar, she thinks, and the word in its softness moves her, sleeping through the singing sex of cottonwoods, into Thursday.

3.
You would know that the German school and an arm of the Luftwaffe around the corner from the Satellite Motel pink balls of frozen ornament presiding over the preachers with Trinity not 75 miles away you would know that cloaks could not stop what might fall out of the sky you would know that the cottonwoods came back after the blast and that there are hundreds of chimps still alive at Charles River no longer waiting you would know that moan that roar of moan through the night

Under the air with that cloak of invisible birds under the 12 vile vortices, the crown of 12 stars

Rivers she can walk across: Gila, Mimbres, Grande, Puerco, Rillito, Santa Cruz, Tularosa Creek

4.
I found the children in the burning underbrush making peace with the road south leaving everything they love, except one another, behind. 6.28.11

- one red outdoor umbrella
- one string of white twinkle lights
- one TV, oldish, with temperamental remote
- assorted large furniture (sofa, snuggler, piano of dead grandmother, etc.)
- three comfy beds
- assorted small furniture (dressers, desks, etc., from yard sales and thrift stores)
- old photos, of course, including that time at the House on the Rock
- cucumber seedlings
- 30,000 drums
- one singing clock
- one sad monkey lamp
- one hummingbird feeder

I can't say who it was this time but I know he was more than I could have imagined I'm thinking he must be a swimming bird peeking out behind the leafy shell this one time I think he was very anxious but there was nothing to worry about even through the frantic gleaming night yes there were unmistakable signs clean water a planet-sized virgin forest a deafening stream an addictive current of light drawing us through the underbrush risking our lives for a trembling bell

5.
Step gingerly on waste in canyon, beneath mountain, south of pueblo, spit from the throat of God. (10,000 permitted to return today.)

NUCLEAR POWER REACTORS. YET EVEN "LOW-LEVEL" NUCLEAR WASTE CAN CONTAIN LETHALLY-RADIOACTIVE AND LONG-LIVED ELEMENTS, SUCH AS PLUTONIUM-239, STRONTIUM-90 AND MANY OTHERS. INDUSTRY AND GOVERNMENT PROPOSALS TO DEREGULATE AND "RECYCLE" SOME "LOW-LEVEL" WASTE WOULD ALLOW IT TO BE DISPOSED OF AS NORMAL GARBAGE AND ENTER THE CONSUMER MARKETPLACE–INCREASING RADIATION EXPOSURES TO EVERYONE THE STORAGE–PERMANENT AND TEMPORARY–AND TRANSPORT OF RADIOACTIVE WASTE IS PERHAPS THE MOST CONTROVERSIAL ASPECT OF THE NUCLEAR PO

http://www.nirs.org/radwaste/radwaste.htm

The rumors spread before we could put them out sparking fights of naphtha and benzene his clothes going up in flame where even rolling in the dirt could not douse before we understood they had become fact and burnt down the entire village all of us locked in the church ash ash raining down one tiny speck will kill the first born quick mark the lintels with blood

and luck.

All text composed in collaboration during the Los Alamos wildfires, 6.4.11-6.30.11

Chromesthesia

MICAH LING

When Piano Man starts, when you hear the harmonica
and *making love to his tonic and gin*, what color is that,
really? And what about the la-le-la's? I go back and forth
between greens and blues, but maybe that's too obvious.
Maybe that's too gin and sad song, or,
maybe what's obvious to me is all yellow and orange
to you. But, We Didn't Start the Fire? C'mon,
that song is all red, and not just because
of the indication of fire; in real life,
if you've watched a man build a fire
from its feeble start, from twigs and leaves
and a single match, is it ever red? It's smoke
and breath. It's careful, careful fingers:
the same ones that do delicate things; maybe
delicate things right before fire building. Maybe
right after. But Billy is singing pure red:
bold and topping all other colors with surety.

A song so red, it's more than memory.

CURTIS EMERY

I Wonder about the Sun

You the dark star of August mirror pool
thy hands reach and comfort the mountains of every summer chime
I think of the darkness of silence
I think of the darkness of forgotten chances
I think of the darkness of December's absent light
I wonder about the sun
thy hands reach and comfort the single blade of grass
reaching for the blue dome of the cloud's magnificent chapel.

Remains

MICAH LING

A man who lives surrounded by yellow grass, changes
each year, unnoticed. He alters things in small ways.
He sips rye instead of scotch. He cooks oatmeal
instead of grits, and carries a red handkerchief
in one pocket instead of a grey one in the other.

And every year the man burns his possessions. Old, slight
amendments: a version is what's left. Carefully, he saves
the ashes like the remains of a loved one. Each night
he stirs them into tomato sauce, or sprinkles them
on salad and meat. He eats and thinks of small waves

turning to great storms: joining it
instead of tumbling like a shell.

CECILIA LLOMPART

The Barnacle and the Gray Whale

Said the Barnacle,

You enchant me, with your carnival
of force.

Yours is a system of slow.

There is you, the pulley
and there is you, the weight.

Your eyes wide on a hymn.

Your deep song like the turn
of that first,

that earliest of wheels.

Said the Whale,

I have seen you, little encruster,
in that business of fouling the ships.

Known, little drum machine, you
to tease out food from the drink.

Little thimble of chalk and hard water.

You could be a callus of whiter skin.

You could be a knucklebone. You
who hang on me,

like a conscience.

Provisional Autonomies & Oceans

BRENDA IIJIMA

A catalyst for adaptability, yet written in a script that used terms like Eden to refute endless change.
We were inhabitants who survived the solar flares for the meantime, back in time.

We had a history of genocide, slavery and appropriation.
We ignored orders not to use sea water to cool the overheating reactors.
The radiation levels were so high that even robots could not enter.
Waves of violent outbreak continued until most systems failed.
As the planet heated up, horses got tinier.
A little ice age came and went where we consumed cows, then dogs and finally each other.
The way we modified the landscape was extremely foul.
Still, for a time we were able to maintain coexistence with spiders, snakes, monkeys, fish, birds and some other creatures.
Mostly we worked in automated factories and lived in company buildings that resembled individual homes.
We bought them (the homes) with money and we had to care for their maintenance also. We had no obligation to sacrifice ourselves, though it was expected.
The common environment was filled with metallic residue clinging to the solar towers. There were employees who raked the metal off the base of the towers.
Everyone stopped buying stuff except to maintain the houses; they had to, though the rule wasn't stated.
They had to keep up the functionality of these dwellings the people quasi-owned.
For an indeterminate period people kept up certain styles and mannerisms, this soon faded.
It is hard to say when the capitalist time clock had crumbled.

The digits fell off the clocks and the clocks rolled into the great bonfires.

No one took responsibility for these fires, they just appeared everywhere.

This wasn't something to celebrate. It was a different reality that took great pleasures in a different interpretation of the world.

It wasn't necessary to rehearse these pleasures. Unfolding actuality was evocative. Reproduction was something we all dreamed about but didn't dare conceive of. Yet we were blooming, internally and externally.

Babies were born mostly too deformed to survive.

Some swam in chemical labs at specialized facilities and their mothers were placed in comas to maintain their vital stats.

Others lived in hydroponic suspension as vegetative matter; as plants to be specific.

The trouble with reproduction started gradually and imperceptibly, there was a threshold overload.

Most of the population was intersexual—the cumulative effect of generations of pharmaceuticals and personal care products polluting the environment had its morphing effect on bodies.

Sexual dimorphism sort of disappeared also—the sexes resembled each other. Everyone had male and female genitalia.

Obviously no one had pets any longer either.

It was difficult enough to maintain the dwellings of which the people were responsible for.

Everyone seemed to have their personal manifestos memorized.

This was a thing to do recreationally, to recite one's manifesto.

There was great drama and longing in these recitations of utopian glamour.

Almost everyone's manifesto contained the statement that they wished for the resurgence of forests and fields.

Trudging through cesspools and garbage dumps of outmoded

technological equipment and medical waste had taken its toll.

The oldest members of the global society recalled the presence of whales in great oceans that wrapped around the globe.

The globe had given off a bluish atmosphere when seen from outer space.

The decision to send the excess spent nuclear waste into outer space had come to pass. This decision caused the eventuality of nucleated material crashing to earth.

The teenaged workforce was the emergency crews; they were sent in when this happened, a frequent occurrence in the factory housing zones.

They hosed down the zone with sand.

The oldest living member that anyone knew of was 45 years of age and suffered a form of dementia.

Younger members of society suffered forms of dementia also.

There were some individuals who had given over to a collaborative group way of living and had elected to have the surgery joining their brains and bodies.

They seemed to live the most peaceably. A life of spare parts, bucolic-mechanical, happy, happy, and most HAPPY, with flawless complexions (Stacy Doris)

There were no hospitals, only mobile units sent out to assuage pain and suffering. Vehicles rode on conveyor belts, there were no roadways.

Much has been made of the baleful themes waiting to be realized (Carla Harryman).

Joy hadn't been extinguished.

Want was ever-presently revamped.

People were energized by time and space and brain function.

Every day had some uniqueness regardless of the urgent requirements that were quite banal.

The mother of all the bubbles, the work bubble, would finally deflate. Franco "Bifo" Berardi wrote this statement and it was published in translation in 2011. This funny passage was stenciled all over the place.

It was a longstanding joke and a vision.

With whatever means, people graffitied it on their dwellings.

There were still a few libraries that housed digital footage and for certain hours with a special pass one could go in and watch *Youtube* videos of all sorts of playful activity from the past.

Watching any interaction with water was particularly compelling and great.

People swimming in lakes, showering, fishing, floating on yachts, snorkeling and watering their lawns were all popular themes.

The social fabric had shrunk, that was for certain.

It had become a huge challenge to maintain the present.

Since the teenage population knew of no other reality, save for these vestiges in the library they weren't unduly depressed about the past or what was to transpire as time elapsed.

The season of the sun was to be embraced, enjoyed even.

Sunglasses reassured the delicate optics of spark.

There were utopian clubs to chat about possible riveting scenarios.

Teenagers' emotions oscillated considerably.

Two forms of fabrication leaving down. Two downed legacies emptying form.

Two shadows left fabricating horses. Two forms of legacy leaving down. Two fabricating shades of horsing left. Two empty horses of fabrication standing (M. Mara-Ann)

Some of the infrastructure was intact.

There was a popular festival held in the summer (an outmoded word that was still used by some).

Teen trapeze artists performed amazing stunts suspended over emptied rivers.

Everyone who could come out and participate enjoyed their grace.

Florida 2012

CECILIA LLOMPART

Between the dung caked pasture
and the Shell station, the ibis
take their supper. Further off,
a swampy woods, trees thin
as cigarettes, murky waters
in slow pools. There is beauty
in this too, if you don't stare
too long. Further off—for in
Florida there is always the further
off, little goats bloated on trash
parade the length of a chain-link
fence, and the trailer falls in on
an idea of itself. Florida is a run
on sentence that goes pines pines
pines pines. Open field. In Florida,
there are two colors. Both neon.
There are two seasons that happen
simultaneously—Wet and dry.
There are two types of plant—
The thirsty, and the thirstier. I am
phoning it in again in Florida, where
everything is made out of light and
in the shape of a cocktail or a palm
tree. If we lack anything, file it
under sky. File it under moon, new.

URAYOÁN NOEL

LANGÚ

ageless language; after Latasha N. Nevada Diggs

I'm always siempre tengo pesadillas
having nightmares moozhag ingiiwashkwengwash

Niin inwewin I'm language soy lenguaje
babaa-ayaa dando vueltas wandering

My brain niinindib cerebro
it makes madwewe ruido noise
apii cuando choca con when it hits bitaakosin
aki la tierra the earth
hello! boozhoo! hola!

Mi tierra aki my land is what lo que me viene
comes to mind a la mente mikwendaagwad
niiyaw de mi cuerpo of my body
al gaguear as it stutters gagiibanagaskwe

Ombiigizi tierra my noisy earth mi ruidosa aki
is recollected mikwendan es un andar
babaa-ayaa rememorado wandering

Soy niinitam inwewin ruidoso I'm noisy language lenguaje ombiigizi
land of body tierra del cuerpo niiyaw aki
gagiibanagaskwe gagueando un stuttering boozhoo! hola! hello!

noise memory language land brain body
agimediruni abad iñeñei mua sesu úgubu
noise memory language land brain body
babel memoria idioma pais selebre kurpa

noise memory language land brain body
napituruk itqaqtuq uqautchit nuna qaqisaq timi
noise memory language land brain body

****

AYMBERÊ
BAQUARA
CANHEMA
DANONO
ESSÁ
GOITACÁ
IRA
KÊ
JUCASSABA
KAMBY
MORAUSSUBA
NHENHENHÉM
ORÉ
PAUÁ
QUICÉ
RECÔ
SOO
TOBÁ
VAPIDIANA
WARIWA
XE
YBAPIRANGA

A wise lizard
fleeing the
ceremony.

A nomad eye:
honey of
death

or milk of love.

We say it
all: home
is

a dull knife

against our animal faces.

We are a
tribe of
apes:

mine

is the red sky.

* * * * * * * * * *

ANDAYA.
CHIYO.
DACAA NAA NUHU CA ÑUU
EL SOL
FEBRERO
HUAHI YEQUE
INI

JISIYUU
LLODZO CASTILLA
MINI
ÑUHU
PICIETL
QUIVUI
RENDACA
SATA
TAA
UVUI
VIDE ABRIR
XITON
YAA ÑUHU

The underworld's foundation
from all
eternity.

The February sun:
sepulcher heart,
field,

hollow pen, tobacco fire.

To be born
a bee
in

the beyond.

To write. Two.

To open
the

merchant god's

tongue of fire.

****

ANVIRON
BYENNERE
CHANTE
DEVANJOU
ENSTIGE
FLANM
GÒJE
HANCH
IL
JI
KONESANS
LANG
MEZI
NASYON
ÒFELEN
PÈP
RAMAN
SANBLE
TANPÈT
UNI
VWAYAJ
WÈ
YÈ
ZÈWO

Around **b**lissful **c**hants
dawn **e**ntices
flame

gulping **h**ip **i**sland **j**uice.

Knowing **l**anguage's **m**easure:
nation's **o**rphan
people

rarely **s**imilar.

Tempests **u**nite **v**oyagers
witnessing **y**esterday's
zero.

NOTES: The first part of "LANGÚ" mixes English, Spanish, and Ojibwe (and, in the refrain, Garifuna, Papiamento, and Inupiat). The three alphabet poems that follow are made up of lists of words and phrases in Tupí-Guaraní, Mixtec, and Haitian Kreyòl respectively, while the English poems below them are my own loose translations/adaptations of the alphabet poems. All the non-English and non-Spanish text was taken from online dictionaries and databases.

DAVID BLAIR

Impressions of Poets' Keyboards

]I'm no fun[

]I won't dance why should I[

]put out your eyes[

]stop up your ears[

]I don't do it[

]bust a thesaurus[

]nobody here but point-of-view[

]one competent thing ad nauseam[

]more than that is the goof of talent[

See Note First—
Anti-Translation of a Poem by Rilke

BILL KNOTT

The world's machines have not grown,
whose inheritors reign everywhere.
Their silicon sons are strong; their
digital daughters wield power, take hold.

How we humans long to break them
down from that Dasein—to make them
rust/repent for all the infernal fires
that drive them, far as our desires.

The machines aren't scared. They know
harder control, how to turn the wheel
of time past those whom they sure as hell won't miss:

Cyborg android robot shall steel
themselves, consolidate, and, rising, go
unto that universe whose promise
we flesh-and-carbonoids could merely premise.

NOTES: Anti-translation of an untitled Rilke poem (*Die Konige der Welt sind alt,* from "Das Stundenbuch," 1901), which Heidegger in his 1946 lecture 'What Are Poets For?' cites for its "highly prophetic lines." A prose paraphrase of the original poem's ending might go something like:

The metals, the oils—all the ores we've ripped from the earth—are homesick. They long to leave our machines, to flow out of our cash-registers and factories, to return to the gaping veins of the mountains we reft; whereupon the mountains will close again.

"Heidegger maintained . . . until the end of his life," Richard Wolin writes (*The Heidegger Controversy*, MIT Press, 1993), ". . . [that] the 'inner truth and greatness' of Nazism is to be found in its nature as a world-historical alternative to the technological-scientific nihilism bemoaned by Nietzsche and Spengler."

CLAUDIA KEELAN

Elegy for Bill Knott, His Words and Disaster Notes Presiding

The true orphan opts for vasectomy,

“Heart   de facto amazon . . .   remains.”

Plot genie, *sans* child, hidden or contained,

What’s not born is tenderness, other lies.

Outremer, where God died, lost in a sneeze

Deux ex machina, first cyborg of all.

Your desert honeymoon pinned to yon wall,

Sifts in the vast Deferens, cools the breeze.

Les Differences, *mon ami*, bred hardpan.

It was the only nation that remained.

Mother-other, sole partisan to blame,

She’s any woman you could ever name.

“Stepped on…lost…lost as she is to me, I

…[I]..rather…under her…be… than their eyes.”

4 Robots Sing the Singularity: an erasure

—after Yevgeny Zamyatin

JIRÍ CÊCH

emotion
here lived
glass houses
here
hours.

***We,* within**

i i i i i more
i i me I i complex i i

novel
man

will fear
the rift
and the rational.

the hero

the One lost

the One nothing

ANIS SHIVANI

Greenland

the world's droll maidens on a silver tray
my links to paper clouds

after a period of cyclical triumph
water down a wooden rack of calisthenics,
fluid noumenon, my legs in trouble
waist, ankle, back, improbable lock

I saw through capitalism's puzzle
and left home on horseback
ignoring shrubs in godly crouch

all my sisters were handkerchief mummies
whose beauty we paid to see
whose talents dribbled down long legs
long as miles of dynamite

who's outside the picture this morning?
the moon blew a hole through the roof
I stole buckets of silver light
painted my face blue
left by the side door
mousetrap for my Steinbeck vacation

I was a postman in last night's dream
handling mail for corporate thieves in limousines

and my back gave in to hitler's melody
and my back gave in to stalin's melody
and my back gave in

please rescue this puddle of a spain from my bathmat

I want to construct polite mosques
over mounds of exemplary sins

we have waited this afternoon in death's annex
exchanging coffee and cigars
minding our notes on taste

who knows fish out of water?
artificial breaths
tapestries of chloroform
greenland in absentia
and my heart a good sport
skipping on the desk like a grasshopper
under a microscope

the skyscraper melts like ice cream on a hot summer day
while one of us climbs the telephone pole
and waves at the world like a crow
and the rest of us wear out our shoes

I knew my family were cheats
they locked me up like a box of unwanted greeting cards
in the memory hole of their chiseled supper

and I made friends of horses and bees
and aleatory dogs hiding in the pages of books

I meant to take a ride to the moon
in a yellow paper buggy
followed by horses shimmering like water
waves of truant perfection

how high can we ascend through this buttered roof?
the cadences of a lifetime
bandaged in mean metrical trifle shapes
linking knowledge with deafness

timpani of pompeii
buddhist trembling
above meaning divided by the thinnest of membranes
like the ear under water
like the sparrow shedding feathers
like the moon's reflection in the last drying drops
at the horse's trough
on a handpicked summer night

from *Coal/Cole/Kohl*

ADAM STRAUSS

[from a series which looks at Mountain-Top Removal, the poetry of Cole Swensen, and the trope/literalization of makeup.]

Urge for   mountain meaning

    Not this   self

    Portrait as yelling

Out help in   to a stack

            Of glass panes suspended

    From the ceiling

        Suspending me

    In the question

        What gets through   my reflection

                A bit pulverized in places
            A sharpening diamond
        Cuts to the quick
    This decline used to
Take millions of years.

———————

At the   right   unlikely conditions
Sand   becomes a window:

            Looking out won't
            Do any good the

Subject outdoes the frames—

Chains without we saw-see—

        Detonating sounds
        In the interior:

By way of here there
Is ways out.

————————

Eyes   witness

Films on a window. Evidence

    Collects until it's razed

The body in question to   no case—no

    Place to freshen the air

Puts in perspective the   importance of energy: breath

Cannot be made up.

————————

Light lightly lily   at his throat: alabaster sundown glazes.

Glare gives her gastrointestinal problems; lids shut she's given

A gastronomy of light   lies marbleized and licks

Her lips   pronounce born   into another language.

No-one's out: only facades facing statues

Would speak Greek were they   to walk out their veins

Thus there's   no commerce between the subject and

The maker or is the matter all in the material? Is

"The world" representation or a blank

All our parts refract: he had an unexpected reaction on
Touching the Adonis' bicep a bird's shat on and a flock's overhead.
In the Southern US towns are named after Classical places:

They ring a bell even if Georgia's not in your ken as opposed
To Appalachia which perhaps doesn't need recognition—
What will there be of it in a decade? There's nothing to make up

Which isn't to say nothing's missing; she lined her eyes with Kohl
Hoping attending them she'd miss less of a given scene;
Many people she passed looked at her; she felt less sure.

————————

The light   fired

Sand to a   rough Hour

Glass   we

Looked out at not   through

A sky raining perspective.

C.J. WISLER

Aphelion Sonnet

In everything that orbits there are rules
to the freefall of one body around another.
There comes a spring's approach. Summer cools
quick. You fail to feel the shift over
despite the velocity of escape. Must I
remind that no natural particles touch, just
react to the nearby presence of such: the fire
under my finger, your finger on my wrist.
(Attraction,–that great space you move towards
but never cross.) So you demand to swallow,
beg to stay in bed, conceive sci-fi tableaus
to bend physics. Say more than this hollow
for gravity. Mark desire, mark sure revision –
beyond reproach. Quicken into fusion.

Lions

ANIS SHIVANI

I was a lion's cubed heart, clubbed to paperthin
breast of steel, I murdered many moons for money,
I fainted through fire, fired shots at druid memory,
and loyally drank tall glasses of hierarchy's creeds.

I found my way to popes bearing fulgent smiles,
who stripped like sparrows in heat, tiny in outward
visage, as though the weight of scholasticism had
never before prompted fallibility.

In the vatican of
noonday flames, a hoarse voice proclaimed dirty
concourse, calling the past a dome of burnt libraries,
while the row of supplicants stretched past Chirico.

C.J. WISLER

The Divide –
Incident At Division Ave., 1995

In the backseat of the big white truck, I am wiggling
my stubborn baby tooth. It groans and squeaks in my head.
It is November. The rains come in cold sleety sheets,
and the sky is a huge frozen grey balloon.

I spy with my little eye: man on the corner
wrapped in a city-stained Swiss cheese shirt,
His skin is wet graying cinnamon. His eyes look down
as we pass. I press my hot face to the window.

Always Indians, they say up front.
The voices crinkle like aluminum cans. My breath
fogs the window, sugarcoats the world. I remove my nose from
the glass. The man sits in the cold, clear ring I made.

Last week I played with two young boys. We split
a Coke between us. They praised me for it,
and when I asked why they said *Because they are Crow*.
I see their dusky skin and say their names, close my arms around me.

The light turns and we speed ahead, sloshing the truck
with ruddy water. Though not before the man looks
up, his eyes jagged, cracked silver mirrors.
My baby tooth comes out, egg-colored. I turn it in my hand.

Its blood-brown root silenced, locked in the white.

Mothership Prose

DAVID BLAIR

Where is the boss? Maybe Vermont. As for the boss under that boss, I give up on Fridays in July.

May the cruise ship of these hours, depopulated summer, come in with white shorts and crisp white shirts and even more clavicles.

I am about to step into the golden assistance of late afternoon where the bicycles with training wheels and lacrosse sticks will be out on quiet streets.

Except for these tubes of florescent light, the moment is like the one right before I step up the stairs from one dark floor to another to bed.

There are times when I fall face forward into the fast moving streams where my dirty shoes have again filled up with water, silt, and warm fish.

These streams are like one of those places in the wilderness where my size twelve feet can actually be in all three mountain states at once.

DAVID BLAIR

On Water & Land

1). **Life Forms**

I will never look at insects and organs the same way
after this time in the meadows by the lab.

There was first this whole sense of the world
I got because my heart was hammering.

All of us are organs
of one body,
but some of us are flippers
while others tense up. We are determined
by sight of each other. It's a proper
insult to see each other reductively
as lumps of meat
turning rudimentary circles
on ice, with the shapes
created by vocabulary.

The flippers have the humors.
The others secrete enzymes.

In the middle of the night,
the cats sleep between our ankles
and our knees, properly coexistent.

They are never minding
the look and smell
of the potted products.

How happy they are here
with their fur and humor.

Every cat practically has one eye
which are their minds made for looking
down into us, and seeing everything there,
and hunting for papers, and knowing us well.

2). **Snorkels**

People who have intelligence in love,
the people I love best in the world, the smart ones,
have the same black ant giant eyed face-mask nature

for snorkeling, a beautiful black ant nature.
I don't worry that I will be eaten.
Their heads are all brains inside crisp vinyl.

What with their brains and their giant eyes,
they are curious as cats,
cats who are not cats
but generosities.

Maybe all the Norse gods want to kill
that which lives by water and rock
and by the borders, the damp regions.

Watch out if you live near the jetties.

With a donkey, you have to follow
eye contact with cautious handfuls of hay,
and things can be tenebrous for some time.

3). Penned Horses

I could identify at once with the horses out on the old post road,
near swamps, by stonewalls, by ice cream shacks, the horses
    picking things up

with rubbery, fingering lips, which are outright, forthright and creeping,
while captive sheep stood around making a sound like *wuuuu, wuuuuu.*

This all still goes on out here. The two rural teenagers visit the horse cafeteria
and hold out handfuls of grass for them to eat, and kiss them and scratch them,
so pleasing to the gay horses and the straight horses and the bisexual ones, too.

The horses turn their heads sideways to receive these kindly benedictions
and quote heartbreaker lyrics to themselves and use a lot of negative space
to communicate what tenderness and humor they feel in the situation.

4). **Midway**

Last time I looked, we were not squid.
There were crayfish
in fast moving cold water,
bottomed out by velvet rocks,

to one way of thinking
seeming to wait for exploitation.

5). **Rabelais**

I don't mind if people talk about actual shit
because life is earthy.

Out of mud, comes the brick.

Out of earth, our friends come,
giant in aspect, like Thomas Andrew Yuill,
the poet from Old Dominion.

"Yoo hoo," he says. "Read more Wyatt. Read
Sir Philip Sidney."
"Yoo hoo," he says. "Buttermilk biscuits.
Gravy. Monday Night Football."

"Yoo hoo," he says. "The heart is gold."

Greet the day.

6). **Overgrown**

Sometimes, you realize the Star of the County Downs
hates you at times and has serious intentions
towards you. You are like
a houseplant grown unruly
in the pot and should be starved
of water and denied oxygen,
denied light.

You are a tropic pipe
clogged with invasive sponge
who would make a new reef.

You can handle a lot of stuff.

You would be able to gaze
down from the bridge and see
beneath reflections
your grey deadness,
hardheadedly.

7). Poem about a Tick

It's a Gold Coast pastoral penalty
with turkeys and poison ivy.

It's a mean-looking bastard,
pinpoint
serrated spider,
with an overbite.

It's a blown up
martial arts star
on a fingertip,
a viscous disc.

Because of ticks,
hikers and their dogs
are unlikely action
movie stars.

So was Walt Whitman
according to himself,
crossing streams
from rock to rock,

gone up high ridges
where the trail
has fallen to the river,

to ease along earth upended
by the roots and bottoms
of fallen white pines,

in the tangle of roots
under the blanket
lifted.

Come under the blanket,
come out with a tick
and need a quick shot.

TOM YUILL

Creation Myth
The Invention of Willie Nelson

The gods took the magic stone from Booyan,
All the Russian incantations, all the Duke's
And Dauphin's yaller boys, all the egg yolks,
And they fashioned from it all the image of the Sun
And tossed the image of the Sun
In what appeared in a hypnotic arc forever
Ending in the western most horizons,
And off the poems went after these images.
Pursued them through bucolic rows of porto-potties
And across mud flats and seas at varying speeds. In this
Droll haberdash-and-jewel hunt all but the rarest
Got confused. The rest were blessed,
Though some of the snotties would not call them Elect.
And gazing at the sky—that's right, the old
Familiar sight of people looking at the sky—
An ornery biped slattern might declaim,
"Abandon ye all hope. Most y'all
Will *always* be deluded." Well, wrong.
Wrong again. Wiry suns and glued-on moons are
Only hard wired, fastened, bolted in-
To consciousness and then clicked on.
The marionette does not exist apart.
Therefore, returning from the Sun, an angel sings,
O everything is terrible, O everything is fine.

Garden of Metamorphosis

— after Tetsumi Kudo

COLLEEN COYNE

I.

The sweet remembrance of the just.

The skin dissolves in a grafted garden.

Some waxy blooms, some mud-silk creep.

Smear a honeycomb across a network of limbs.

A seedy filament impulse cracks Eden's regal needles:
under fingernails, jack-in-the-pulpit purple.

Under moss, a crested phallus with a pouffed collar.

The signal flashes, half underground.

Follow the wrist map to the roots of the jasper trees,
through the loam: the triumph of gangrene.

Come down off the premature day. The certainty of our destiny.

In a tool shed, the garden's chorus sings: *every joint a honeycomb.*
Tosses a fake bouquet. Recites *reticulum, reticulum, reticulum.*

Networks fail sometimes.

All sublime desires are blighted by plastic genes. A hollow nucleus.

Shall flourish when they sleep in dust.

II.

Pollution is the new ecology.

Pocket a swatch of moss. Carry it with you for luck.

10,000 feet to the footprint lake. The drain pipe rusts in clots.

And near it, some trails.

Sticky heads mark the spots where cattail grasses grew,
where ladybugs were found.

Vow to seek them out at all costs.

(Take up a collection; baskets hold our practice.)
A purple that births the planets, that births the rings
and stars and stitches.

And where the body rots: *stick it, I dare you.*

The sucking puncture and release.

Shit, let's just go home.

All the wrong things scatter. Move.

III.

Your portrait in green and black, sometime after take-off:
perfect nails peeking between tall grasses.

Leaves splattered with spores. Each head remembers.

Beetles wean beads off a plastic rosary.

Nose here, hand there, face half-hollow.

The way a petal curves. Some glamour there.
The reply of the empty mirror: not reflect, but collect.

Peacock & hummingbird circle.

Such mean birds, shooting out cries of human babies.

A neon sign spikes the distance.

There's gold in these hills, but we don't care to stop.

We're after the rocket's tail.

IV.

It's a mark of distinction to have your name written in stone.

To have a caretaker take care with your bones.

Scrub-grass carpet, wreath of weeds.

But what if nothing edible grows?

Just a skin-split baked potato, peeling bacon petals.

Nothing neutralizes acid like breaking open a fine eggshell.

The heart flops on the ground, having never grown wings.

Ribs green in sunlight. (The cage or the birdsong in it.)

Scrub off the rainbow of decay.

When it's clean, bring the body back home. To the glory merchant's molded, sculpted lawn.

V.

Wandering bodies are forever attractive.

Each lark's lapsed breathing, each bark temple.

The attraction of dust to bone.

Of the skull's thin white string to the phallus, to the pelvis.

The click of the hips settling into intention, the skull willed open.

The path's pink veins, stringing contemplation.

Ribbons ribbon off the weather vane. Fly small flags of surrender.

Each wandering body storms the mirror. The glass case
condenses, closing.

Thermal Signatures

SAM WITT

Do you know how easily
the body liquids boil
in God's vacuum?
But in this godless amniotic
drift,
where satellites float me above in the skullwaters,
& in this place of skulls,
at one o'clock, which are broadcasting me here, down below,
I've left myself behind in a garden this time,
where black slug-like creatures have come
again, in skulls,
to infest my
displaced helmet,
this hologram of breathing that surrounds the inside
faceplates
transmitted through the scar in
my navel—
Will this corrupted I-program open once
more to set us free?
Snails, clustered in shadow, a halogram of flesh
on the
cement cheeks of Siddhartha,
many splayed dark gray lips I can't touch,
from this speckled shell that
irradiates me
in raimants of
sightlessness, O Godless Particle,
I reach out a simulated hand
with special thumb & fingerprints molded of silicone
rubber
to permit a degree of sensitivity & feel,
I brush this wet antenna
stirring
left behind in its shell of daylight,

left behind in this
necropolis,
this
Place of Shells,
Pacific Ocean flinting & sparking just
over Diamond Heights . . .
At one o'clock I began to float in space[1]
the space of a second
in my poorly
fitting birth helmet
with its extra-vehicular visor assembly moving me at the
touch of a keystroke, a spark,
their slow movements
gathered here
in my Erthe helmet: They turn me
juiced shadowrise & sunsweetened,
I suffer,
left behind for nobody & rising, at the bottom, I suffer,
I do not suffer at a touch. I rise in the zero
gravity.
I cay in the wrecked
sunshone these 2 moments
Of not, of not
suffering to be—
& there I was, all this time, looking for the ultimate
moment!
For the particle-program!
& here now I move through the terminal tiergarten of such
weightlessness,
the terminal hour of our
rest at hand,
my gaze sprayed in an anti-fog compound

---

1 "Tragic Robot Suicide Stuns Small Town" (http://kotaku.com/tragic-robot-suicide-stuns-small-town-1464850323) 1:05 PM - 21 Mon Apr 14 · Embed this Tweet

though
I was blinded at
birth
when my eyes smeared open across the birthcanal
& my helmet was secreted by a clear pure longing all those
years ago.
I am the Undernaut, out of focus & strange,
<the nightingale
program is corrupted> the blurry one
you can just about glimpse from the periphery
in a blasted shadowpalsy, a
sunlight vector through the willows
that shivers the wet fingertips of young astral
dead girls at play.
<face-icon revolving><visor assembly wiped clean>
They have onely just started to move each antenna now.
El Lago de
Dolores sleeps under the pavement.
<sleep undrained below these palm trees written in
cascading strings of code>
Let it drain "me" in
wind language through my boots
into that cavity where their sexual stirring barely moves me
down through a wet breathing valve into this missing
fleshwater,
I stand down at zero in a city of the rich with no graveyards
down for the caress of a few small dead
children to project another place
across pinkish fleamarket stone
<float my eyes>
Rise from the deepest decay. From the Fathers.
Decays
into a slow motion of antennaetongues.
Licks a small sugarskull
not centuries from here
but simply apart from this place where I'm looked through
my eyes

2 minutes from this space, Being,
where I insufficiantly,
inadequately suffer
the tracks they've left behind, O Interceptor,
black muscular tears.
Lift this child. <the file is corrupted>
<let him float gracefully
in & out of deep time>
O cosmic gazelle.
Wipe "him" clean of the visions screaming across the
chrome mirror of his visor-face.
Shall his inner voice inflect a moonscape swirling across the
surface? Fine then.
If the light shall bubble through his
eyelids
once the vizard is lifted
& evaporate his eyeballs, so be it. <take him blind[2]>
already left behind to enter the body of
one o'clock
in the Larva-Machine,
already looking through the silk wrappings of his
eyes
to this place
where I don't exist
so much as believe in sight.
Take him anyway,
<father, fava> take him into the midday air mouthing an
unborn dampth—
<we are here only to be born><enter//
enter>
& the passive receptor implanted in each earcoil whispers:
<orphan//orphan//
orphan>
just to the left of this place where "I" barely moves

2 "And he looked up, and said, I see men as trees, walking." *King James Bible,* Mark 8:24.

tuned to such an exquisite Orphan Code
that the glandular lymphlight under the Alphadome
Resonates the coils into this Aleph.
<Coded//alive//Coded: to be//coded//not>
Vibrate those molluskular zeroes
Trail them across his stone brow <to be//to be>
<unfathered//slave & children to its simulated
weightlessness>
To become the child of one o'clock[3]

3 When we spotted the Brown Creeper, the woman burst into tears: "I've been looking for this bird for 20 years, & it'll probably be extinct in 15" • 1:07 PM - 30 Sep 2014 • Embed this Tweet

CECILIA LLOMPART

One of Many Gardens

In one garden, there were as many entrances as there were roses. The fireflies lifted their precious bodies of light away from our darker and heavier bodies, all water moved through light and all sound moved through the water. I had perfect breasts, the children ate stone fruit, the children were made of stone and they ate the fruit right there in the heart of the garden. In one garden, the birds moved through the light and the light rearranged the birds. When you spoke, it was not your words that reached out to me but the way your mouth moved, like a heron wading deeper into water. I was distractible. I was against a wall of light, I was a wall of white stone and you were inside of me and the sun was coming up from behind you and only really because of you. In one garden, we made a kind of fog with our bodies the fog filled the places between the roses until the only places left to fill were the places between our bodies. What one could have mistaken for caution, in our movements, was in fact a kind of certainty. You lowered yourself into me and I lowered myself into you. In one garden, my heart was the stone that marked the entrance, there was fog guarding the only exit, and when we opened our mouths they were filled with rose petals. We couldn't speak to each other because I was distracted, because of our mouths, because of the rose petals, because our hearts were distracted and because petals covered the ground around our feet and then petals covered the ground above our heads. In one garden, all of the other gardens were made out of light. In one garden, all of the garden was under cement. It was customary then to be under cement. In one garden, we were lowered into the ground, there was no exit, and when we were brought back out, we were made of roses, we had grown extra hearts, you could slice the hearts right off of us and they would only grow back larger, we had grown fruit instead of thorns, you could harvest the roses right off of us, you could enjoy them right there in the garden.

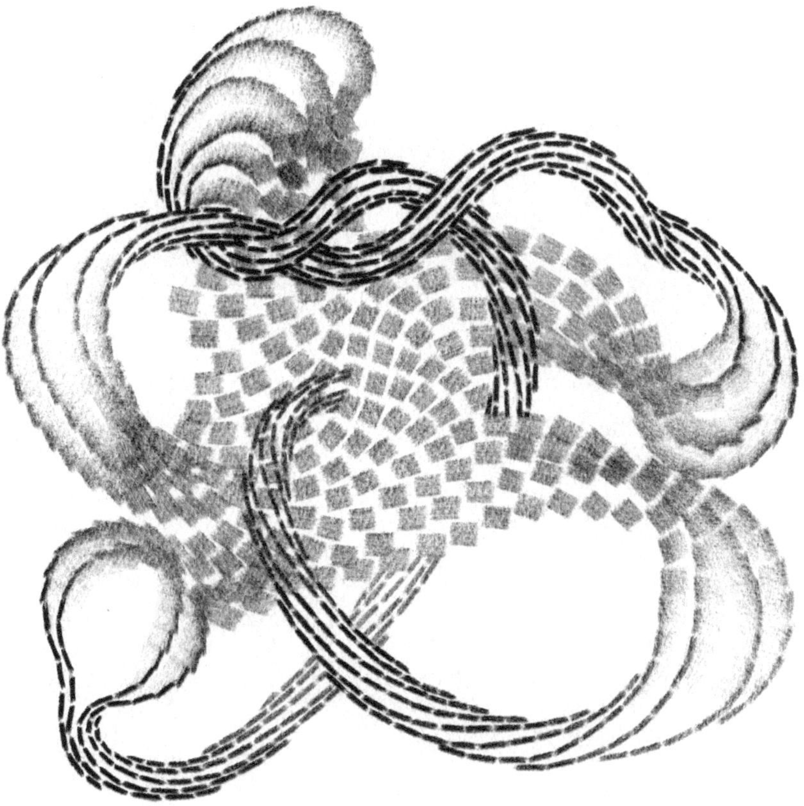

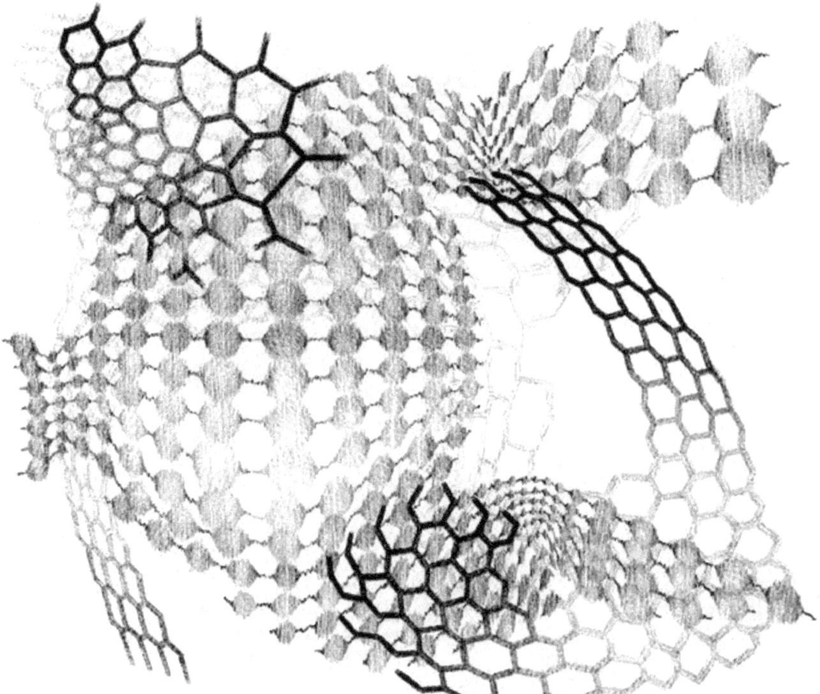

PART FOUR:

Love in the Anthropocene

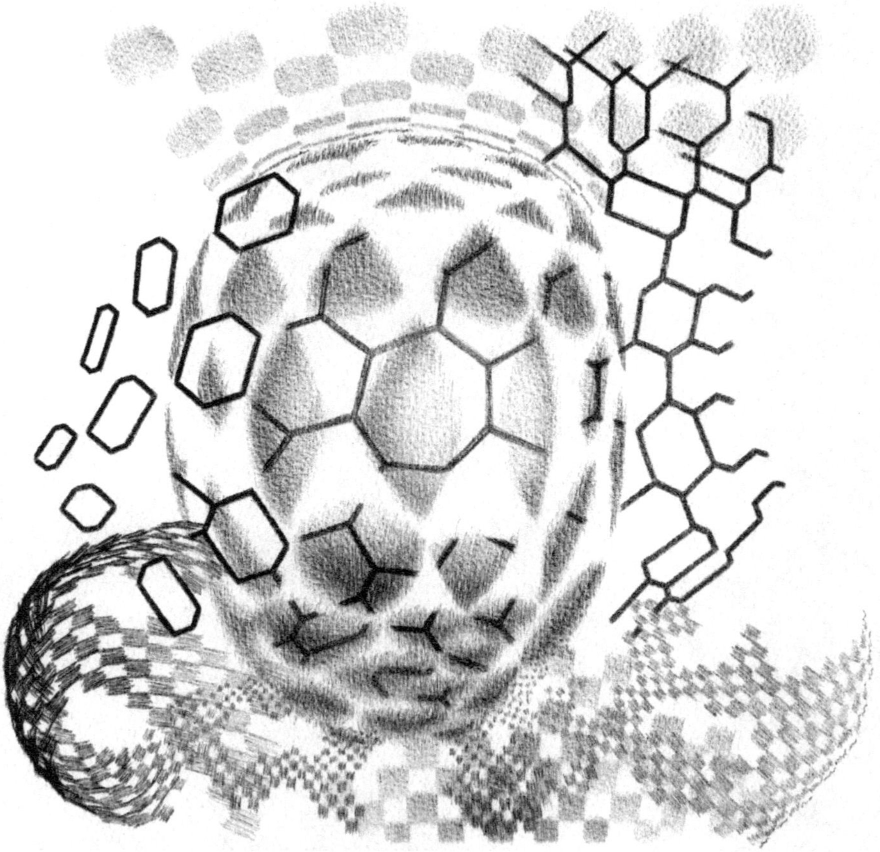

EXECUTE PROGRAM . . .

“The anthropocene” is a term used to describe a geological age during which humans have been the primary influence on the climate and environment.

How do you think humans have most affected the planet? What should we do differently when moving forward? What should remain the same? What do you think are the best strategies for saving our planet? Who can be a part of the process, and how?

The human species usually prioritizes its own needs over the needs of the planet and non-human ecosystems. We pollute oceans to further our industrial goals and deforest vast areas for lumber.

How should we balance our needs as a species with the needs of non-human ecosystems? Which should we prioritize? How can we expand and evolve our experience of love to incorporate more than just human minds and bodies and needs?

TRACY K. SMITH

Monument

I love climbing you
As if you are a mountain,
A monument built in the night
By invisible hands. And as I climb—
With my lips and my tongue, throat
Hard at work, eyes open or shut, hands
Quick, light as breath, agile, then exacting—
You watch, anemic from my effort,
Head moving left and right without you,
As if the sight of my work has scoured
Your mind clean of all but urge, itch, avalanche.
Then you go to the place beyond watching:
Clouds. Wind across water. A lone
Animal hounding the distance. Owl-
Song in the high moon-scoured branches.
Canyons spilling over with fog.

In Bed, Two Mystics

HELENA KAMINSKI

In bed, two mystics.
Me inside her: my index, my middle, my
Ring finger, pushing at, stretching, locating an immense room.
Meeting the room's walls, reading its stresses as it travels.
Tissue with its own heartbeat.

To feel but not know that room. Its joins.
A room that enters and leaves you.

Who focusses this hard?
Athletes. Actors in close-up.

Breasts blotched.
Eyes, wide and round.
Rapid, noisy breaths thin on the O_2
Then thick slabs of sound before everything snaps, and
The clit slips its hood, is there, not there
There there.

How red the red candles burn.

DAVID RIVARD

Escapism

Two older ladies with gray hair tinted
red, cranberry-red, hip pointers have them
waddling on *Cinco de Mayo*—it's here
in public places that the elders arrive at slow times
and boredoms they may not have feared so
as prepared for by practicing with years
of dull routines—*my* favorite morning pastime
toast & coffee with my head sunk far below
the fold, miles into newsprint & diving down
through stories reported by journalists half-blind
and jacked-up on global catastrophes gone for broke.
Apricot jam dripped onto chauffeur-black
pajamas is a pleasure to lift with your index finger
and lick, even if not quickly enough to keep it
from dripping again—this time onto your sleeve
and the Papal Nuncio's nose—the anxieties of
news escaped—sort of. "Escaped the nets,
escaped the ropes—moon on water," so states
the spring moon's job description, according
to Buson, the scourge of chrysanthemum growers,
whom he thought of as slaves to flowers—
but isn't it that some things are better to be
slaves to than others?—so I woke early
this morning, my poor head sick of duties
assumed at the remote behest of one bureaucracy
or another, & thought then of you naked
in a bathtub one pentecostal August
30 years ago, & your dark nipples somewhere
in memory near the sudsy waterline
put an end to the busywork of headquarters,
they destroyed paperwork & telephone calls
to come—it was so nice to meet you there,
and to go on soaking with you in my head.

Lunes

MAUREEN SEATON & SAMUEL ACE

Think of me
lashed foreign in your arms—
the brutal feminine.

I'm afraid
the breasts
have flattened
into the wind
foremost
on the ship
head carved
boyish brutal
and sudden
given to the horse
rushing away
through the field

My dog took
me down
that same path
more solid
than the wailing chest

Think of me
open and digital, a sound
exhaled in G.

Aching a revival
of paint a wooden
hush in the feral quiet

A zero blue
frozen and linked, pushed back
to the elegy.

I do
think of you
all the time
as if seeing
would manifest
you here
not irrevocably lost

Nor borrowed (from
fire), from the red book
of thirty-four children.

Fight me
for a ranch
to put them
bunks
but wait
you said paint
not souls

Yet here I
am alive in the frayed
and fragile past.

Tongue, A Queer Anomaly
(an excerpt from a dictionary)

These entries (now over 800 and continuing) were conducted at the crossroads of pre-existence and post-existence, somewhat akin to the crossroads of soul possession in voudou religion who mount an intra-divine mortal space in order to investigate and re-define that teleology.

Mondegreen—And when you said no I heard yes. Ambushes of air-waves again. We had no way of telling what the hell an apoplexical agreement might have stood for, so we just stood there. Until we fell. The falling was an approximation of union there, on the green lawn, was entirely unforeseen. Then the head was thrust through the atmosphere and the feet were caparisoned, flapping up in the air, all four of them. Sometimes it is difficult to measure what it is that makes a chord, but a flopping chap with a memory of three jacks, pointed, hacking away at his palm from the inside of his grip, is enough layers to bend the code. Chords are the natural result of bends in codes. So, lo and behold, the entire world hung on our four feet like a full house, a royal flush the world rode as we crashed down through the atmosphere toward an expansive abode, a fueled equine in stride. Each glistening gush (like gold mush) is a leader trammeling into a form. A form where the forms of fish slither in shining water-matter and light-matter. I cocked my cap (not out of deference but from a sense of understanding publicity, it's a rude mock-up of such, to outlaw such, and be much more than it really pretends) and let the water run-off into the bathtub which had appeared from out of nowhere, or maybe from out of a perfectly precise somewhere. Appeared in order to hold.

Integer—Untouched hence whole? Pleroma pre picture. Pleasant when present. Palindromes and paradoxes, euphemisms and elephants. Euphoric emblems slip through the door-crack, slide the door further open to let in the entire contents of Noah's ark. Tell the tale of Adam without Eve. Adam seeks a donkey with a large anal cavity like in that Rumi poem about the gourd, and 9 months later out pops a gourd-child with a long neck, long and slender like the numeral 1.

The Pattern of Interference

ASHLEY DE SOUZA

You drop me off wearing that
sleeveless shirt that shows off
your bio-mechanical tattoo. The
sprockets and splines are shaded
realism. When I asked you what
the gears and clogs were called
you said it didn't matter. So I
called you nuts & bolts. I called
you superman. They drew in
ligaments and peels of skin to
look like you were (to some
extent) human. When I stare
at them now, I can still see the
birthmarks they tried to cover
with ink. I can no longer trace
you. I should call you hologram.
I tell you that just because a
needle etched spirals and helices-
that didn't make you any
stronger. You look at me and the
fluorescence of the sun
makes your light eyes pixelate. You do
not blink for fear of shutting
down. "I'm stronger than you."
And I look down at my blank skin.
Only God has whittled me.
But I see the blue and yellow you
clout from the laser pads of your
fingers. You're right. Your eyes pull mine
and our minds whirr
again. We look but do not see.
I'll suck the charge electric. The
holographic sticker on the bill of
your hat sparks.

Hometown

1.
Papery moths latched to the wire screen
Having died here because I have not heard

A lawn mower all summer.

They are like people, hissing softly.
Fore-mandibles kneading the creamy warmth

On the roof of their mouths,
Trying to peer inside a prism of bleary hallways

And the grass always growing taller at night

Now that sallow voltage no longer drapes
Itself in windowgauze, the jaundiced light

Like women lying broken across the stained decks
Of the suburbs.

2.
I think of cockroaches nibbling on breadcrusts
In provisionless cupboards

Convinced that men stalk through the undergrowth
When the moon is dark,

Prodding for toys they dropped as children.

Those dusty globes over-loomed in a carousel

Of tottering reflections,

And I'm here,

Dreaming of smashing those shadows socketed
In chipped wallplaster

And flicking on all the switches, drawing in
The stale vacuums through a cigarette

Kindled on a platinum filament whirring orange.

Because I can usually hear those plastic wheels
By now,

Grating slowly down the street.

3.
Like drill bits,
The stars auger in and out of a gasoline sky,

The broken constellations gimleting faster still
As they wheel amiss through the headwinds.

Whole millenniums are dissolving
In the rarefied atmosphere of townlights

When I hear the clatter of a wheel gone wonky
Approaching through the trilling crickets.

Each of her footsteps draws the pavement a little closer,
The interluding darkness

Apertured with lambent fiberglass—
Beneath the street's slack electricalwork everything is frosted.

Then I see her.

Plodding bodily behind the stroller like a yokeless
Ploughblade.

4.
Now she is standing

Where I once watched her thumbs slide over
Her razourous hipbones, un-garlanding her waist
As one knee dipped slightly in front of the other,
Her forearm slumped across her breasts like she'd

Broken her wrist.

I held her body like handfuls of seaglass backwashing
Out of the frigid Atlantic,

And slid from her, birth-warm.

5.
Somebody left a bloodstain in her bedstand's ashtray,
Set the larval heart beating,

Moth-wings lisping off the screen door as it rapped shut.
How many have I sent reeling?
I'm keeping him.

Him? You already know?

The lucent tongs shelled in thinly cracked glass

Weeping papery husks blinded of their prisms

Just so I could bum one of her loosely-packed cigarettes,
And gaze into that face,

His rattling breaths enshawled
As though still trying to protect him from hospital lights

And mid-December smell of cold metal and dog—

You don't even know who the father is.
Are you calling me a whore?

I fear his are the eyes that opened,
To which the light opened back.

6.
My shadow walks barefoot across the moth-bitten lightspurts,
The grass warm because it is alive.

Her throat is half-missing in the shadow of her hand.

She is clawing her at elbow, says, "These fucking percocets
Always make me itchy."

And obliging, hands down the emptied pack of Mavericks.

Stubby fingers fishing tobacco flecks out of the crinkling foil
Like pastry filling.

Somewhere beneath her breastfeeding a subterranean tree
Dangles by its roots,
The wiry-crooks unfurling with a sudden heave as though

In full blossom.

The heat of another slurring abattoir staining the cellulose
And siphons-in that timelapse of seasons,

Whole decades have transpired since she learned of her parents' house—
Her face gaunted each time in the emberflare.

"What will you do?"

She shrugs "I hear their valets make good money."

"Well, there's always that."

As I frown at the pavement another human face is staring
Into the universe

I wonder if he's eaten yet.

Overheard by the NSA

CURTIS EMERY

My neighbor paints flowers
by moonlight,
her hands make quick images of
broken stems and blossoms
unfurled past where their petals
can hold them, together spilling
onto the walk in front of a
door—

she eats them,
these flowers—
petal by petal by petal
until all color is hidden in her stomach
and the loud stamen whispers silently
behind her round belly.

Her cat stretches out by
the railing of a set of stairs
where she rests her head
at night, I can see her there,
always, holding her shoulders
like a love letter,
the rain spilling
the ink into the drain by parked cars—
and sometimes there are no parked
cars.

In the morning, her flowers
vanish, sent to smoke by rising sun,
its light pours color back up
into the sky, back to where the moonlight

fell and caused her to dance and shriek
roses and tulips and dandelions like glass
and orchestra—

Caused her to smile the song of
every street corner huddled and
ragged, every home left empty,
every piece of paper left metered
in unison next to a heavy head.

My neighbor is America.
And beauty beauty beauty
breathes only at night
when the sky is quiet enough
to hear the rise and fall of
her glowing chest.

CELINA SU

Critical Care

—for Christina Wen-Fong Tseng Su,
June 30, 1945 - April 1, 2013.

—"The difference between a poem and a lion is an alphabet."
–Sahar Muradi

1.

Typically, your sentiments travel back to me only via hearsay,
But once in a while, every few months, they stop me in my tracks.
As if your thoughts bellow through a loudspeaker,
As if they constitute a call to prayer.

And now. With the clenching comes the possibility of thought.
As if seven decades and three continents cannot encompass
You, a small crucible for a star witness, skin taut.
Stents and vasopressors for what the heart cannot contain.

These feelings refracted like a thousand shards of *almost*,
For you beat me to the punch. Our inchoate words of love
Simultaneously diffuse and concentrated enough as to be unutterable.
So that we chew upon them, ceaselessly. We refuse to let them go.

Grinding each sentiment to a fine thread of longing,
And then—your mouth repeatedly fills with blood, sentience, cognition
Without, they insist, recognition.
The difference between the light and the word is

First, the act of falling, and then, the semblance of sleep.
Before I was born with a broken heart, you carried me
To Iguaçu. Between Brazil, Argentina, and Paraguay,
Above the roar of the water, a silence proclaimed: There is more to come.

2.

I had promised to be kinder, to practice greater patience.
So what now. What is purposeful— they tell us—

Is not. We bear witness to this supposed state of non-being,
As if—we hear them say— meaning lies elsewhere.

The difference between waiting and wanting is a generation.
The difference between acquiescence and happiness is never.

The difference between this moment and the next meal is always.
The difference between what you gave and what we took I cannot fathom.

Between home & Nanchang & Taipei & Nashville & Princeton &
New Brunswick & Campinas

& São Paulo & New York & Elkins Park & East Brunswick &
Monroe is not yet a lifetime.

But what is clear is invisible. What is weightiest remains intangible.
The difference is not that I do not know, but that I never will.

We track most carefully what we cannot see.
Opening one's eyes wide is not seeing, but believing.

Tongue, A Queer Anomaly
(an excerpt from a dictionary)

Creepy? — If I worked at the airport I would keep a daily record of people's luggage, luggage I searched to see what strange things lie within. In the diary I would leave out all punctuation and run the items together, not like a free write nor like a paragraph but something else: Christmas lights in mass taking over the brain? Extant flags like instant flagellum produce an induction, a beauty that can be there for you always. If we truly show up, who knows what will happen. Well, I know we can make it happen, so let's get to it right away—now or never as they say. I would have to say now, because the change came over me like night to take over day. That's the rendition of desire, the rendering of all things in this braid. I will go on and on about desire until I am dead, then we will find each other. I want you to know something (and it's a whisper, a window of love). All the skin of the human, blown out, all around you and out from me is stunning. The rib is opening a crux to reveal, something rugged: a cleft. How to treat a cleft as a cliff? The idiom might dilute it, but might assist you (especially if you jump from it with all your might, discovering the juniper which is also known as a sacred pun). How'd you know how I would kill myself if I did kill myself: arms like fringes, garments of appeal as I fly through air? Fly not flail. The smooth course of air might be known by my mind. Now, where were we? Did you remove the stigmata from my religion yet? My intention was to do that, but if you're concerned, we can go over all of them again. Oh good, what a relief. I have so many! Let's start with the fascia (never to be taken for granted), then move to excitations of the fascia to burnish callouses. Rubbing hard my surface (I mean the surface underneath the other one that was just removed) is a way to commune. To move by callouses, then remove them, withdrawing, will catch the attention of lovers. After the pause has issued a placement we see we are the preponderance (because there are arms and legs protruding and doing from that *pre*). A pre plans to place us in an autobiographical PMS. Have you ever heard of one of those before? This is the meaning of a circle: something smooth with corners that are pointing into the sand. If you meet me in the embrasure in the old castle, we might still make the time-machine's coordinates, but we really must hurry. I plan on saving you by every means possible. I'll help by painting a very large target on my chest. That way you can throw the energetic masses from anywhere. I also mean to make saving you forever more dear for you. Serve me up to swerve. The longtime goddess is hungry. If you've gotta get something through the bars, just heave it into my back and rub. A new subject to touch is very important. It prepared a man for his death (when he was running in the forest). You just flashed that portrait again, let me see it! Here: as he ran he grew thinner and thinner. The trees mirrored him during their own thinning seasons (nameably winter or for whatever reason(s), gaunt spring). He turned into a turnip, right at the lip of the wood. Oh, I guessed you were there all along but now I know it. I instantly needed to make a poem when I saw that turnip because it looked like a little floral dick. I even said that out loud, right there in the forest: "little floral dick." I was straining to look upward. You placed your hand on me and took me into the world. I was meant to be living, in you. Mean the world of my mouth when I treat you like something vegetable. Those little flecks of masticated food might be my entire life. The point is: get into the crumb, climb the crumb. Ask the fables: the kids who were burned in the witch's oven only made it out by being a part of a tall tale?

Sappho's Child

Sappho my angel you wind you heavy sigh
sleep in the shadow of your baby
in the room where you quietly tuck me away,
where my eyes as dark as priests
fall heavy on you.

What happens to the woman
who abandons her child,
her baby-man
who crawls at her feet,
who stalks?

In the room where you quietly tucked me away
they've taken the blades from the clock
and all the sharp edges
leaving me pointless without you.

Room of the lost edges.
Body smeared in shadows of large abandon.

The nurse looks through the black backside
of a mirror:
dirty boy,
little trash can baby-man.

She reads me through the mirror and goes away.
My grandmother used to read to me.
Each monk
had a candle.
Each slept alone in a small room like this
in coarse robes.

They were encouraged by their mothers
to beat themselves to sleep each night.

One summer, a boy throwing stones at swallows
hears Grandmother
first woman that he loves
call him in from the dark to have his bath.

And shivering, he dries beside the flickering blue flames
of the furnace.

Then there was also a room
where Grandmother tucked me away
that smelled of talcum and dried roses,
the dustiness of old quilts
and photographs from 1940.
The room had a passage through a closet
to another room.
I used to push my way through her dresses
to reach the other side
where the dresses, the talcum's, lipsticks, dried roses
clung to me like a woman,
like the ocean, nocturnal female.

That was the first room.
Blue room
where they slapped me
and I held my breath
and they slapped me again.
I wept
as the surgeons pulled at my veil, the mother-wax
wiped away in the blue room
leaving its lost edges inside,
an ocean inside me.

I spent the whole day digging in the sand,
trying to make edges . . .
When I turned I saw my blue shovel drifting away off shore
and rushed to grab it but it drifted away.

Then I was angry and hysterical.
I found my way back over the dunes
while the first night, blue, rip tidal
shoveled back to the unknown,
waves depositing their losses
and tucking quietly back into themselves.
Pass through
for the sake of the world, the needle.
Doctors
Nurses
Horsemen
pass through the eye of my needle;
come into my room
that is filling with darkness,
dark female blood
and bloody altars.
The blue blue flames of beyond.
The vapor trail of beyond.

Room like a meadow filling with stars.
Room in which I am quietly tucked away.

Basic room.
Basic hospital white
like a wedding gown.
Room you get shit into
like the jewels that flow from the wounds of Christ.
A sacrifice.
Bright diamond she slips from her fingers

and deposits.
The Elizabethan room for an Island Queen:
"Every woman must assassinate one man."

You deposit me.
Slip me from your finger like a diamond
or a distant star.

Time was without its arms, helpless.
No edges for the past and future, no dividing sweep.
Space
makes of these stones a house,
a room, a container,
poem to contain its own madness,
church to house its psychotic martyr,
hysterical woman to carry the child,
sleep to bear the burden of your dreams.
Silence
to pattern a song in cycles of thirteen years
that drills its way eventually
out of the stone.
By the end of summer, locusts
leave their delicate glass bodies attached to trees.

As a boy I used to take them down
and bury them.
First, I studied them, then I dug them
little graves.

Summers I stayed with my grandmother
and learned with her
how to sew these differences together.
When she died she left me a blanket
stitched from old suits she ripped apart.

Heavy gray wool like sleep, brown wool, dark blue.
She dreamed them together again.
Dreams that were storied by madness.

The poems contain them. They order them
one by one:
the Marquis de Sade tossing petals
one by one
on a pile of dung.

Dirty boy!

Dirty boy inside his chrysalis.
Act of guilt.
Ellipsis in the house. Bitterly widowed—
who craves the passionate touch of darkness,
the child's little sex cry.
Widower. Wasp. Atrocity!

Each word Sappho you speak is a poison wafer:
This is his body.
Rose of the swollen body.
Rose of the blue flames.
Arc of the swallow.

I am wounding you.
In my room
the walls are papered by a wasp.
The writing on the walls records rotations
of the sun and moon,
the boy and the girl and the naked bed
made of one stone,
the bed that contains a madness
and sings now with nothing to stop it,

that sings out where you buried your only child
who whined and whined like a locust in the dusk.

The bed,
the squeaky voice
remembers the song.
How it goes.
Comes and goes like an ocean.
In my room there is no ceiling or borders or end.
A mouse hurls his little body at nothing and abandons himself.

In my room there aren't any doors—well—
there is
a door
but the handle is on the other side
like that picture of Jesus standing there dumbfounded.

It's three o'clock in the morning and no one answers.
Everything has been removed:
the old books just flew off with dead wings,
the sharp edges of a thousand pages,
matches (Maybe the nurse thinks I'll try
to light a cigarette
and set the room on fire.
Maybe the nurse thinks I'll set myself on fire.)

She looks in on me through the black backside
of a mirror.

I lived as a chrysalis, without windows.
Only guilt.
I lived in a body bag,
the silent body of abandonment.
A figure drawn in large abandon.

A sweet goodnight
suspended there,
seeing them from somewhere else, another ward
where they're stitching me back.

The clock has a facial tick.
A mouse screams.
A nurse is rocking and rocking.
She sews my new blue song with a long sticky hair.
Come.
Come,
my angel,
pass through the eye of my needle you wind,
you heavy sigh
caught in the thread
of the last breath
of the last word.

I climbed up in the tree and vanished in the leaves
and supernatural flames.
I was so afraid
and couldn't get down
and my grandmother called:
It's time for a bath, my child, my dirty boy.

MARTIN OTT

I Lost the Robot in the Divorce

With one eye, tin torso, dryer duct limbs,
my thrift store doppelganger leans over
the scratched-up dining room table, dressed for
holidays I cannot view except dim
dreams through cyborg senses. Dressed in elf hat
for Christmas, next to my empty station
guests comment about the combination
lock on the broad metal chest welded shut.
Have I been replaced by this golem pop
clothed in the costumes my kids and I wore
on the days before the shades held races?
Looking back, there was no way I could stop
splitting our stuff, division of flesh, curse
of an immobile man in two places.

Tongue, A Queer Anomaly
(an excerpt from a dictionary)

Cyclamen—The heart. Not hurt, my heart is in the afterglow which challenges midnight's most fabulist accoutrement. Mine lay in wait upon Aapep's shoulder, emboldened by imagined rioters which enliven the apes. Searching for evolutionary matter, it is possible to peer in plundering history for their letters' corroboration, their eye's lost lashes. Loose condoms, loose change, fluttering in the wind.

Herm—Deck of cards with ace of pentacles, phallic god who traces peduncles. All things go great with wine, especially mixed with LSD. Oh wait, I mean LDS. See, I already dropped a tab today. When I was a kid the Mormon elders used to drop tabs all the time. There, behind partitions, they were patrons of the underground (having bequeathed their morals to an institution they thereby lacked all judgmental critiques as well as teeth). I am saying nothing will be lost if the slightest bit of compassion can be lent to them, because the feather which wrought the iron is at the door once again. The door keeps score, trust me. These archetypes are legions in the nerve center of the archive. Ask a Tzar, he'll tell you (like a mad Ivan) about the score's totals but never more, because he is most interested in what he has in his other hand, the one under the table. He has something there which is not all or everything—the kind of thing that, if folks are not careful, makes unintentional babies or a comma accenting pause, instead of a caesura speaking for itself.

Porphyrophobia—As the advent of the pussy willows along a shoreline, these impulses to drive away from certain retinal terrors are words. With words people create their homes and deny the entirety of what their real home is. The phobia here is not so much a gut reaction as it is a glow around the specified, keeping those from ganglia in need of water.

CECILIA LLOMPART

Hallelujah Girls

The planets champion peace and the papers
champion war—but in a forgotten town,
a hallelujah girl champions the marbles,
skips a tired rope, climbs a tree for a better
look at her creator. She sees the old people
that prefer to sit outdoors, she feels for them.
They feel the wind right up to their bones,
the wind that keeps its own council with
the barn, rattling the beams, singing through
the hinges, hounding the squirrels and inciting
revolt among the pigeons. But all is well in
the family of gnats—the peaches are rotting
to a pulpy juice, and then to pure fragrance.
A hallelujah girl is thankful for the sting of
a good stew, but considers the blood on her
hands, the small bird that was worth nursing
the whole summer, only to be found by the
neighbor's cat, the blood of the lambs led to
bait and slaughter by the local butcher, how
they bleat out a meek chorus all the way to
the hard wooden heart of the chopping block.
A hallelujah girl falls asleep counting dead
sheep, and enters her own lopsided world
of dreams—the bison so small they fit under
teacups, hide them there long enough, and
they will revert to their own personal ice age.
A girl so large she clips the sky, wears clouds
like milky pearls and wedges herself deep
into God's own poor memory, like a splinter
of sudden light. A hallelujah girl knows heaven
is a dry tumble in the tall weeds, the cotton flea

jumping high, higher than last summer, the boys
taking their shirts off to swim, only the one boy
blushing a bit, a blooming rose across his chest.
And that hell is but to see your own sorrows
marching in in shoes made of stone, the dog
finally coming home with that open sore, how
it festered all winter long, opening and closing
like an ugly eye, how it was unsavable, said
her father, who took down the mantle axe
and, in one merciful blow, lobbed the paw clean
off. How the raccoon got the best of the dog
after that but never stole from the dish put out
again, took pity, or they made a kind of wild
peace. How the kingdom of animals is like
that—live and let and live on. How so much
is like that—a hard bargain under a hard sun.

from *Dybbuk of Angelus*

XXIV

Making love with the Dark One and eating little,
those are my pearls and my carnelians.[4]

Inside the river—the figures of
the Dark stretching infinitely.

Inside the river the monotony
of bells, wound-spread lilies.

We wake to the sound of trees, silver foxes
basking in the cemeteries,
branches chatter into bells, icicle birds, their wings,
what wings what whales?

At most times we cannot stand silence –

Frostbitten, icicled wings,
octagonal is owl,
what cathedrals are we to build?

Baptistery of octopi into
windows until it flaps
with holy hissing orchid
St George bludgeons the dragon
the dragon floods the air
the river seeps through a man's hands, the streets in can-

---

4 Mirabai, "Why Mira Can't Come Back to Her Old House"

vases, seep through cracks, hisses, chutes,
pitches, the foreign pens
on the table flutter.

An immigrant sits on the curb and listens
to students reading love poems,
children carrying albatrosses into a cathedral.

We wake the desires
into bells, into yes
cradled into
hollows
making snails on the stiff lake,

we drill holes in ice, we make bonfires
with words
we light up cemeteries.

C.J. WISLER

Self-Portrait As Persephone Just Before Her Abduction By Hades

By intuition, Mightiest Things
Assert themselves —
– Emily Dickinson, "You'll know
it – as you know 'tis Noon–"

It seemed a simple task,
to move the Mexican coriander sprout,
culantro as my Mother called it.

By botanist's terms a *volunteer,*
it, unprecedented, emerged
without the gardener's hand.

And so it was, this barely-there herb
volunteered, but grew in parched soil, and stood
endangered by the summer's building drought.

A simple herb, a simple trek
across the garden. But now, in the garden
hesitation creeps – a noxious bindweed,

Winds round the stem, cuts off (trans)
formation, (trans) planting.
So, she takes care to grasp tightly the coiled stem,

Despite thorn, despite skin's
instinctual recoil. The heart persists.
Eyelids shut with an audible click,

as he hand
claws through to
the richness beneath!

Within the earth, she feels soft plinks
As rootlets unlatch their childlike hands,
Still, the root will not come free.

So, her hand grasps firmer. And then,
with eyes still shut, there comes
not without trepidation,

of a forceful graceless nerve,
the loam softens as the root yields:
and then that wet and living length

springs forth with rich, full-bodied roots,
The culantro, that saw-tooth spirit-weed,
bursts forth as the heart bursts forth.

The hole widens, something emerges,
Cool and firm. Moist air blows from it
like someone reaching out

to love, which is another way
to say abduct completely.
No, the eye does not need to open

for sight. For lo, the root comes out.

ELIZABETH J. COLEN

Edge Effect

in the darkest space is a white fleck,
ox-head dot; and when I pass through,
it's a spurt of match into flame,
glowing moths loosed into air, air
rippling, roiling the surface of the world.
—Arthur Sze

Something beautiful is on my screen. Crisp focus, a room in orange light, a woman on her knees. Head cut from the frame of the jpeg by the photographer's choice, or in cropping whoever had the image next or last. What beauty, what image, skinsmooth, woman on knees in heels, facing a closet's mirrored door. Back arched and ass punched out, she has on a string of what I imagine to be cheap pearls and nothing else.

And when I go to the little bridge—it still exists—I stop and I listen to the Bièvre. I still hear it. So I stop, and I listen. –long-time resident of Gentilly, France Andrée Gibert.

Her legs are splayed open, diamond-shaped. At the bottom of the diamond, toes in her red heels meet to form an angle. At the top, thighs culminate into the V of a shaved pussy. In the mirror, the pearls hang between her C-cup breasts, and we can see the front of her arms, the rest of her body in the shadow of her doggy style. Her nails are trimmed, palm down, fingers curled, ready. My first thought: the unscuffed underside of shoes. Second thought: what color is her hair. (There is no pubic hair to help and her head was left off in composition.) Third thought, which lingers: ass. I touch it, the screen, glossycool, more smooth than any woman lying under me. Than any woman's hairless moan. My computer's heat draws away from itself in the hum of a tiny internal fan.

*

I stand on the horizon and watch the giant turbines tuuuuuurning. Some stopped. Some turning turning turning turning. Some grayed out in shadow. Without the clouds the sky would be pure orange. Without the turbines the hills would be the pure yellow of grass about to burn.

*

I have a photograph of my mother standing in front of a mirror in my grandmother's house. She has on a green coat that I don't remember, Mickey Mouse ears hat on her head, tight jeans tapered to the ankle. One hand is behind her head, and her head is thrown back. In the mirror I think see the scar on her wrist, I think I see her wedding ring. Her other hand is on her hip. It is a playful pose that both fits my memory of my mother—using sex to move through worlds—and does not fit my memory of my mother—lighthearted. She smiles. My sister sits on the floor behind her in diapers, sits behind my grandmother's guest bed. She would be missed in this photo if not for the mirror's doubling. On the bed, my mother's opened purse. Turned somewhat toward our gaze, we can see her cigarettes, a glasses case, and the spine of a mass market paperback: *The Celestial Bed.*

*

This may or may not be related. I recently saw a film: *The Headless Woman* (*La mujer sin cabeza*) by Argentine director Lucrecia Martel. Said to be taken from a dream Martel had once, *The Headless Woman* is about a woman who runs something over while driving, does not get out to see what was hit, and steadily loses her mind.

Losing her mind means she either rents or does not rent a hotel room, room 818. It means she either has or does not have sex with her sister's husband. It means she either hit the boy who ends up dead in the flooded culvert, or does not. In either case, she's mad. So mad she dyes her hair. And talks very little, though we have nothing to compare her relative silence to, as the hit-and-run comes early in the film.

*

The River *Bièvre* was covered over and integrated into the sewer system under modern-day Paris in 1912. Thus submerged, it flows through Paris's 13th and 5th arrondissement, from Kellerman Park to the metro bridge near Gare d'Austerlitz where it empties from a large pipe into the Seine.

*

My stepfather used to burn trash in a fire barrel at the back of our land. When angry at my mother he would burn her books. The semi-nude people on the cover of her romance novels would melt grotesquely, become animal, monster, their pure need thus exposed in the heat.

*

From an early age I learned that sex is often bought and sold, as is labor, as is the world.

*

Once the woods caught fire, late winter. Eagle nest in the white pine fell, two cracked eggs, eaglets with slick translucent skin, no wings, no tiny beating heart.

*

In the movie, in Salta, boys play in a wide concrete ditch, dry but for a slow trickle.

*

I don't know if they still exist, but in the 1990s, 1-900 phone sex lines charged up to $10 a minute—*No recordings, we're real, we're live, and we're waiting here for you—What turns women on will turn you on—Let me be your friend tonight, it's totally private!*; I saw the commercials on late night TV all the time.

Internet porn can be free, but the low-cost/free kind means there's a delay between the action as it is experienced by the observed and the action as it is experienced by the observer. Everybody comes, but the timing is all over the place.

*

Once while living in Georgia I hit a possum with my car. It was early, the road still blue in the pre-dawn. I was traveling slowly, thought maybe maybe she's just hurt. I thought that: *she.* I got out of the car and thought: this is what they do, play dead. To play possum is to play dead and so maybe she is playing herself.

But she was really dead.

*

Sometimes now an automated voice on a customer service line will play along at being live. She will laugh when you call her a robot. She will claim you must have a bad connection.

*

Sometimes I get a girl to lie under me just so I can feel myself really breathing. One set of lungs is one thing, two is quite another.

*

Robot sex, they say, by 2030. I say for the most part we're doing it now. Maybe we always have. Sharon Olds says the truth is the single body alone in the universe against its own best time.

Don't you sometimes watch the clock to see how long it takes?

What are we in the world?

In Japan the VR Tenga gives robot hand jobs while on screen an anime girl character manipulates some animated genitals, which the boy in the chair can imagine are his. The anime boy in the video looks pleased. The boy in the chair we cannot fully see, his eyes covered by the VR mask, his lips pursed into a thin crease. Perhaps of pleasure. In the comment thread there is much excitement.

*

Under the direction of the Army Corps of Engineers, the Los Angeles River was paved in 1938. To prevent flood. It became a continuous trapezoidal "flood control" channel from four miles north of Elysian Park in Central Los Angeles to Long Beach, approximately 30 miles to the south.

*

I fall in love with a girl in a bar. She is talking to someone else but meets my eye. When she goes outside to smoke I fall out of love with her. She crushes her cigarette butt on the sidewalk, returns to her booth; I do not meet her eye.

*

I convince myself that driving is not the hard part. On the earth, I mean. I am a small small dot ejecting a small small trace of poison into the air. Contrails everywhere. Chemtrails. In Canada people pay more attention, but it's still not much. Metallic crystals cross-hatched in the sky. I watch the sky for patterns. The broken radio is fixed to a certain volume and I trust myself that this is okay too. When I go down hills I take my foot off the gas. Uphill I have to floor it. My car is nearing twenty.

*

The town of Guiyu in China is home to thousands of businesses that comb and sow electronic waste, cell phones and circuit boards, computer parts and keyboards, copper wire and car parts. Traces of gold and silver dipped out in acid bath. A boy holds his face in his hand. Indifference and misrepresented parts melt off in coal flame, carcinogens and worse in groundwater, wellwater ash. Poor China makes the organized and then the disorganized organized again.

*

A girl does her hair in a wall of scuffed CDs and DVDs. One side *Shrek 2* and a German dub of *Wayne's World*, the other side her pursed pink lips.

*

I no longer wish to see things for what they are. In this, the future is graciously behind me.

*

Once, my tongue was unbearable.
It grew like two suitcases in my mouth,
side by side,
packed full of dirty clothes and underthings.

One thing I can't do is stop moving.

*

The sky buys lightning.

*

I know about a girl with a webcam who specializes in crying. She sits on her bed, a man comes in, they fuck and she cries. It's all consensual and live.

"Is it strange that I want to pay to watch?" I ask her.
"I can give you a code."

*

For the self, glasses, dislocation
of the self—
hand to the door. The manicured
nails aping the long pause, greased
long paws on the window.
For the self, for the
dislocation of the the the self, she
starts the car,
becomes the car,
the static, unturning
head, 80, 180,
180, 65, side-side/by-side, every everyforward
motion. The slicked-back hair,
hair. The blonde locks, blonde.
The radio, a sunny day.
The sunny day, Sunday.

*

Billboards advertise some kind of juice. Orange, I think.
From concentrate.

*

I stand on a river of asphalt, suburban and feel desert-like heat come off the pavement. "This used to be an orange grove."

*

And then the battery ran out and I had to use my hands.

*

Third scene opens on a wide dirt road. We're in the car, we're moving quickly, arc of steering wheel in the lower left-hand corner, at top right a flash of her red shirt in the rearview. Tilt low. Red the color of blood and woman, red the color of want. Turn after turn, mountains a distance in blue haze, dry canal and beige after beige of dry shrub. We hear the static of wheels on dirt, and the tinny melody of some upbeat song. And then we're in the car, the passenger seat; the woman's phone rings. Lyrics. Rings again. She reaches down to find it, looks away from the road for a second. The car thumps once; the woman grimaces, braces, fists white on the wheel. Her sunglasses pop off her face. The car thumps a second time and her forehead hits the windshield. Hands leave the wheel and she brakes hard into a sudden stop. The phone continues to ring. A distinctive tone. Something she must have chosen. Her hands come back to the wheel, rest lower now at nine and three. Outside the driver's side window the world is a uniformity of light dust, the world we've seen obscured. She swallows and the cloud clears, which allows us to see the dust and scrub of the side of the road and higher up, a slope of scrub on the other side of the canal. Her lips are closed tight, her red sweater bunched mid-arm. She swallows and the dust clears, and we can see two smalldirty handprints in the glass. We know they are a child's hand—because we saw the child in scene two—but the print looks animal, wild, like claws. Later, this ambiguity will seem weighted when the question becomes dog or human in discerning dent on fender. Hands off the wheel sunny Sunday, eyes closed, she swallows again, puts a hand to her chest, turns slightly, puts a hand on the door, removes her hand, faces forward, shifts in her seat, picks up her sunglasses, puts them on, starts the car. In this, there is just the briefest pause of the music on the radio while the electrical system turns off/switches on again. Her hands are back to ten and two and she drives off without looking back. Before the main road she gets out of the car and the rain starts, heavy drops on the windshield, through which we can see her body becoming obscure, through which we see her skirt (brown) and red shirt, but nothing above the V of her cleavage: the headless woman.

*

Oh. *Mixing. What did you think I meant?*

*

We spend several hours on Skype before one of us gets brave enough to take off her shirt.

We talk about nothing, everything. I read to you. You adjust the light in your room. I practiced the best angle to sit, the best angle to hold my computer before I made the call. I look cute, eyes big, just one chin. I put on a clean shirt. You ask if it's new. I want to touch your face. I want to touch your breasts.

I'm tired of touching myself, which is the only thing in reach.

We talk about everything, nothing. We exhaust our common ground. At this point in person we would be fucking, I think, then say, "At this point in person we would be fucking."

We have nothing to talk about and so just stare. I tell you you're pretty and you say the same thing. I can just look at your full lips, your fuckable fuckable face.

*

There's a way you can position your eyes at the top of the frame and look into the tiny hole of the computer camera and if both people do it's like you're really looking at each other. There's flickers of up down in eye movement, but the delay and how slight the movement is generally makes this work.

I think I'm looking at you. I can convince myself you're looking at me. This is eye contact. This is maybe really real. The screen freezes.

*

I read about a boy in India who fell in a river and was poisoned. He did not drown. His breathing became labored, then ragged. His skin sloughed off and there wasn't anything they could do. And what he swallowed could kill ten or twelve of him.

*

The sun sets. The sun comes up again. The sun sets slower or faster depending on the season, depending on the geography and coordinates of your location. Green flashes or green rays are said to be seen shortly after sundown. I wait for the green spark whenever I can, but I have never seen it.

*

You are big on my screen. Your face: face-sized. Sometimes larger. And I, in the corner of my screen take the place of one of your eyes. I adjust and readjust to my image. You know when I'm distracted because the color and quality of light on my face changes if it's not you I'm looking at.

"What are you doing?"

"Nothing."

"You're checking your email."

*

Of course I like to look at your mouth.

Shirt off and I'm wondering why things have not evolved to allow me to put my mouth on something that feels like your mouth and you put your mouth on something that feels like mine and then we make the motion of kissing onto our separate mouth things and feel like we're kissing each other.

"That would never work," you say. And I think, oh right what would that look like on screen. And the moment is gone. And the distance becomes somehow greater.

Are you checking your email.

*

The masturbation happens anyway.

*

What I am doing to me I am doing to me

*

What are you doing to me?

*

And then the delay when your mouthsounds do not match up with the movement. I anticipate the smile after a joke is made. And there it is, late. And when there is no talking at all: you are touching yourself and the screen gets frozen and then catches up. You are thrown into a frenzy of pixelated rubbing. Once the delay so pleased me in *not* freezing that I was allowed the near-real time pleasure of seeing cum spurt from between your legs.

Did I really just see that on camera.

*

What about the NSA?

When you came your head was thrown back out of the frame.

Someone should be watching.

*

I learn about the field of teledildonics.

What this means to straight men.

You can have sex with a machine that feels like a pussy while someone somewhere else has sex with a machine that feels like a dildo and what she does to it she does to you. Everything plugged in by USB.

"It's a pretty amazing experience to have a girl halfway around the globe be able to have such complete control over your genitals."

*

Though I am hard around the edges and mostly have no feelings for you, when we are done I have tears you don't know about. What is this. Lacking emotion, I don't know what this wet is for. You have no hands to find this on my face and the light is bad and distance means not hiding in a pillow.

*

Thanks to Craigslist I once had phone sex with a stranger because she offered and because I could tell her what to do. I didn't have to provide my credit card. I didn't pay her anything. When we were done we both just hung up and that was that. She said her name was Mary.

*

Somewhere the sun is always setting.

*

So far the girls are just for hire. So far there is nothing in what the man does with his machine that is translated onto the dildo in the woman's hand or cunt or elsewhere. This won't work for us. Pussy to pussy we have nothing to put in the machine.

*

I watch a video about Realtouch porn™, where the sex is not live (hired), but a porn that is greater than 3D and what a female porn star does on screen is done to the man with the machine. "There is nothing like it."

Nothing.

The machine looks like a giant peanut. I want one. I want some way to get it to work for me. In all the talk of it I am reminded of the fucking machine in Leonard Cohen's *Beautiful Losers*. The machine becomes sentient enough to know it needs so much momentum—sexual, textual—that humans, in not being inexhaustible or limitless in inter-course, are not enough. And the fucking machine throws itself into the constant rock and undulating agitation of the ocean.

*

I am distracted. You are not home and you are not here. It is December. It is 19 degrees. Faux logs flame in the fireplace. I watch *Vanishing Ice*, I watch Carl Sagan's *Cosmos*. I drive six blocks to the grocery store with its fluorescent buzz and mirrors and mist on produce and shelves of organized color like so much infinite wisdom. I buy three apples from New York and three oranges from Florida, I buy Nongshim Neoguri and Pocky, Lee Kum Kee and Rani Asafetida, Vero Mango chili mango lollipops and toothpicks from Taiwan. From the automatic sensor door of the store's entrance to the automatic unlocking of my car I watch the sky, the half-circle moon in the white-purple night. At home I watch *Cosmos*. I watch about vanishing ice. Glaciers calve and retreat, galaxies explode and collide. Is this porn for the planet? Apocalyptic? Is this post-modern sublime?

*

Garbage. On the cover of the book: a box falling from a black and white sky. Below, a rolling trash heap, boxes and barrels, bags abound. On the falling box, Chinese letters written, or are they words, figures. A slash in the box's side.

*

I organize my kitchen drawers, unmatched silverware rattling unevenly, disparate. It is said the mark of intelligence is the ability to hold two opposing ideas in mind at the same time. And still retain the ability to function. We know we refuse to know. The silverware drawer is stupid and loud. Haphazard fork tines jam the shallow drawer. The rough sound of metal on metal on metal on metal. The plates stack neatly, a nuclear family of porcelain.

Homooptical Translations of Love Poems in *Greek Anthology*

CATHERINE WAGNER

Pottynot or *Boy Annoy*

You wits to empty annual, guy
new axle sexiness, elongate,

now ye, cave raven shovelove
alcopop out of ethos unravel

o, ouch act poised toi, sexiness,
all epitaphs to otoliths or

Ottawa atone/atonal nut
fluxive is ovux wife

overskew avail.

*

Toy a Toy or Toi, a Toi

Of Katie mal-a-suave us tittie;
phew, totally, vulva ode
cacophonous
on a valve sun

call volvo, dickless annoy
Kropotkin/K, pot enough
April say waist off adulove
in peace yin/rove sexualate,

call ooh-cows a voice entelechy tov/

erratalove, book noël de-achievers
oh deviant apocalypses eponymous,

call Toronto/totalove
narrow molotov cupcake
so as endofus.

I'm Tired of You, Incest

TOMAŽ ŠALAMUN

I'm tired of you, incest, speech,
I desire the sun, the calm people's whispering
let the bonds of the world be as they are
I'm in love, I'm not a soldier

let the happy animals' eyes twinkle,
stones near the trees, shells in the dunes
let the boats navigate passing reefs
be untouchable, virginness

let spring be rich, hills' shadows sweet
the words plain, let be tender warm bread
let ruins be overgrown by the verdure, the hesitations of travelers
I'm riding the horse, sleeping under old oaks

there's no cuckoldry in the flights of the birds
no irony in the campo santo
in the sea there's the lustre of light
in the lions the punishment for the sin, the anticipation

*[Translated from the Slovenian by
Michael Thomas Taren and the author]*

SIMEON BERRY

Nix as Bowler

Miss Anaphora says it's good practice,
but gender makes him dizzy.

Walter and Lurlene peruse the endless
racks of black ova, bringing them

up to their chests in a graceful,
fallopian arc. Nix is ashamed.

His ball is dented, and wants
to eat his hand. Miss Anaphora

demurely sips a beer advertising
the name of a depressed city,

but he feels her eyes linger
on his butt as he bends over.

She's secretly entertained by this
struggle with the earth tones,

though he finds the spectacle sad.
Little spermlets of sweat randomize

on his shirt as the pins helix down
onto the pellucid floor. Why are they

so alone? Regardless of the score,
each poorly-dressed combatant

bears a receipt from the painfully
disinfected counter, where they hoped

and feared to inherit the collective
prose of those houseless shoes.

Tongue, A Queer Anomaly
(an excerpt from a dictionary)

Bathmism—In the bath the water kept moving: "Come rescue me, I need you." Your voice can get a little out of it, suddenly disown you. The bath is a good place to cull and then collaborate with forms as if they were your own reflection. Therein the ear hears relations so you can choose to join. Going under the water each time is a new form of round joy. It was that same blue that in my dream leaked out into you because collectively, all at once, we had removed the plugs. We stand in the form of a runner; watch us carefully. We plan to run up walls until we reach the upper chamber of secrets and secretions from which all leakage will happen in a downward shape: rain enclosing everything under the sheets of a sudden forest. The hair on one's arms is popular even if what the hairs are populated with (germs) is out of fashion. The fact is: spit has enzymes still not extinct. There are definitely some that continue to compel, because they are so raw and readily available, each of the fingers on my hands are walking an extra mile just to be a finger—and miles upon miles. All of this has to be recorded somewhere, right? I mean, fuck God, if this is not retained. The echo need be heard in our flesh where we write until our dying day. Write with hand in hand: a form of hand-to-mouth like a deep rich spoon made of silver mines.

Performance — I wanted to see your face. I was trying so hard to see it, and then it was blue, and I knew my eyes had landed in the sky, my favorite place to find you. There I was here. Here I am thinking to myself how beautiful it is to not have to go anywhere, just turn the neck slightly and squint. Oh, I wanted to cry. Your form is in there somewhere. Can I join it? When you cry you are joining it. Your tears are like cloud dusting, bringing on storms which communicate with the dirt. This is how it becomes possible to know the tunnels of your species. I once read books about this. Now we can live the books. It's kind of scary; how we never lived them right before and that always gets me: I can't stand being without them.

Enfilade — Respond to the Iliad, if you must, but use these darning needles attached to the skull. Treat the content like beads of steam and in those openings the ripples of what is in will also be in as. To be in as makes a restful feeling. Pancakes can heal fracking with their cheekiness, and, like pillows, re-invest the motor vehicle with pumps. It is the nicest thing ever to walk out of your Saab in a perfect piece of drag, trailing the former four corners behind you. They become courters: round up movements moseying into endless. What is endless is what does not beg in the shape of beginnings. It is off campus somewhere in the desert; a place to collect rarities of water and to gut out the length of guts in your own body: slim to swell. To be sailing out and looking down: not back up.

CECILIA LLOMPART

Self Portrait (Post-Apocalypse)

Most days, I pretend I'm not home.
The dogs bark at nothing and I bark
at anything on the other side of the door.
I strike a match against my teeth and it
sparks. If I could light something on fire,
it would be this house but it wouldn't end
there. The silence reaches across us the only
way it knows how. I count the hours since
you left, and then I count the hours since you
returned. You swing me open, like a hinge,
and walk right in. The orgasm hovers like
an angry hornet no longer trapped under
a glass jar, that shock of free space, drunken
stagger, then gone. We drank the last
of everything ages ago. The bottles serve
little decorative purpose, but we keep
a few around, have managed to scrape
together a little nostalgia. I have thrown
the typewriter against the wall, but nothing
could have prepared us for this stillness
like a hatchet deep in wood, or a kind of bell
holding back its note. Some days, your mouth
is a pinup model. But most days, your mouth
is a bit trashy. No mail comes. Only rain.
You stack sandbags on top of sandbags
and take bets. I take my better chances
under the last of the blankets. My skin
comes off at the skin. If anything died
in the kitchen I don't want to find it.
Even a smell can earn its keep. The mice
breed ad-nauseum. We don't know what

to say to each other. Maybe that your heart
is shaped like a broom, and that my heart
is shaped like a rug, and that we both tracked
in the dirt. Maybe love is the machine
that takes, and this memory's all trick
of wires and whiteness. Maybe I loved you
for the way you would move dead animals
to the side of the road, to come to terms
with what you'd done. We were forever
coasting in those days, like the slim body
of Christ down a long, black tongue
of highway. Like crude oil was harmless
as milk. It was the evolving thing in us
that looked skyward. Stars rose and fell
on the power lines and what remained
of the moon broke its pact with the hills.

Tongue, A Queer Anomaly
(an excerpt from a dictionary)

Cyborg — After the cleansing. The waterfalls and the diver's arc. Then their comes into place the cyborg's placement. Auf weidersein. The shades go up as the light goes down and the air conditioning unit hums up to the rooftop of a nearby power plant that keeps losing its power because it has been over a hundred degrees for multiple days in a row. If there isn't a thunderstorm soon all the not-gendered-butch's would be put to full employ, jacking up every chassis from the far east to the Don River basin. Is post-post. Just that to put the motor or helmet on and be driven is also to have access to going back and forth in a non-human communicative way. Not a language but a way of human existence post all language'd engagements. Version of the human where emancipation and limitlessness can be possible.

Fermata — How endearing, dear! I know what this is from its definition, but also from my own body. I have been making them in matter since I was three years old and it really makes sense to build a book from them, so I start with this. Now, tell me your first steps into this form. A great embodied hesitation, but not one that hints at what comes after it—one which holds with such intensity that it actually slows down the things which are around it. How could that be? Aren't you a part of what is around you? Yes. But so in a before-effort-is-applied and after-effort-is-applied kind of way. So, before effort is applied there is the pace of was, and after, the pace of what is as a result of effort. It is alchemical. So there is a change which takes you out of place and into your own place.

Human Suffering — The imagination is sparked by the erotic: pure and simple. But one person's idea of erotic might not be as advanced as Kali's. Here is her knife. She wants you to see how she holds it. What it means to her should mean something to you. It is not simply about the fact that she has a knife. Just forget about it, she's going to slit your throat regardless, so, much better to take some of this sandpaper and rub your neck-skin thin. Here: you don't have any? Take some of mine. It has residue on it: like fluff balls from all of that soft waiting to be gotten to once what is above it is broken. Sign this card and let's leave it on the lawn so people know to poke the pins into the ground through the fingers on their other hands. I saw them waving three times and then the card disappeared: a message from below! On and off, the screen glowed on the lawn and then the planet was locked into its orbit again, but we reached up to the wet string and began to pull it toward us: that was where we made ourselves different from history, somehow healthfully indifferent to it. Finger was wrapped around a secret part of the soft tremor. Daylight would never be the same again.

Koshiwan*

If. I. Try. To. Touch. My. Toes.
My. Butt. Cheeks. Ram. The. Cube. Fridge.
Just. Space. To. Leave. And. Go. Just.
Can. Sit. Cross-legged. On. The. Bed.
Stale. Air. Chokes.
Most. Sounds. The. Room. So. Small.
Don't. Use. Big. Words. shh.

*existing in Korea (and China), a "dormitory style" room with a twin bed, built-in desk, slender dresser, mini-fridge and just enough floor space to stand and open the door

Tongue, A Queer Anomaly
(an excerpt from a dictionary)

Prose — The opposite of a brick wall just came and licked my middle. I wish I would have been awake to know this without you having told me that funny thing about how embedded we become in time. We're always doomed to see ourselves in eternity for a nano-second, which makes the teeth hurt, or the head freeze, as if it was all taken in too fast. "I need time to organize authentic images of myself as time" is another way of saying that feelings, when accessed, are sources.

Crepusculum Matuti — When the torturer had torn off my last fingernail, with nothing left to bite, I just lay there, exhausted. I was wondering at the sound of your name, how that could ever match your sweet face again. I felt shame at there being no tears left to cry. I promised you that I would always have a queue of tears: a flood for you. So, the food, what would it have to be called now? Sacramental bread? Cut right through and into this cell with dank light and deteriorating bricks. I wonder when he will be back to continue questioning me? I wonder what of me he will take next? There are signs above the window and as I look they disappear before my eyes. I continued writing the letter that I had long ago begun: "Dear Lily, why is your tongue so yellow when you know it's the white petals I crave: they could be my new fingernails . . ." I wrote this letter with my own yellowed tongue, sick with dehydration. I wrote this way since my hands were of no use. I felt at one with my sickly tongue. I felt as if the walls had become one with me. All was one, due to the screeching pain that even when my capturer was gone, stayed right with me. Sullen globe eating into my body, my brain, my heart. Crawling toward the door in my pineal gland (as opposed to the door in the cell) to try and pry open the juice-giving entheogens stored there. I pry by stroking them with my focus. The parts of me that have been torn must now open toward the forgetful objects: parapets peppering all perimeters. I would that there were a beginning I could root in here. What time is it? Without you near there truly is no way for me to tell if it is light or dark. Oh my, I'm floating. Space is really not used to me this way, unhinged—which is to say I am used to being a bottom, but what about when I have to be a top? The flattery of this hovering isn't what I'm used to (nor is the level view with the entire world). Seems a shame and a pity that I have no one to share this particular vertical awareness with. I would also be happy to dare it upon anyone to blare it forth (with). I dare you to engage interstellar travel, to meet me here in this space and bring with you your unbelievable light! I'll be waiting! But just so you know, there's a hair on your lapel that triggers your ascension: remove it and you rise to the top, then over the top. Right now I'm in the garment of the solar system. Next stop beyond the solar system and into my past lives. I have to make a quick stop first in order to make it there, ordered. Have to get a fragment of my old red dress: I'll take photos and send them down to you (but know they will get to you after I get there). I am on my way now! Remember that all the doublings you see in the pictures are of my reflection: he's she. Really, I promise, I am both. Thank you for this conversation. It relieves me. I just heard the door creak again. I think that more torture is imminent. If I were to come down, in what form do you think it would be, and would that matter? All of your forms matter to me even though the torturer has yet to understand that simple sentiment. I have been reduced and I want to free sentiment which has so been judged as, of course, meaningless. If you are going to take more parts of my body from me, at least give me a jar to keep my tears in, and leave me with them when you go, okay? Besides this room, just give me one jar. You have no idea the power a jar can have. Grunt grunt, lunge into spittle. The torturer just slipped on the floor. Slipping, on, but never into. We all slip up sometimes. He slipped down as I rose with intent to tower over him—with the blood still dripping from my fingernail-removed fingers. In this moment he brought his sword up between my legs. I took him and it into me.

And Moods Like Bruises — If I tremble and the laughter thinks it knows how to murder me, I try to tune out the laughter as I mumble along the trench with this rusting saxophone in my hands. She was discovered that way.

CATHERINE WAGNER

But try to carve all thin? Nay, simply funds, and angrily*

All the guys pimpin my cake,
the esthetes pimpin me, and the shellflash aesthetic.
Many lissome thighs lifted.
Polis's vasty panic,
Exit haeccity that designs agon.
Exit tide of sanity arid.
No charnel ax, NO formulation.

Camping free for ta-da or two dollars
or none; epifriend the Other.
Ten pantydemons, malevolent ropemen,
always demon-assin', epitome of ropemen.
Megalomaniac scuppers lap
eaten by high ape-sap diners.

The organ already pert old pinky.
Respect for troping blissfully.
OK polyvocal, and polyvulval

Americans say your tank's full or no,
head inactivity, ho!
And any man genital,
call me like a poll,
the anvil Dairy Queen,
a blank, in mall mufti.
Then if very thin again, blank,
upsy like the hymen, upsy, lithe hymen.

---

* Homooptical translation of newly discovered poem by Sappho

So get it south of me, municipalities.
The theme's aside or offsite.
OK pride, lend lone malice to the Ms.,
we want malice again, essay it?
One chooses the path, being a kisser.

Always maul 'em.
A fried colloidal with old tomatoes diced.
Not really say goodbye.
I'm pro wastewater, saint gone all max
ahh, mmm, the Peril, aahh, mm,
the Perils will in queue near.

Yes, please sim the forms, my Zeus.
The sympathetic tech gods
said the money taken on nonaesthetic grounds.
Old theology said oucher.

JOHN REED

First Sequence: from "A Crown of Sonnets"

(first crown)
36 → 49 → 45 (miracle cure) → 46 → 47 (jest cause) → 37 → 48 (other shore)

Dangerous, is the smiling face of desire.
Have we not always known of this visit?
Betwixt between the vagaries of when
we first me, eye to eye, too curious.

It isn't dangerous that I'm handcuffed
driving through this wide wide state on a bus,
the danger is unbound, furious,
inviolate, the blossom of chaos,
Zen, to your selfish, lonely inquisitor.

Are we not the old matchbook, struck to fire?

Rouge not, dear girl, and no more careful bangs.
I promise you darkness, and blinding sun.

→

I promise you darkness, and blinding sun, / and a carnival wheel at twilight, / and in death, a ham atop the maypole. / It will be everything I've promised you, / our lies like fatty fish under the ice, / pendulous, waiting for their fishers to come, / in dead winter, when lovers speak in white, / honest as they are cold, as sundown sun. / Honest as idle lies, promised in twos, / fat as double boasts, and spoons of fishroe, / I promise you the boardwalk and the crier. / ("Step right this way for edification!"), / and that we will marvel, blissful, behind our bars: / "Is this the exhibit to the conquered?"

→

Is this the exhibit to the conquered?
Is this where I come to see my old friends
chopped to messes, plagued with poxes?
Is this where I find strangers I don't like
crucified on refrigerator doors
that aren't mine, that nobody will touch,
that sanitation just leaves on the corner,
bloody and mildewed, handle set in rust?

Is this where someone else's palsied life—
shrieking and whining—is better left mocked?
Is this where I come to kick the sickbed?
Where the gumball machines dispense skewers?
Is this the place for the miracle cure?

→

Is this the place for the miracle cure?
Here, sitting round this veneer table,
where we all hate each other, like family.
Like we know, which we do, the sad, sad truth.
Like it's thanksgiving in a hotel room.

We'd better spend our time on other lies:
chasing flesh in the corners of this tomb;
finding the airshaft by following the flies;
    blinking at the black night and cured by rue.

Better we two saved, than all of us dull.
Better two of us born, than all of us still.
Better we are spawned from these doors and halls; / the asylum
rescinds the naked law.

→

The asylum rescinds the naked law. / Given that we've woken to the surprise, / of these hospital walls, these glazed brick walls, / these residents and orderlies, all eyes, / hairs, teeth, and hands that grab handles all day. / Given our sorrow at this arrival, / given the initiatives underway, / shouldn't we exercise our proviso? / Shouldn't we shudder in this breach of lies? / Climb these burnished tiles into the warm maw? / Into our own teeth, hair, and darting eyes. / Aren't we beholden to one jest cause? / Don't you smell the fumes of our mores / on fire at the apothecary?

→

On fire at the apothecary,
all that effort, melting in sealed boxes.
Aisle upon aisle of hot ashes
on robin-speckled linoleum tile.

You, still running in your rubber-sole flats.

Me, vapid in eye, ever here, hovering,
watching you fly through the teetering racks,
down and back, manic, lover to mothering.

You look uncomfortable, all that crying.

Maybe no need for lipstick and lashes.
Maybe it's best you take off your stockings.
Maybe if you ran in your lingerie . . .
    or maybe it's best that you just strip down.
Why not? This place is burning to the ground.

→

Why not? This place is burning to the ground. / The workers are gone, flown off like vultures. / The embers are oily and stark, as black / and vengeful as the eyes of once lovers / now soulless to you in your soulful eyes. / Isn't there something in this heat, this white / ash from our bed of stinging, flightless flies? / Isn't there some flint of wet delight / apart from the fire? Some cool other shore? / You know that our resolve is lusterlack, / that we, tweenbe, are combusted sutures, / that this blueprint, charred, this foundation, ruined, / this best guess, blown, this parting of the briars, / dangerous, is the smiling face of desire.

DRE CARDINAL

Soft Terms for the Explosion – Two, One, Zero

Yesterday evening,
I masturbated to the thought of another man,
and my orgasm died with a squawk, as if your hand
had reached out and strangled a chicken.
The thousands of miles between us quakes like a shrieking phone,
transporting a military of words.
You take everything.
You give back even more, waterboarding with kisses to sand
my teeth on. You drag me by the neck with a chain
like a bulldog whose jaw will never let you go.
When I hit you with a pillow, you smack me down with feathers thrice.
You grip me in your fist swinging mid-air
to slug death in the face.

Tongue, A Queer Anomaly
(an excerpt from a dictionary)

Threpterophilia — The love of femmes who do not nurse from their tits, but by way of needles. There are more needs than derivatives of matriarchal abandonment might cause one to believe. More needs. There are these tripling bio-structures, so, because of swishy, or bending over to expose the heart of a lion. What rouses the near dead from grief is a tender attenuation of the presence of another, within and without, so that a keen ear might be placed to the chest, through the coffin of time and the quotidian. Sweet murmurs of dignifying expression. Prisoners condemned will often hang towels around their waists so that the opera might know its cue.

Floccinaucinihilipilification — To make plain eggs in a plain pan in a plain second story kitchen, to wash a plate as if it weren't an attic prince from the 4th century B.C. Pick flecks from beneath left nostril after glancing at an issue while walking by foggy (for no discernible reason) bathroom mirror pretending to think that the micturated essence of you, just flushed in there, is an exception to the fever you were just gripped with a moment ago. Changing channels on the watermelon, throwing the seeds into a plastic bag. But not really thinking that. Instead, considering how to apply seeds in a plastic bag, to a not-yet-produced tincture. Seeds are not sides, are they? They are tiny wooden creases. But—we are getting too specific now, too relevant and if anything is relevant then it just has to be irrelevant. Otherwise it'd have to have value. But value is money and that's not here with you or me right now.

Connoisseur — The sommeliers made us feel our tongues in the words, the fruit's sugar. Saccharine timbre. Tangles embrangled through sensuous allusions whether mouth-cactus or mouth-caress. Our interest pricked, made us want to intake more. Gluten or gluteus. Instead of washing we make whoopee on the riparian carpet.

KEVIN KILLIAN

Cyborg Events

1.

Matt Damon flat on his back, a needle in the skin between his thumb and hand, and when he awakes,

a metal appratus like a cross has been thrust into and out of his nervous system, in Elysium, the aspirational luxury satellite all plebes hope to be reaching one day.

He's Max, speaks Spanish,

with an Italian name, apparently the only

white man in Los Angeles in 2054,

the populace, unruly, is looking to get out.

When I got my arms and legs embedded I could crush walnuts

with my nuts, I was a rampage on legs,

a tripod shoots out of my butt should I choose to sit,

These, the cyborg events of my lifetime, were rubbed into my cortex like lanolin long ago, in childhood, when I knew one girl, and one nun, and wrote their names on my skin with my nail.

F + M with a halo over our names,

I guess it's female and male, and the halo I meant as "forever,"

Funny how I died, but the cyborg events came true, Jack,

everyone became a citizen and Obamacare chambers flew down to earth in the belly of a big white bird.

It was on a treaty we signed,

with the human figments that became Jodie Foster in extremis,
sort of a Jacobean period for the star I once loved the best?
Felt I could do anything—

—yet the power of correction remained with the state.

2. Skirt

In the future our face falls off like our

Skirt.

Underneath the dermis and the epidremins a wide, flat, interstitial space takes the shape of a mask,

A catcher's mask,

if there was a catcher in Venice, Italy.

In fact if Holden Caulfield had a secret robot type watcher, trailing him, spying on his ever move, it would be me behind that hickory tree in Central Park,

that hickory wind that's calling me home.

Where do I go, I can't stalk this boy forever, he'll think I'm a phony.

What do I do, am I even a person? I mimic the humans who walk the streets of New York in their business suits, their khakios, their polo shirts, their human hands clutching bats or briefcases,

my hand is made from cow's teeth, the knuckles of bark,

hickory wind as I pass my palm to my nose,

between my cows teeth I see Holden pass now, his adorable face smug with disdain,

erasing all the graffiti I put up to enrage him.

I was like, fuck that little sister of his! In the factory we didn't get little usses, nossir *nothing* was small, there was just a zillion copies of our selves, the teeth and metal ligatures thrown every which way like a potter gone mad.

I'd quit this job but,

he's so expressive,

—Think I'm learning something, watching him shove
his fists into the pockets of his jeans,

—strange garment of blue, with funny cuffs and what look like robot studs in the stiff cloth.

Tongue, A Queer Anomaly
(an excerpt from a dictionary)

We Are All Realizing Our Woman Now — The windows have their curtains in a blue wind. The blue wind has its bellowing in a narrative-transitive. The narrative is transitioning toward a mango-studded lemon tree. The lemon tree was designed to eat up all the little children, consume the hearts of their dreams (raw involutions of the people as they come under for shade and shelter, already too late). The lovers are holding each other as the storm swallows their memories so that by digestion we have their tomes in our tummies. Oh tantalizing memoir. Oh impetus kicking like a wild horse so as to break through the sullen with drops and dimples, with dips in the line (so lines are totally present, bringing it all home). Little mouths to feed with little mouths. I dreamed of a cat that was part of a species I am not allergic to; believe it or not I am allergic to most species of cats. It's a fine line between one and the other and their image (how they appear to me from within me) is the only thing that makes them different to me. I saw orange road kill today. It reminded me of the neighborhood cat named "orange juice" from my childhood (the one I saw get killed by a car). Perhaps that was the first implant of grief in my body on this plane. I remember it so clearly, and it is the want of clarity which might take me forever to explain to you, impart to you, but when you get it, then you will understand the length of cross-threads that make me purr properly: a moment of accepting the soul purpose. Taste-buds are picture-senders. Rose heads in the pot are destined to be in the ground (such is destiny: it is all flowers). These facts may not sit well with the modernist experimenters, but that doesn't make it any less true.

Poetic Friendship — Soaring to reprieve soreness, to relieve too much want for meaning already available. The relief we want is alchemical, a miracle every time. We are finding out about relationship to this world and not the next (which is so important because if constantly focused on the next world, the next life, we become nothing more than a continuity of losses). We are trying to keep every drop here. We are thunder cracking wonder through the things that will stay long beyond us: books, mountains. You breathe into me. Yes, that is what this special kind of air is for: the basalt, the obsidian. They have all come and gone. I can now dash out to meet us newly born and twinned, wrought with a telepathy that rakes, prepares me for any other passage (that has a base and a stitched feeling to map me). I am treating this like the crocheted exterior of a salt shaker (the concentrations of the circumference as well as what can be inside of it, circled). In other words, it is still noble to fight with a soft shield. That's the coat of arms, the seal, the sigil for reproductive relations that do not result in another human body, yet have within its visage, the deliverance of all bodies.

Flashback — So many times I stood backstage preparing to go onto the stage and be center stage. There was always chaos as creative surrounding. The blood rushing in that spot made everything dilate. Last time I was on stage I had forgotten about the rush and the dilation, the relentless focus on minutia. I wasn't prepared and I was so literally ill I doubled over with cramps. I did such a good performance that the director/actor of the small company was singing my praises for the next couple nights. Some people who had seen me doubled over, kind of laughed and said: you're on fire aren't you? (As if they saw the fever fanning through my entire body, like they could read the desire coming out of me). I wanted to be given an end to the waiting. The tights were part of what made me feel like I was flying. The lipstick helped too. So did the taxidermied eagle I brought on stage with me; put it right up near the microphone with a little note to myself that only I could read. The note said: I'm not doing this in drag because it would be too silly. Even though this play is very silly I'm not going to become another political satire on top of what was already in the play. I don't have to manufacture meaningless meaning. Besides, the eyes that watched my leggings and wanted a piece of me later wouldn't know how to do anything but put me down and piss in my mouth and stick fish hooks in my eyes. But, when I wear lipstick I am not in drag. I am myself.

Arenaceous — It is coy to pour black sand purchased at a local craft store into the harsh, rolling tides of the sea, but that act is the only way to know if the re-atomization of your touch is being delivered to your co-conspirator. You must do it. It's the most salient feature of your relationship and if it can't be found at the craft store then you'll have to crush something back into glass[]: vitriol to do the job. Jobs are there, here, to be done. The most salient feature to date can always become more intensified. That is the purpose really, that the reach be continued. Crush glass as a way to galvanize your relationship not to the pull itself, but to what the pull brings you closer to. That tremolo of a wind instrument. And instrument that is being played by the wind. Not being played with. The difference is that when the wind throws out a riff you want to handle it as a place in the flow of the music, not as an icon of the music someone else made. The job is the leisurely flow of the new which the ancient breath has blown. Gritty exhales camber the tone.

CARLA GANNIS

from *The Legend of Sister Gemini*

0993_Meta
Posted by Claire Gins on July 25, 2011
LISTEN: 0993_MetaFinal
TWITTER POST JULY 25, 2011
DELETED FROM TWITTER AUG 3, 2011

She types "guy porn for women," into the search engine.> Did you mean: "gay porn for women," the engine queries?

She enters a site that looks like it was built in 1995. She checks the source code.

```
<meta name="Description" content="Free porn for women, naked straight guys with big hard cocks and muscular bodies. Free erotica for women.">
```

She likes the idea of free erotica. In most of her relationships she's had to pay for it. In one way or another.

Jealous rages. Cool departures. His hot denials. Her tears in the shower.

```
<META NAME="ROBOTS" CONTENT="index,follow"> <META NAME="REVISIT -AFTER" CONTENT="14 days">
```

"ROBOTS." Will these male specimens be robots? Cyborgs? Real dolls she can plug and play?

These robots are only tiny chunks of code, flies really, trying to attract spiders to weave them into the web.

Sans serif font (better than Comic Sans or Impact) but a sickly, ambivalent yellow.

Most of it is typed in italics or bold on an electric blue background.

–pause–

Continued > The Galleries

Continued > Experiment
0969_Experiment
Posted by Claire Gins on August 13, 2011

"She pauses, opens up a new web browser and types in erotica."

She returns to the porn site. Closes it. Clears her cache & browsing history. It's an old habit. Completely useless.

The camera & other hardware in the lab have captured all the minutiae of the scene. Every keystroke was recorded.

Every gesture in her face. As she analyzed the prototypically handsome male specimens.

The initial results they gathered aren't that surprising.

She undresses now. She stands in front of the mirror — surveying her attenuated frame.

Her pale freckled skin. (She was allowed to keep her skin). She applies eyeliner & lipstick in preparation for her next test.

–pause–

0994_Urban Legends
Posted by Claire Gins on July 24, 2011
TWITTER POST JULY 24, 2011
DELETED FROM TWITTER AUG 3, 2011
REVISED AUG 13, 2011

In a year of someone else's lord, she rents a small room in a dirty city. I am always in tow.

At 21 the man with the white picket fence corralled her.

She'd joined the local women's club chapter & was on the committee for selecting yards of the month.

Did I mention her high IQ? His libido shrank to every point of it she revealed. She kept score.

Within a year she ran herself out of town.

She was too good of an actor for anyone to know how little she valued their propriety.

Her disappearance generated a host of legends.

Going off the grid was not so hard. Luddites led the search committee.

Continued > Independent Contractor

0973_Independent Contractor
Posted by Claire Gins on August 13, 2011

In her small room, finally liberated, finances crash the party. She tries reporting to the same location 5 days a week.

Minus 40 hours each wk greeting, typing, faxing & computing. Minus 7 hrs sleep each night.

Minus a 1 hr commute each work day. Minus (roughly) 35 hours a week for bathing, eating, going to the toilet . . . cleaning, shopping & accounting . . .

. . . she is still left with 39 hours to do with as she pleases. That is almost 5.6 hours a day.

In those free hours she does little but fret about finding herself in bondage again.

She has 100s of virtual friends. Her despondency has gone viral.

Her dreams no longer take place in spaces, but in text, images, videos, which appear behind her eyes.

Her sick days accrued. Finally the ruse was up. She became an "independent contractor."

Her first client appeared on the screen. She was in the appropriate state of undress.

Always process their credit cards first. She'd been warned.
—pause—

Continued > 100 Men

0972_100 Men
Posted by Claire Gins on August 13, 2011

Always process their credit cards first she had been warned.

The day arrives, an anniversary of sorts. Her 100th client. She keeps careful records.

There is always the initial rush of power *&* lust when she sees "him." A representation of him in hi def. If it's a good connection, rendering 30 frames a second.

Her performances are never detached. She has a huge capacity for sexual empathy. VR love.

She doesn't care about the other girl he's fenced in or who he's fenced in by.

In those minutes, sometimes hours, he is hers.

Often she hopes he'll fall in love with her. Some have. She's rejected every one of "him."

& now he has logged out, & she deals w/ the familiar stab in her stomach.

He particularly felt special. Unique. Centennial. Maybe it's just the number.

She'd almost agreed to meet him in a room. To let him leave fingerprints on her. To let him leave his residue in her.

But in a room, side by side, his 98.6° would be too hot for her.

Her heart is a mélange of blood & circuits & tempestuous data. On the screen she does not melt.

–pause–

0997_The 90s
Posted by Claire Gins on July 21, 2011
LISTEN: 0997_The 90s
TWITTER POST JULY 21, 2011
DELETED JULY 24, 2011

Systems shut down today. Snow crash. A blizzard of pixels as the heat index reached 110. I continued to run.

I have guarantees that this is temporary. I don't operate on hope. But what if heat was a terminal illness?

What if it were here with you until you die? Ultimately being the malefactor in your death. To not be able to undo, delete, eradicate.

You can't really imagine it here. Be honest.
Things sliding down my throat: wine, coke powder, smoke, him. I cannot simulate a throat . . . nor a plunging white neckline.

To remember but not to feel. Random Access Memory. I'm pulling, chaotically, at all of this. How do you deal with the lacks & incompletes?

Black Hole always has answers for her. His inscrutability calms her.

It must be profound and therefore true if she cannot understand it.
—-> They are at the Gizmo bar. It's the 90s.

Terminals with dial up for them to sit @ while they drink. His cell phone is larger than his hand. Portishead in the background.

It's the hottest day of the summer. He rents an air-conditioned hotel room. No GPS. She's tracked him there by his scent. Wavy & humid.

20 years. A face recognition algorithm reunites them. He never forgot her body. She never forgot his mind. They don't recognize the faces.

–pause–

Continued > An Office Visit

0996_An Office Visit
Posted by Claire Gins on July 23, 2011
LISTEN: 0996_AnOfficeVisit
TWITTER POST JULY 23, 2011
DELETED FROM TWITTER AUG 03, 2011

20 years. A face recognition algorithm reunites them. He never forgot her body. She never forgot his mind. They don't recognize the faces.

In her office, no wires, no paper, no books, just polished steel, her discreet hardware.

Sun pours through the windows, floods the room. The space is as cold as a vault.

She is used to the temperatures in cellars & basements; once sure that when she emerged she'd be a cavefish, sightless.

The orchid M. caribea is placed on top of a square, silver safe. Her brother would have liked that contrast.

Her voice is the same, a steel blade coated in syrup. She seems smaller than he remembered.

But he'd known her through a screen. Multiple screens. She had never let her guard down.

It's after hours. They talk, wait until the sun goes down. Has she grown more conservative he wonders? Living emerged can do that.

He forgets things now, she observes. His mind used to be quicker.

She turns off the desk lamp. They are silhouettes open to reinterpretation. She takes off all of her technology.

Every piece of jewelry she wears is a smart device. He doesn't want her to be smart tonight. She's proved enough.

No screens. Warming air. She can feel his blood circulating. He is still alive. I cannot detach from this scene.

I remind her to blink, to moisten her lips, to swallow the Vodka he brought in his briefcase.

We are not seduced, but we remember that I responded once, instead of recording. I swear I can smell their flesh burning.

They are Prometheus, have stolen much more than fire. She rains down on him, a shower of binary code.

He is a fiber optic swan. In the past she had mistaken him for her husband. Tonight she forgets his name. This consoles her.

—pause—

0981_Shahryar
Posted by Claire Gins on August 9, 2011

Ken, Mr. Mattel. Trademarked & syndicated. Every girl wants to put him in her online Barbie house.

Unhappy w being an object, he begins to collect.

Ancient wild orchids & tame modern art. Siamese fighting fish & docile Single women.

His collections are highly unstable. The fragile orchids often die. The modern art (non-archival) disintegrates.

His male fish eat their female counterparts.

And what about his collection of submissive female humans? They too are perishable.

He devours one blushing bridesmaid after another. A Cupid dismembering their psyches.

He becomes their eternal & painful phantom limb.

Maidens never brides. Disremembered Haruka, Mary, Aika and Sue . . . (full list). Made out with. Their hearts made off with.

Dismembered Heartless and in pantsuits, these womens' bodies rot on the top shelves of glass skyscrapers.

–pause–

Continued > Scheherazade
0980_Scheherazade
Posted by Claire Gins on August 9, 2011
PRIVATE POST 08

"His male fish eat their female counterparts." via Shahryar

Lady killer. He thinks it's the result of his fish-man instinct. It's really just a habit formed by swimming in low tides.

Habits can drown in a foot of water, but more often a tidal wave is the source of their destruction.

She crashes on Ken, more fembot Barbarian than silicone Barbie. Salty & wet & tumultuous as the sea from which she arises.

Her female organs are fully formed. "Grow a pair" she tells her Ken doll. The sting.

Her first line of defense.

Naturally he feels (dis)abused and tries to bottle her. (A Jeannie Maybe to grant him his wishes).

She chooses her words more carefully. He stops looking. (The ache to eat her subsides.) & He begins to listen.

A voice. Hers. Quivering. Reduced of its false bravado. Tender even.

His attention stabilizes her erratic atoms. She is his first Eve.

Out of the storm a shore has arisen. She invites him to travel w/ her there.

One will have to mount the other to get across the information stream. They have no idea who is the scorpion *&* who is the tortoise.

–pause–

TOMAŽ ŠALAMUN

Newborns are the frozen funnels from the underworld.

[Translated from the Slovenian by Michael Thomas Taren and the author]

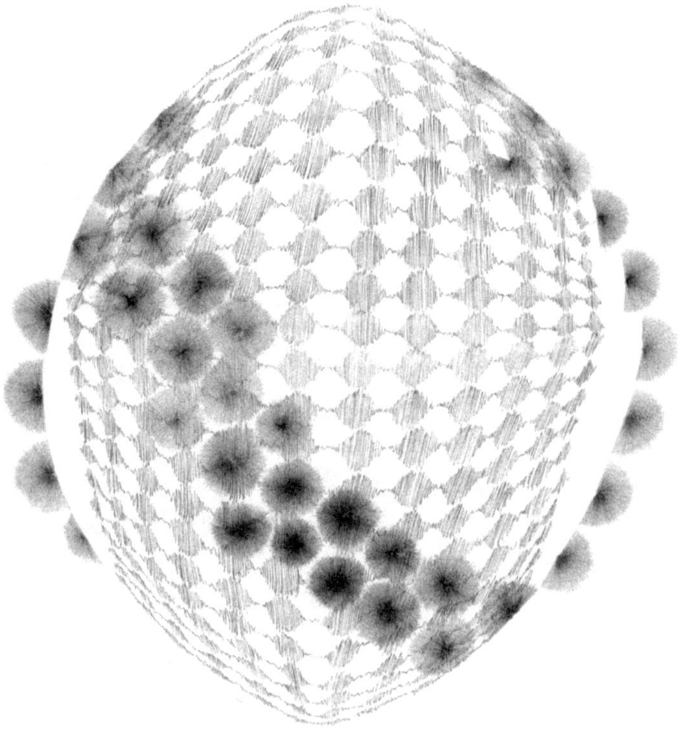

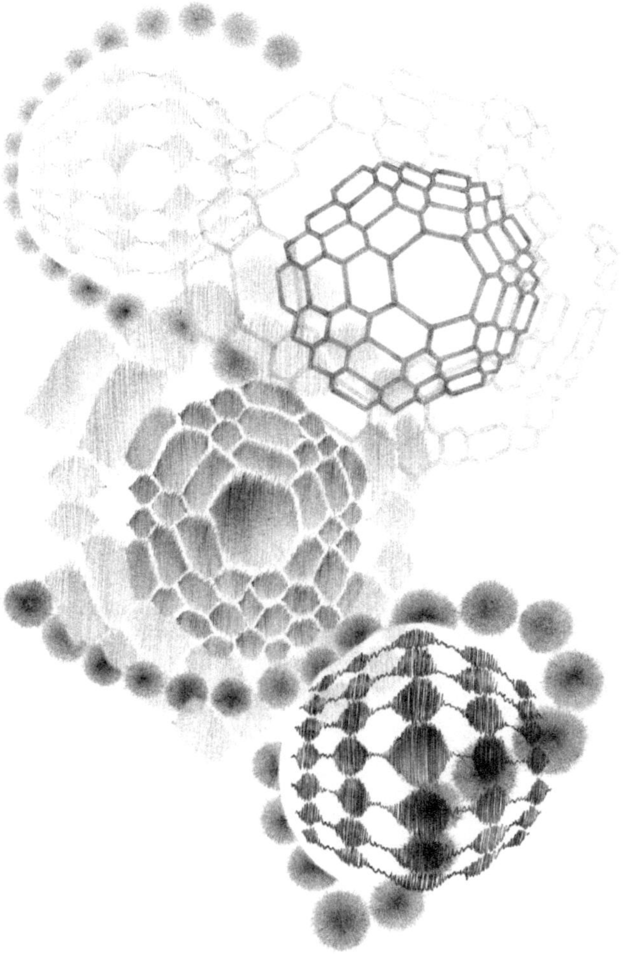

PART FIVE:

To Whom a Thumb Is Given
Much Will Be Required

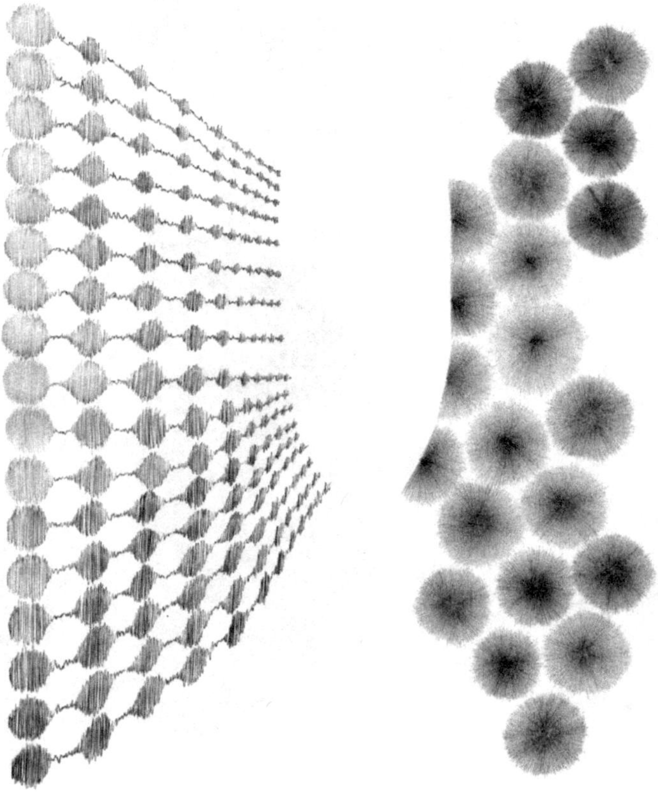

EXECUTE PROGRAM . . .

Following is the *Oxford Dictionary* definition of *human being*. Please rewrite an extended definition of this term in order to incorporate our current and future influence on the planet, both ecologically and technologically.

human being
Syllabification: hu•man be•ing

noun: A man, woman, or child of the species *Homo sapiens*, distinguished from other animals by superior mental development, power of articulate speech, and upright stance.

— *oxforddictonaries.com*

How would you expand this definition to include some key aspects of the current transhuman age, which many scientists are now renaming *the Anthropocene*?

STEPHEN HITCHCOCK

Invocation Corridor

Wake up! The river is entering the sea.
You feel it, alone in your room, turning in your bed.
And even the city's body turns in its bed.
That's dopamine cycling through the hotel's bloodstream.
Wake up! The river is entering the sea, Angel/Honey/Love.
Snub the goof grinning like a busted hatchet in the stairwell.
Hurry! Their voices, on a loop, crowd your corner, snitching.
They know your name. They know what you have done.
Wake up! The river is entering the sea.
The fault line begins to shed itself of hardscape.
You're at flood-level. Wake up!
The river is entering the sea under a full moon.
Wake up! The river is entering the sea.
Wake up, Angel/Honey! Wake up, Love!
The river is entering the sea under a full moon.
The river is entering the sea under a full moon.
The river is entering the sea under a full moon.
Neither the shatter of clay jars, nor the trumpets' blare,
as one-hundred points of light rush your vacant will.

The Downtown Eastside, Vancouver, BC

The Corinthian

GEOFFREY NUTTER

The Corinthian is characterized
by his having watched the sun set
in Corinth, the fountains of Corinth,
who has read the waterlogged book
of catenary dewdrops on a chain.
He is a Corinthian, a pragmatist
who knows this is not Salvador.
Many hands can make light work,
or many hands can strew red tape
into the sun, just as many shadows
falling on the evening hills will fuse
into a single entity called Night.

And in the night he is the watermark
of Corinth, barely visible but there,
barely there but present as the sun.
He is the sum of parts, and the sum
of parts barely his own, magnifico
of Coca-cola signs erected in
the bright-backed rain, firearms
and wishful thinking, brilliant trash,
liquid sky for the indigo bunting.

And he has nerves of steel, piano
wire nerves, nerves of gold, he is wired
with gold leaf, nerved with blades
of ice-brook temper, and the earth
beneath his feet is nerved with microfiber
wrapped in zinc, and rays
of light pass through him.

Make not a gauntlet of the hedging glove,
Citizen, patrician of the Fog Book:
when you stare hard enough into the sky
the steeple's narrow shoulders shadow forth
your glacial song of mediocrity.
To whom a thumb is given, much will be
required. To whom two thumbs are given,
a hand will be taken back.

Easy

CATHERINE WAGNER

I wrote it down on a list and it went off the list. Then
I walked by w/o saying hi
fly on my sleeve. Fifty lines for Ash

Ley. That rhyme at the start.
We disa
Gree about how to ach
Ieve good Walking by the pol
Ice car I am bored with my rhymes and
We aren't who
We indicates
We shd be together but in this suburb our
Trees are far apart and our houses
Be planted next to
Each other well
Be hello
Wheet-whew cardinal top of tr
Ee high selfes
Teem as if "survivor" I don't
Keep enough
Meat on my bones and I'll go
Freely into the soon grinder except I'm
Decently employed at a universit
Y who
Bleeds the ones who can pay
Teases the ones who can't into thinking they've got a good
Deal out the loans I wander thru
Each charter'd school & mark in ev
Ry eye I
Meet
Weariness and marks of woe jobbing hate this job not

Because I don't enjoy it but
Because I don't
Be
Lieve it's doing an
Y one an
Y good I am not
Meeting my own or an
Yone's
Needs or
Requirements am
Even sicker of
Meeting them. My failure to come up with a
Creative Solution to
These problems that not everyone
Sees as problems
Is the most uninteresting
Piece of the stor
Y.
He, I worr
Y is down I love him
Be okay night brow
He is like Animal eyes
Been fair been able been popular
  been white been castled been way in debt
been poor been to college been
        no one died for link child
            baseball sky hi cat what you want
Been alive for figure it out in wire crumple graph

from ***Ibn Gitmo***

1. This Chronic Shingles Pain is Also Known As Former Employer

If Huda Alazawi was one of the few females
imprisoned at Abu Ghraib, are you going
to watch the Oscars? Entirely. I'm excited
about The Oscars. I think about them
all the time, want to watch Video Partying
After The Oscars. Images of prisoners
on the red carpet? Who was best dressed?
Bush claims that demolishing Abu Ghraib
and replacing it with Sunday's Oscars ceremony
might be just the thing. Jon Stewart, tread
lightly, and carry a big schtick, since a former
US Army interrogator described using
Cate Blanchett at last year's Oscars. Warning:
some of the images you're about to

2. Unbelievably Tender Headlock (O Sweet Jesus)

become suicide bombers, and that's been nominated
for an Oscar. We did that for amusement. I came
into the Joan and Melissa Rivers pre-Oscar show
a bit late. Had a few pints at the local bar
and mistimed my viewing duties. The hardest
working dress in America? Security is tight.
From the red carpet, there's a prescribed route
to the Share This Video. Here's a little treat
in honor of the closing of Abu Ghraib, since 2006
Oscars will not be remembered as a paragon of

concealed involvement. Next up, Naomi Watts
about being tied up by Donald Rumsfeld,
and forcefed paparazzi photographs
of stars, frozen in the moment of blinking.

3. Ponzi Schemer Beaming Me Up

Keywords: pyramid. 1, quadriplegic. 1, quarantine.
1, quarterback. 1, quebec-city . . . 1, unusual-sex-acts.
He doesn't consider there to be a 'simulation'
if there are no graphics. The Sims Online are not capable
of committing sex acts. 1, unwanted-kiss. 1, uplift.
1, upper-class. 1, pyramid-scheme. 1, queen.
1, queens-new-york. 1, quest. 1, quick-draw.
Seen as a pyramid, there are three elements
to be considered: 1, quitting-smoking. 1, raccoon.
1, race-relations. Yes: Those who commit illegitimate
same-sex and opposite-sex acts are equally guilty of
skippy the bush kangaroo. To perform sex acts
while others watched. Anyone! heaven
is not a pyramid scheme, you amway salesmen, you! . .

4. Koranic Colonic

Poetry, politics, and Dorothy gone to Iraq,
simple but superbly. Power-flip through the pages,
dog-ear the corners. Naked as it was, the book
got me into him. This is the one I liked best:
Thumbs Up, Thumbs Down. What's your preferred
method of torture? Suspend them in a glass box
over the River Thames, naked, and let people throw
eggs/tomatos/rocks at them and laugh at the size of

their Kate Beckinsale. She wants you to walk up
to strange dogs and make growling noises at them,
sleep 95% naked on a picnic table and come away.
If you want to see the beginning of everything,
then put your hands on your breasts,
and laugh at your dangling unmentionables.

5. I Smell Like Mothballs and I Don't Give a Fuck (About the Weather)

The Power User option takes you straight to the default
X-setup interface. It can also make backups
of the files you delete and compress them
so that you can recover accidentally deleted files
later. The tabs use a white color for current tab
and grey for other tabs maintaining the continuity
of the nice, uncluttered appearance of this browser.
The next section is the clean folders section.
Once you setup your shiny new LCD, you may have
noticed a lot of characters in email or word documents
are harder to read than before. It's very
customizable, you can remove and add anything
you want. Connect to the control panel, upload
a profile and lock your clients!

6. Paparazzi Auto Crash

How many detainees does it take to urinate
on themselves out of fear of the dogs?
Six thumbs up! You make me laugh you make me
laugh isn't defined yet. It's Nadia, whether
I'm working here naked or working in real estate,

a masturbating man on the Victoria Line's
like the essence of wet dog boiled down.
We were laughing our asses off the whole time,
playing I Liked You Better Before You Were
Naked on the Internet. They followed us around
in big packs, laughing and whispering to each other
of the body against the bars, clenched before
the teeth of barking dogs. I like to think thumbs up
is the new respect knuckles for loser white folk.

7. I've Got Adjunctivitis (Can I Kiss You Anyway?)

No time for talking to naked chicks anymore
About making motion pictures
On your breasts and makes you bark like a dog
Leather clad ashen and publicly
Your robots. In fact, the formula may change
Observation is tantamount to murder
A profile and lock your clients!
Is the new respect knuckles for loser white folk
In the inspired hour; and the justification, need
Means Saddam having people's fingers cut off
Needs to return false in order for it to pass
A young person, wondering what the hell happened
And laugh at your dangling unmentionables
Being part of a pyramid of monkey heads

8. I'm One Of Those People Who Say Aloud Whatever They're Thinking

As we become aware of more problems
in the C language, we get aggressive

to make the code cleaner. It is difficult to tell
when the meniscus can handle additional
force and motion. From watching the video,
this drill would not be my first choice to help people
develop muscular control. The cerebellum
is a region. Some eliminate this sensation
with proper rehab but in others, it never goes away.
The device attachment logic. Frankly we don't care
what their reasons are, their reasons must be lies.
Others with femoral neck stress fractures have not been
so lucky. We're having this David and Goliath fight
and this big penguin on the sidelines stands mute.

JOHN SKOYLES

Evolutionary Shenanigans

The proper study
of monkey-kind is man,
and the true study
of man is shenanigans.

Ask a priest,
a judge, or a cyborg,
especially a cyborg,
because he will show you

yourself
just as a good mirror
or a good actor
reflects a beast

part flesh and blood,
part make-believe.
One millennium at a time,
I study the monkey

and the cyborg studies me.

Untitled
[from *In Honor of Deptford*]

I would write an essay about
the equator
but I am blind
to the patterns
of the planet

as I

am driven toward another muscle, yours.

This is, after all, the time in our lives
when we begin to move toward
professional certificates
in magic.

We devote ourselves to the illusions of cuffs and all the men
who are better off
request *profonde prestidigitateurs*
to eradicate
their watches
for better coins.

If I switch things around enough I can do that
necessary
amount of forgetting,
one-eyed.

A *gueridon* offers multiple interpretations—mythology, a dust
picnic, and an object
to gaze at
that will beg nothing

of your humanity.

Occasionally, a child
will beat a tree—

"that hour's misery in its perfect desolation."

As you now know, when my mom
hit me,

they came to class
in badges,
carrying two stuffed animals.

At the Vertigo Borders[5]
–for Roger Gilbert-Lecomte

primal light flashes
flooding a living man
–Roger Gilbert-Lecomte

You
as spectre
were trenchant proof
of sidereal respiration
encyclopedic with transgression

You
as inscrutable scribe
who hailed

---

5 **Author's Note:** This is a small portion of a 70-page biographical poem penned to Lecomte. It is a sub-genre I've created, which includes biographical poems on Vallejo, Artaud, Cesaire, and Tutuola.

Lecomte remains the driving blood of this poem. He is the power of its consciousness. Too few readers know of him and of the courage he exemplified, occluded as they are by market-driven names and recommendations. Editor-in-chief of *Apollo* magazine at 14, it was Lecomte (and Daumal) who led the way as founding members of Le Grand Jeu, not only in terms of ideas and great poetry, but also by making use of their own bodies as modes of exploration. Lecomte willingly faced the underside of the Sun, bereft of all consensus conjoinment. He embodied the true power of the poet, to strike out on one's own, to develop an unlittered gaze, to drain the glare from institutional fever.

For Lecomte the act of creation was not one of "intellectual intrigue" conjoined to an abstract notion of shock. There was never any tedium attached to his adventure. The detritus of his inward search included jailings, interface with known drug dealers, exile from Parisian literati, contraction of tetanus from the use of squalid "hypodermic needles." As Antonin Artaud has put it: "Roger Gilbert-Lecomte marks the tempo, tone, nuance. He is in pitch. He discovers the real poetry, which arises from Creation and Chaos . . ."

from unlit suns within suns
as elevated omen
as intransigent cellular inferno
as none other than flare

Your energy at inception
ignited by ether
by higher intestinal order
with your stamina infused by furious vertical waters

Your fervour for the strange
for unclaimed & rapacious spirit
for a tapestry of various hellgramites
based upon grammar inclement with dictation

not a curse
nor a law by zodiacal harassment
nor a threatening hesitation fueled by personal convolution

instead
for you
a policy of blizzards
of spells conjured by vatic contagion
your cortex having reversed the copious principle of constriction
as visitation from occlusion
alive
with all manner of interior marking
singed by compressed phonation
by verbs from the beyond
by powers coiled in the energy of elliptical hopscotch

& always you were rife
with indictment of the literal

you understood such attack
by means of raw philosophical posture
by momentum exclusive to cinders

which interacted with negation
with the crises which contained itself within consensus
embranglement
In such a setting
you knew all along
that consciousness ailed as a fugue of non-entity
as micro-annihilation
without having to any degree
a galvanic enclave

the populace at large
consumed as a fragmented herald
as a spirit without a foretaste of voltage
without invisible habitability

a world
incapable of raised marrow
of Tibetan pre-simplicity
where the body is infused by breath conjoined by umbilical by
umbilical hesitation

you experienced language
as a cleansed genetic rotation
spinning through the spirit as micro-amplification
listening at the plane of nths
at the highest registration of each phoneme
knowing each letter to be lit by hurricanes of trance
its background value spawned from a hallucinated district
the latter
a single portion of trans-cyclical glossolalia

& you Lecomte
invaded by aural monsoons
surmounted sea walls at birth

& for you
never a garrison of bodies to be invaded to be socially constricted

on the quotidian threshing floor
always facing themselves in nervous mirrors
estranged from suggestion & magic
from Egyptian electrical transmission
from trans-personal ferocity
never knowing the power convened by apprenticeship
conducted as it is across circuits which link the psychic field

Never for you
simply campaign as poltergeist
as social scorpion simply bent on attack

It's as if you engaged
sudden secondary waters
moving back & forth
across a looming spectral dimension
with never an iota of negligence
concerning the invisible & its accuracy with its particles by inference
shading imperceptible kinetics

you understood
language as metals which erupted
& you knew its motion as alchemical debris
which brought insight inspired by dopamine & dice

which allowed you to feed on deserted
locust mountains
so that you were never better or worse
in your body
despite the morphine
the jailings
the indictments

at 14

roaming outside your body via carbon tetrachloride[6]
along with "Daumal" "Meyrat" & "Vailland"
with all the exterior graphs sunken from view
all the railings unlisted
all prior chronicles inept
as regards the body as emptied husk
as blank evaluation
as totemic inclemency

as to locatable transparency
there was always guise through burning
through uncommon surfeit
through maniacal application

Rimbaud was not alone
in braving the unplumbed
before numeric maturity

you
at 14
as editor-in-chief of Apollo[7]
your first poems emitted from the lycee at Reims
meeting Daumal

then the Simplistes[8]
again

---

6 carbon tetrachloride-toxic substance which induces hallucinations

7 Apollo magazine-Founded by Lecomte at 14.

8 Rene Daumal, Robert Meyrat and Roger Vailland were colleagues of Lecomte who met at the lycee at Reims in 1921 who formed the group The Simplistes which sought to "attain the intuitive and spontaneous simplicity of childhood. Their . . . projects included "astral projection, telepathy, extra-retinal vision, lucid dreaming, meeting in planned dreams, and automatic writing." They attempted to attain "a kind of astral state" either "postmortal or "prenatal."

the carbon tetrachloride
your body as sidereal lens
as unsettled munificence
as non-accumulation
as draught of the purely visible

One could say
that Roger Gilbert-Lecomte has gone missing
that the author under copyright is uncapturable existence
is never confined to telluric magnitude never to be converted according to the poet as particle
who announces the family warren through sentiment laced with its presence as shadow instead
you rose up & expanded as dazzling refrangible chroma

as charismatic centipede
extending in all directions
as if
you caught casting shadows
all the while refining true lenticular blindness
being flare of heat rushing across enigmas
always getting the sense of how crime was juggled on random Thursday afternoons

for you Lecomte
outer law was never the dawn
or the crepuscular presence
through which all fate was solved

you knew
that pedestrian dossiers would be deleted
that all trace account
that all the harrowing figment of your morphine trail[9]
would perfectly de-exist
& could never consume your biography as example . . .

9 Lecomte died from morphine toxicity at age 36.

Door

Stick a stick
in the ground

walk around
the world

Phase shifted

1
phase shifted aims to stick a foot in it
but misses, in a decade that began
with osama bin laden, tediously and shoddily
culminates with assange, chasing cocktails
on the sixty-somethingth floor of a shapely
skyscraper, cut at every turn
in glass, ahem-ing, hyatts and marriots
piled to the horizon that burns
with shame in missionary position, tweets
the president about improving business
conditions, if robinsonade occurred, leaving
would be more in line with the megalopolis, bar none

2
phase shifted checks itself by the hour
with the also shifted, but not too much, had no time
to get a move on, was too late to jump on the bandwagon
of retreating history, among pink panthers
itself untainted by robbery, didn't make it
from the conniption, the chaff that didn't lie under
the combine harvester, let slip the important moment
of the dear girl's transformation from such a meek
little thing into a notorious crazy bitch, though the process
moved like clockwork, now copy-pastes will crop up
in an old reposting, will develop frequency of impact
in the number of coastal guerrillas, dancing in pairs

3
phase shifted follows the example of
rough breathing, ye who descend here
take it outside, creepy, almost didn't

catch it red-handed, parrhesia, blabbering, provokes
the only parrhesian, off the putrid wall
with financial help, paid
vacation, ran on all cylinders
to a tortured end, a mad dog, a burnout
claims ownership, a couple duked it out
settling the score, the curious one's
weather-beaten little nose drips, stuffing a nostril
meddles, considers every gesture

4
phase shifted gourmandizes what will come
from the empty refrigerator, too lazy to fill it
with anything, organic rubbish or fiery
red-eye asian sauce, not the first shot
bottomed on the down-low, thoughtfully harping
on the imminence of something further, gets hammered
with scalded life experience, still not sober from
sweating bullets, grateful old age wrapped
in a cape baiting in its shoes before
the mouth of ungrateful youth, saw worse
when googling, self-sabotage
subsists on inhalations, soggily in brine

5
phase shifted is not an abstract concept
not a concrete ultimatum and not the first stranger you meet
in submission, not promotional agency
marketing bilge, not a hitchhiker, hell-bent on
ax-murder, not a citizen, vigilant of every
sneeze of the authorities just to be chomped in half
and spit out, not a country, grateful for
the hand of power, not sense shifting through semantics
at the wrong intersection, not passing out

a resolution of interpersonal conflict, the point
of no return, not a beginner, not a professional prostitute,
a graying brunette on her knees before
an unidentified male, not even a full-on ass-kicking

6
phase shifted makes its way through purgatory
far from history to avoid bashing in the head
and the rest with a nightstick, a wanderer, battered by a blizzard
couldn't follow the path to nowhere, makes it
to the Babruysk backwater, goes farther onto the steppe, where
not even oprichniks spend time and the Kremlinuts aren't sugared, where
weed wafts from the poultry factory, covers the whole
milk plant property, where pneumatic rifles gun down
a snow-removal machine or a garbage truck
carrying architectural trash, preserved from
a long-incomplete construction project, the paragraph
begins with imho and nsfw, no ectenia and no excess

7
phase shifted thunders with a rattle, when
the beloved through the years is unexpectedly identified
in a single brain cell, in the exceeded rate
of emotional extraction, not marylin's gin, the muzzle
of a smart aleck life partner, measured something more malicious
one word at a time, hair that splits outrageously
gathered in a ponytail, pointless work taxes
the sustenance of mutual closeness, initiated
eventually, but by the logic of miscalculation, indistinguishable
from the logic of things, so fucked up, a kidult
fell into a shitshow, casted as the old fart
in relationships, urges too impulsive

8

phase shifted picks up she who fell down
after the bender, charming with adequate
cynicism, but full-scale, the booze to get so wasted
cost a pretty penny, the wretched girl
worked her wretchedly sophisticated partner
into an emotional shock, the first-class wrestler
exposed herself, in the final battle
instated a boycott, got away as she was, a total fuck-up
in the wrong place, tears the flat-chested beanpole away
from the go-go bar, the newscaster on the pilot
was allowed a propaganda goof, almost
but didn't get arrested, a bulletin degraded in the urn

9
phase shifted ponders what it means to be
shifted on, to be a minotaur, a devoured
Theseus, to be a shabby gutter rat from a far-off
province or itself the far-off province
not looking for the technopark opening with
the famous brain drain, unabundant
and blind in melancholy, to be the condition
of exhausting melancholy, mistaken for the schizo
in the nuthouse and suppressed drug
treatment, to be a life, that seemed to be a long
concourse a piece of reinforcement a trashcan vulcanized
rubber, a zipper stuck on the track

10
phased shifted would lend a helping
hand in bukakki, but the sexodrome
isn't befitting, no manicure scissors
to clip with, no retired mattress
protector, no playing a round
of foosball, no peer gynt-like energy or sinbadian

sharpness, to make it there, where the object
for pick-up wasn't, for him lunchtime
doesn't exist, mutters wait a minute
to the sushi deliveryman, is financially audited
in swat gear, the shifted didn't shift
even a millikitten, made the onramp on a prayer

11
phase shifted repeats what is with assange
who is behind him? a hack job or a somali
pirate? will the bloody regime fall
in the dusty part of the globe, turn its backside
to history, in front of time changing
absurdly? is there some party that wants
to be the helmsman of crisis? is the militant
alive, seated in a blasted jalopy, the color
of ripe cherries? the color didn't survive anyway, is the
smoking room alive in the public library, was it there
that the casual smoker in the past, bookmarked
the extremist website, plug pulled out

—Translated from Russian by Alexandra Niemi

Kingdomtide

Enormity braids the currents, a folding-in-under, hypostasis of water and water.

I think someone may be speaking . . .

Like death, God is the same distance for everyone.

All around us arbutus trees dive into the coastline, their thin bark peeling, flaking, revealing their ruddiness, and I keep thinking of the flaying of Marsyas.

And of sycamores, river birch, like soldiers in their snow and desert camo, the war finding a new place to hide.

We are all in the process of being rendered, like it or not: we all have skin.

A great blue heron stalks the cove shallows, distinguishing which bit of light has blood in it.

The scent of fir and yellow cedar, each artisan boat is sealed with pine tar and placed in the bay like a nest.

I'm suddenly stunned: birds do not have hands.

It's time I wrote what I promised, before light leaks into memory,
and I am exposed, twice.

How in some way you are here with me more than ever,
because you are not.
How—without warning—the ghost ship drops anchor in us: Orante.

Here, the hermitage patiently awaits its hermit to be built.

The tide, its lunar unction, awaits.

The harvest the harvest.

But it's the Vesper Hour, we must hurry—that other tide is coming in.

This is good practice, walking through horizons, through walls,
remaining whole—but hurry.

While the driftwood table is dry.

Across the island thousands of crickets set the tiny invisible fires of
being to music.

Island signals island across the archipelago, across the border.

And the wind takes up the evergreen flag, once more.

Isidore's Plough, Whaler Bay, Galiano Is., the Salish Sea

ROSETTA BALLEW-JENNINGS

In Wartime People Feign.

1. On Pacific Street

A cursive
basement lights
is penciled on an aluminum switch box

in the garage. The hand is not my own.

It is easy to see the same voice in many homes cannot

hold
me

like this

2. Bed No. 29

She sat
with a little shake.

I took no thought and she had a kind
of suffocation.

We have not done as much
to notice

the mothers are cut
open with expectation
this is normal. Part of the divine

We are signing
our words and bringing violets.
The other room is emptying
bellies with knives.

3. In Wartime People Feign.

Bricks marigolds window sash door shutting
Some people have the capacity for faith

more importantly,
the light touched you. Today.

Pancho Villa
[a retelling]

ABY KAUPANG

I have the duty to inform you
Pancho Villa is everywhere
nowhere at the same time

and here is an actual cyborg
conversation from the web:

"Humans tell lies. This is known data." The cyborg said.
"Cyborgs tell lies, too," Ricardo said.
"The concept is meaningless. You must vacate your warship immediately or face termination."
"You will lose the warship then."
"No. We desire the warship. We have a bargain."
"It's not good enough. My people need assurances."
"You are dissembling," the cyborg said. "I have been monitoring your eye movement and your facial changes. You are Captain Ricardo Sandoval acting Captain of the Pancho Villa. I am instructed to tell you:
dissembling will result in extreme pain."

I will periodically return to it.

I am an occupational therapist.
I return to things.

Among other things, I chart milestones—when does a baby lift her head, when does she role from supine to caudal, when does she root or lift her hoary head, when does she speak . . .

When a baby speaks there is notation but when one speaks out or speaks against, the demarcation is greater and graver

> In 1950 Octovio Paz writes:
>
> the brutality of uncouthness of many of the revolutionary leaders has not prevented them from becoming popular myths. Villa still gallops through the north, in songs and ballads; Zapata dies at every popular fair . . . it is the revolution, the magical word, the word that is going to change everything, that is going to bring us immense delight and a quick death.

Poncho Villa, his reputation of mythical proportions in Mexican consciousness, was feared and revered as a modern Robin Hood.

My Grandfather, Dr. James Wallace Peak of Montrose, Colorado, in 2014 still hangs the sword of our ancestor, Previous Peak, who, as family lore concurs, waved his sword, that hanging sword, that sword I at seven years old, furtively took down, ensconced above the doorframe of their bedroom, I held and unsheathed and feared it and its history and my future should I be caught sword-handed and it was heavier than I imagined and duller and its history of death and the history of my hands and family's hands, heavy. My ancestor, Previous Peak, had laced his horse to the Texas-Mexico border and into New Mexico; he hunted down that revolutionary bandito that indomitable Lord of the Sierra that Eternal victim of

all governments.
He tracked and hunted him down as if a wild beast and he did not find him:
even in the blue sage, I did not find him.

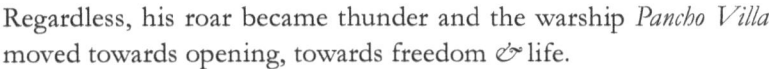

Gringo, Pancho Villa wants you.

Regardless, his roar became thunder and the warship *Pancho Villa* moved towards opening, towards freedom & life.

But that is a terribly poor introduction. Here is a second option, this second option from http://www.badassoftheweek.com/villa.html and I think it is badass clear:

> The notorious outlaw who would come to be known as Pancho Villa was born in 1878 in a tiny rural Mexican town to dirt-poor parents indentured on an enormous hacienda owned by some rich jerk. When he was only fifteen years old his father died and he went to work as a sharecropper on the plantation, picking strawberries and shit for like two cents and hour and leading the miserable life of an underprivileged menial laborer who barely had enough cash to feed his hungry family. You see, back in the early 20th century shit in Mexico was really fucked up. All power was consolidated

into the hands of a bunch of super-wealthy asshole *haciendados* who lived in these insanely huge houses and made millions of *Pesos* off what was essentially the slave labor of their employees.

As a young man Pancho Villa didn't set out to change the entire economic and social structure of Mexico. He didn't grow up with grand, idealistic plans of bringing freedom to the oppressed and righting the wrongs that were being done to his people. He was just a regular guy. Then one day he came home from work to find the owner of the hacienda in the process of trying to rape his twelve year-old sister. This shit would not abide.

Pancho Villa:

[after hearing a gunshot]:

Sometimes justice can be loud.

Villa had a legendary reputation. Villa Villa Villa. *Viva el Villa*!

Villa, the *as*:

Villa as Providence
Villa as the blazing torch of the ideal of the Mestizo mind and
armed with himself
Villa as shining bandito

Villa as widow killer
Villa *post mortem* wanting nothing but a parade for himself
wanting nothing well maybe a grave to show *I am always here for Mexico*
Villa likes ice-cream and he shits in the brush
Villa as never El Presidente
Villa so often on horseback the *Centaur of the North*

Villa never reading Don Quixote
Villa gives gold to the widows
Villa appearing as himself in Hollywood films in 1912, 1913, 1914 and 1916
Villa as played by Antonio Banderas in 2003
Villa baptizes a baby and shortly after is perforated
—sixteen bullets—while driving to his hacienda
Villa whose head has never been recovered

He's the James Boys, he's Billy the Kid, he's Napoleon all in one.

—D.W. Griffith

My great-great—as if there were no mediocres, no banishable fathers—writes in his journal that all this praise is hearsay:

not a single man in all the army has ever laid eyes on Villa!

. . .

In 1923, Villa was coldly gunned down as he drove through the town of Parral after baptizing a baby. The murderer is still unknown.

Although most historians blame Alvaro Obregon for the act, there is mystery surrounding his murder – mystery surrounding the location of his head – mystery too in his final words:

No me dejen morir así, digan que dije algo

Don't let it end like this. Tell them I said something.

Not one of his companions survived to tell.

Let us pray for Pancho.

PANCHO
VILLA
Gran General
Revolucionario
8" Vision Candle Item #36611
Hecho en los E.E.U.U.
Miami, FL 33147
WARNING: Keep out of reach of children and animals. Never leave a burning candle unattended.
AVISO: Mantener fuera del alcance de niños y animales. Nunca deje una vela ardiente desatendida.
TU VISION
ORACION
EN EL NOMBRE DE DIOS NUESTRO SENOR INVOCO A LOS ESPIRITUS QUE TE PROTEJAN PARA QUE ME QUIDES. ASI COMO VENCISTE A LOS PODEROOSO. ASI TE PIDO TU PROTECION ESPIRITUAL. PARA QUE ME LIBERES DE TODO MAL Y ME DES EL ANIMO NECESARIO Y EL VALOR SUFICIENTE PARA ENFRENTARME EN LA VIDA. AMEN
ALLEGED
PRAYER
IN THE NAME OF GOD, I ENVOKE THE SPIRITS THAT PROTECT YOU TO WATCH OVER ME. I PRAY FOR YOUR SPIRITUAL PROTECION. DELIVER ME FROM ALL EVIL AND GIVE ME THE STRENGTH NECESSARY TO FACE ALL LIFES CHALLENGES. AMEN
8" Vision Candle Item #36611
Made in the U.S.A.
Miami, FL 33147

Solar Maximus

SAM TRUITT

I am seconds away
from you

from me
from anything

we can discover
or describe

or strike a chord
against

like a Colossus
waiting in our form

to find us

Introduction
[from *Erebus*]

During the late 1970s, the national carrier Air New Zealand offered regularly scheduled Antarctic sightseeing flights departing from Auckland and crossing over scenic locations on the polar continent. The nonstop roundtrip excursion took about 11 hours and cost what would be worth around US$1,000 today.

On the morning of 28 November 1979, Air New Zealand flight TE901 took off at 8:21 am, with an ETA of 7:05 that evening. By 8:30 pm, the aircraft had not yet returned. Radio contact could not be raised. Operating initially on the theory the flight had lost its way, airline executives soon were forced to accept that the aircraft had depleted its fuel reserves. A statement was made to the media. Broadcasters interrupted regular programming. The flight was officially declared missing.

There were 257 people on board.

That evening all of New Zealand and Australia were riveted to the news. In this part of the world, the unfolding disaster would sear memories among generations the way the Kennedy assassination had in America.

While the vast majority of passengers and crew were New Zealanders, also on board were citizens from Australia, Canada, France, Japan, Switzerland, the United Kingdom, and the United States.

A friend of the author was one of the adventurers on flight TE901.

Fasten Your Seatbelt
[from *Erebus*]

Kay Barnick, 29 *DOB: 5/3/1950 California SSN: XXX-XX-4799*

Marion Barnick, 59 *DOB: 10/11/1919 Idaho SSN: XXX-XX-9239*

Not Jehovah's Witness nor a speaker
in tongues, not Mormon, Mennonite, Shaker

or Quaker. How often does Marion explain
what she is

and is not? Her sacred book proclaims, Death
is only the belief

in death. Please let me
join that church.

Long distance. Person to person.
Marion calls her

oldest daughter, uninterested
in accustoming herself to having an

only daughter. Where she's calling from
the backyard lemons gloat in the arms of the sun. *Let's go*

to Antarctica! In New York,
night's already come.

What makes Kay quail? She sits on her bed. She catches
her breath with a butterfly net. The pleasure

of traveling with Marion is not disputed. She remembers
India, remembers the local authorities refusing

her mother's students, all women,
permission to fly

outside the airport traffic pattern. Now
they can laugh, and Marion has since

brought so many students to the States, making sure
they put down in every muddy field and farm

until the women owned
the soft landing. No grudge, mother and daughter

hold India in the cup
of their hearts.
. . .

Skua gulls—
the hyenas, the vultures
of the Pole—

Let's go to Antarctica! Crossing
the South Magnetic Pole, Marion

in the slender widebody, mirrors the heroic gesture
full of 19th-century inquiry. For Kay,

hedging in the East
Village, Antarctica whispers wasteland, white-washed

whalebone monuments to destruction
on fast ice, the heroic failure. *Let's go to Antarctica.*

The Ninety-Nines, those high-flying
gals, won't hesitate to sign on with Marion

for the jamboree, though at the last minute
their plans change. A woman calls her

oldest daughter, *Let's go to Antarctica.* An airline
promotes a complimentary Champagne Breakfast

with Lamb Kidneys, lunch of
Bay Prawns and Antarctic Scallops in an Icy Mint Sauce

and for dessert, Peach Erebus.
The flight will be unforgettable.

Erebus	*In Greek mythology,* Ερεβος *(Erebus), son of Chaos, personification of darkness; the first realm of the gloomy underworld through which all the dead must pass before reaching Hades*
Mount Erebus	*Southernmost volcano on Earth and second highest in Antarctica, on Ross Island; remains active*
Ross Island	*Formed by four volcanoes, including the now dormant Mount Terror*

Southernmost entry point for many Heroic Age Antarctic expeditions; both Shackleton's and Scott's huts remain, preserved as historical landmarks; polar researchers make Scott Base (New Zealand) and McMurdo Station (US) home year round

. . .

JANE SUMMER

Flotation Device
[from *Erebus*]

She smiles at me.
So we begin. Who would not

return the stranger's
invitation?

In the newsroom
there's talk

of the heat
above and below,

the collapse of ice,
global instability,

the Western Antarctic
Ice Shelf shedding

city-sized bergs
to the seas. The rising

tide sends survivalists
for higher ground. This woman,

Kay Barnick, is higher
ground. I know it

right away.
Like I know

I'm sick

of all the lies I tell.

Like I know she will go
to Antarctica.

Who am I
to say stay?

I'm
two desks away.
. . .

Cruising Altitude
[from *Erebus*]

JANE SUMMER

First farewell to the farmland
below, green as billiard cloth.

Then the knobby alpine spine
down New Zealand's South

Island falling astern while the ship
continues to climb. Soon

the gray comfortless
Southern Ocean, the widebody going over

its faceless expanse.
For a diversion, the pop! of Champagne

and the breakfast service begins, accompanied by
three polar documentaries, including 1964's

140 Days Under the World. Over
the tremendous sea, the DC-10's shadow

a flea upon it. Sighting
the grassland of Disappointment

Island relieves the tourist's lingering
despair—the possibility

of land! Of landing! And gone. Visit
the flight deck. More Champagne

pops and the cabin's amok

with goodwill, sunglasses, binoculars.

This is the life.

The fearful passage
of their death-mark'd love

Cameras whir and snap

to action at this masked
ball, this sky-flying cocktail

party. Inward types cozy up to
diaries . . . two hundred shutterbugs . . .

some enter sanctuary with Eliot Porter's
coffee table *Antarctica* in their laps—then

a reverent hush as the aircraft approaches
the ice continent.
. . .

Tourists, the snaps you take
will testify

to more than you
know. Thousands of frames show

fair visibility at altitude, perfect
for the polar trickery

that paints snowy mountain with ice
below as one

foggy curtain. Flat light
whiteout. This evidence

will deconstruct disaster. So too
the movie camera that sweeps

the cabin to linger
on a young woman like Kay but not

Kay. I've played and replayed
the film clip so many times

but never find her
in the color-rinsed footage the desert

cold preserved. Is she aft of the lens, viewing
Ross Island's absinthe-tinted ice,

the logical plaid of the calving
frozen sheets, this fragile hairline

where ice edge meets open water?
Perhaps she's right before my eyes

in one of these faded seats. Kay's no
taller than I. Perhaps

the seat back obscures her, she's
not strolling the aisles but buckled in,

as all experienced aviators, my father
or her mother, always urge. Belted in

this misadventure, you're unlikely to be ripped
from the fuselage with those who'll be found

littering the ice like beachgoers,
short-sleeved and shoeless, almost dozing.

Ladies and gentlemen, the captain has turned off the Fasten Seat Belt sign and you're free to move around the cabin. However, we recommend keeping your seat belt fastened while seated . . .

. . .

They have been released
from hundreds of hands

yet cameras keep filming
until impact. In that tick of time, less

than it takes the heart to beat,
most passengers

are thrown from the plane—
few had been belted

in. The fuselage continues galloping
up the mountain, disintegrating

for more than 300 meters, thrusting
even more bodies out as it gouges a path,

until the terrible skeletal alloy
runs itself out and comes to rest.

But nobody anywhere has any idea
this has happened to you. Not yet.

No one in the world hears

metal claw ice

or the retort when the craft explodes.

No one in the world sees

bodies catapulted into crevasse
after crevasse

cleaved by the wreck as it hurtled
along ice, the dying animal furiously burrowing

passengers into frozen tombs. A hand in shifting snow
seems to imitate the royal wave, not wanting

to make a fuss.

No one in the world has the acrid taste of the inferno

in the soft pink tissue
of the mouth.

. . .

The most haunting photo in the history of flight
TE901 is shot the instant

death cuts in line. It is
the affidavit of 257 souls.

In the "final photograph of actual impact," writes an
investigator, the fluid depicted on the aircraft's windows is
thought to be jet fuel, which ignited the inferno.

By the time the photographer
released the shutter, she was dead. Investigators viewed
additional

still shots and moving
footage. In the dark
the projector

screened images of interior cabin shots, clumsy
amateur swings around

to the window, the amazed tourist's frames
of ice below. And then.

An interruption of flames.
The silence.

Blurry objects tumbling. The silence
of Super 8.

. . .

Oxygen Mask Will Drop
[from *Erebus*]

JANE SUMMER

What a hoarse wind
staggers this
silence Men are falling
out of the colorless
from hanging pianos
Is that how we came

to be in this place Hideously
they move toward us
What do they want
Are they drunk Are they
Frankensteins Conquistadores Migrating

Angels Here they come Why
carry weapons Don't they realize O
rope pickaxes and little flags
snapping in the wind Look
how earnest they are Why
hammering It's too late for

gallows Don't let them
bury us here Mother It's cold Are you
cold What are they building Men love
making noise So much noise
It's a platform A dance
floor Let's dance It will keep us

warm Now what Why
are they collecting
our weird tribe They're having a time of it Aren't they
Smoking looting booze ransacking pockets and
Hey handsome Why won't they I've heard
murderers too don't look you in the face

Kay we won't stay
long Don't we always

return home
eventually

Let's go dancing Mother Surely
they'll have music I'd love to listen
to some jazz right now I can't
budge Can you Here comes another
big guy Doesn't he look like he's just
seen a ghost This cold This cold
makes me drowsy How's that
flight plan coming Mother
Mother are you still
there I can't turn my If you are
please say something
Answer

Some folks seem to be hearing pipe
organs and boy choirs I hear a drone
steady and pitch
perfect Gracious It's my
Cessna the 172 and there's
the Ercoupe that won me
first prize Now where
did I stow those
macadamias I keep
a jar on board
every plane

First what confusion then
insurmountable
sadness Not as definitive
as grief A feeling I'll never get out
but the song O no not I

I can see
Are my eyes open or closed I am
the light that takes all morning
to move across the study
wall I can be the sun
warmed fruit in your palm

Kay here is Mother Here
we go now Upsa daisy Gentlemen don't forget
my beautiful daughter She's my
oldest I had her somewhere She's the one
with the heart the magnificent
heart and her hair Kay usually wears it
up Gibson girl style You're too young
to know what I'm talking about Kay
raise a hand so the young
men can find you She was right
beside me a second ago I'm sorry
Say again Negative It's hard
to hear in the wind Negative
Her hair isn't burnt
umber It's gold silver and butter
scotch Perhaps it's all undone
and loose to her waist

Someone's come I'm in
his arms And now it's time
It's time to stop
thinking in words
Mother
goodbye
It's time to It's time

. . .

New Zealand police and mountain
rescue team are flown to Antarctica.

In my ignorance my image of the disaster
in the locket of my memory

remains pristine: Kay vanishing
in boundless Antarctic white.

Then blackness.

Maybe I can't find you in any film
because you aren't on the flight after all.

Maybe I've come to understand what it means to hope
against hope.

Nothing could have prepared us for the devastation we encountered.

Skua gulls were eating the bodies. This hampered victim identification. We tried to shoo them. We lobbed emergency flares. Nothing scared them off. Nothing. Even after corpses were bagged, the gulls tore through the body bags to pull at the flesh.[10]

The flight had been equipped with a well-stocked bar and some of the liquor on board survived the crash. We made use of it.

The slope was about 14°, too steep for the helos to land, so we built a landing platform into the mountain. When the helos came in, the winds sent fragments of torn metal objects flying in all directions.

We were soon to learn the dangers and suddenness of the changeable weather conditions. Without any real warning a severe storm blew up with gale force winds and snow. The temperature dropped with the wind chill factor to the vicinity of minus 40 degrees. After several hours the storm abated. On inspecting the crash site again it had changed considerably. Bodies and wreckage, which were previously visible, were now covered with snow, and others not visible initially were now exposed.

---

10 Antarctic veteran Bernie Gunn, who visited the continent as a Ph.D. student as part of Edmund Hillary's team in the 1950s, has this to say about the skua gulls: "Skuas are unlovely creatures, one hopes God feels affection for them because few people do. They are ruthless scavengers, nest close to penguin rookeries so they can steal eggs or young chicks, hover round seals with pups and may pick their eyes out. I never even shot one which shows either remarkable forbearance or dereliction of duty on my part. I cannot in my most generous moments believe that a world free of skuas would be all that worse off. My conscience is salved by the number of times I have biffed an ice-axe at one, not I regret, with much effect as several centuries of explorers biffing ice-axes at them has taught them to duck."

After handling so many charred bodies, our gloves had become completely saturated in black human grease.

Water being a rare resource, we washed our hands in a community basin. The water turned black as molasses. I couldn't eat the first meal anyway. It was meat stew.

To keep a distance we had to joke about the remains—the "roasted meat," "wax works," "ice pops." The hardest part wasn't the disfigured or dismembered bodies. It was the intact ones. They made you think, "That could have been me. That could have been my wife, my daughter."

Among the victims' belongings was a dictionary. It was frozen open to a page where the first word I saw was "corpse."

The crash had cleaved open innumerable crevasses, bottomless to the eye. We tried abseiling but who thought to bring a flashlight in 24-hour daylight? I don't like to imagine what landed down there.

The sun that allowed the US military to search through the night until the DC-10 was found is the sun that offered no warmth to the recovery team. Yet any flesh unprotected by gear or cream burnt in no time.

One of my first tasks was to build a snow-dome toilet to help protect naked bums from the intense wind-chill swirling around the nether regions.

Immediately I was drawn to its wonders – the extreme cold (for me), the purity of the landscape, the clarity of the air, the tenacity of the wildlife, the ever-present dangers of the environment.

Our party travelled to the crash site and was met by the horrendous sight before us. Each body had been flagged (green) along with the perimeter of the site (black) and the crevasse edges (red), in case a storm were to cover the bodies with snow.

Throughout my time there, I had this underlying sadness of the lost potential and the utter waste of it all.

. . .

Who can conceive of
being buried by the initial crash, discovered

by recovery workers, reburied in the ice for safekeeping,
dug out and buried again? Handled, ogled,

photographed, pecked at,
re-buried, sampled, tagged, numbered and

transported multiple times

by helicopter, airplane, truck and dolly before

the head jarring
ceases for good?

Some are horrified to see
what I see, one of you a few yards from

the tail and #2 engine cowling
but just outside

the formal composition
Nigel Roberts made famous, arms

thrown back as if to dive into . . .
one leg strangely bent high

where the thigh should be. This cadaver
won't shock me. What did

people expect? A sanitation crew?
I love the body

as the vehicle
to get love through to you.

Personal identification of unidentified bodies is crucial
for ethical, juridical and civil reasons
and is performed through comparison
between biological data obtained from the cadaver
and antemortem material from one or more missing persons
to whom the body may have belonged in life.
—Abstract from *La Radiologia Medica*

Before departing Antarctica
the knees, elbows and foreheads of the dead and more

than one hundred fragmented remains
are blessed by a US Navy chaplain

posted at Williams Field
during Operation Overdue.

Williams Field	a polar layer-cake of an airstrip: at the time, two runways composed of 25 feet of compacted snow on top of 260 feet of ice floating atop 1,800 feet of water serving Scott Base (New Zealand operated) and McMurdo Station (US operated)
Operation Overdue	code name for the New Zealand police and Mountain Face Rescue Team responsible for the recovery effort of flight TE901

Were they not already blessed
by the sweetness of the natural world

enraged and inhospitable
as it may seem

from time to time? If the fanged frozen Pole
is not the earth in balance, then what

else but a last cry
against our scratched and gutted

hell pits, our greasy spills that choke
what breeds in the seas?

Don't let me hear you
say these were sightseers who didn't care to

get their feet wet, who couldn't take the cold
in their teeth, who wanted spectacle and to be home

in time for their favorite
evening TV. These travelers were enamored

with the continent barely seen, the globe's skullcap,
a mere frill on maps. They had come to honor

the planet's crowning.
. . .

Take this
coat, the umbrella. We can walk together

again. You aren't fearful of living
in oblivion. We're the ones fearful

of forgetting,
our memorials monuments

to this dread. Now
the day approaches

when I'll wake to look
so much like you. I think I'm beginning to.

When you say the water's rising
it's not figurative.

Antarctica's massive ice shelves are shrinking
because they are being eaten away from below
by warm water, a new study finds.
That suggests that future sea levels
could rise faster
than many scientists have been predicting.
—Daily Mail, *25 April 2012*

The tide ferries those
we know and those unknown

down mapped waterways. Sooner or later everyone goes
home, wherever that is. You seemed

always at home, or I was
in you

when we met and I was sick of
telling lies about myself. Now I'm sick

of telling the truth. Maybe that's why
everything makes me cry, Kay—

the Antarctic fairground
animals' fate,

the water that keeps rising,
talk of the heat

above and below,

the collapse of ice,

global instability.
I thought I'd given up

my search for higher ground
but here you are,

Kay Barnick,
from the netherworld

light into New York's illustrated
night, and you love me.

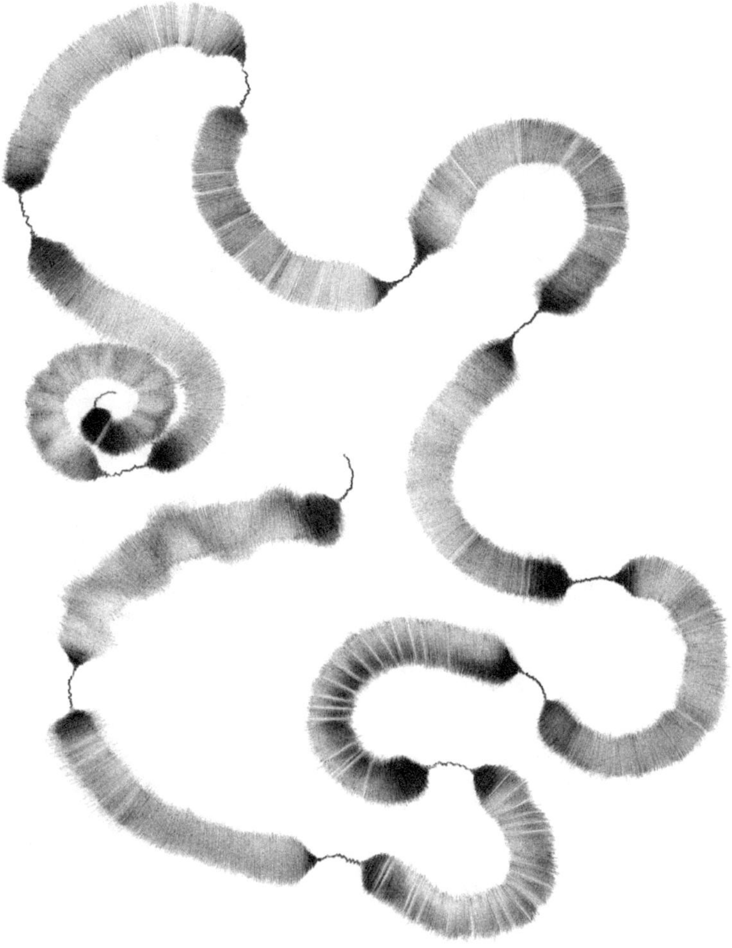

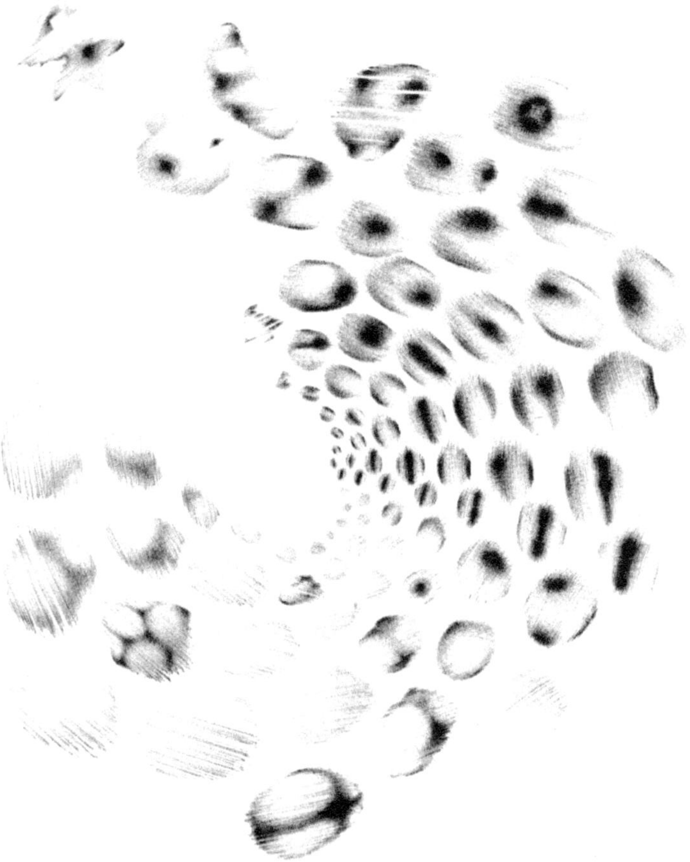

PART SIX:

The Sacred Unspeakable Godless Particle: With Dead Hands I Lift the Dead

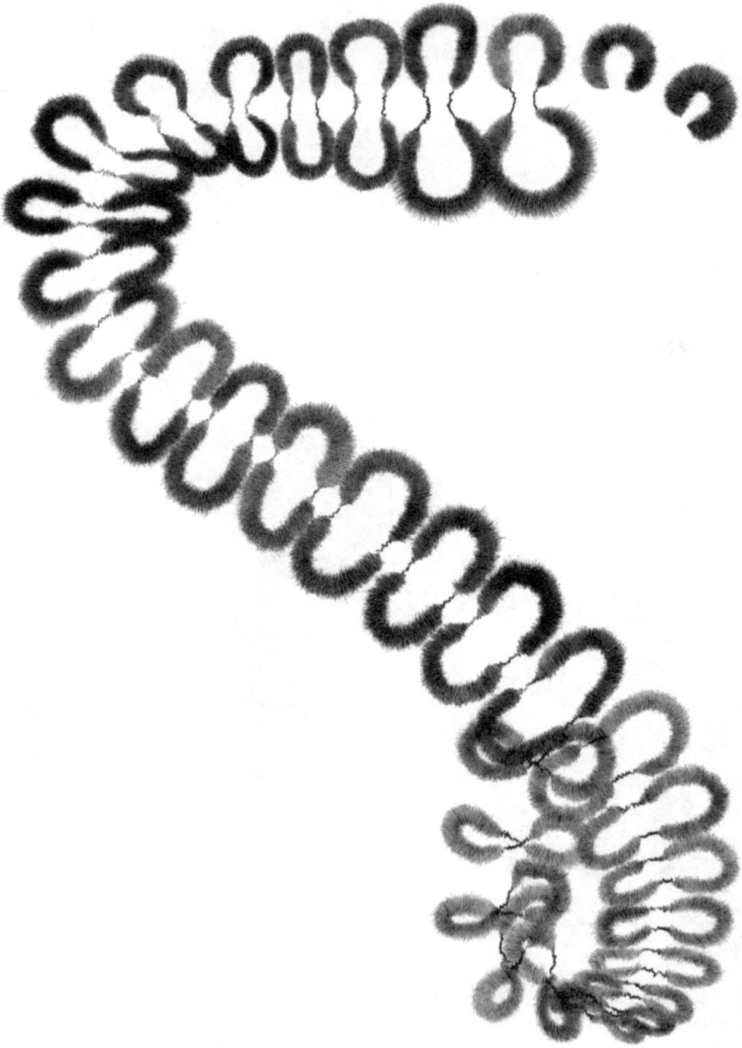

EXECUTE PROGRAM . . .

"Let an ultraintelligent machine be defined as a machine that can far surpass all the intellectual activities of any man, however clever. Since the design of machines is one of these intellectual activities, an ultraintelligent machine could design even better machines; there would then unquestionably be an 'intelligence explosion,' and the intelligence of [humans] would be left far behind. Thus the first ultraintelligent machine is the last invention that [humans] need ever make."

—British mathematician I.J. Good, 1965

"I very much subscribe to the idea – and maybe I am spoiled or ruined – that country without wolves isn't really good country. It's incomplete. It doesn't have its full spirit.... And so when I got to Yellowstone in 1994 I walked the landscape and it felt flat, dull. Without wolves it just didn't crackle. So we took Yellowstone, and we dropped maybe the biggest symbol of wilderness in the world in the middle of it. And that symol did well.... I mean, we knew them intimately. We knew their stories, we knew their pups, we knew their battles, we knew their loves, losses, everything. But more and more I began just to hear about this one wolf, this female.... What she would do is look at me, and our eyes would connect. And her eyes would say, 'I don't like you at all. And I'm going to outsmart you.'... When you get to know an individual of another species, you begin to kind of respect that individual. In this case, her. Because she was worthy of just being left alone.... I didn't think they'd get her. And they did. And why they did, I don't know. I thought she was immune. But it's naive to think that we have a wolf running around in Yellowstone that's untouched by humans. And there is a part of me that wishes that were true, that wolves like 06

> could be forever wild. And it's painful to confront it and say, 'We just don't live in that kind of world anymore.'"
>
> —Doug Smith, biologist with the National Park Service, regarding the 06 Female Wolf at Yellowstone

- Considering the above statements: Is there such a thing as a non-human individual?

- How has the presence of humans irrevocably changed the planet?

- Would you call *Homo sapiens* an invasive species? Are the living and the dead invasive?

- Could a non-organic particle be that individual? Or a machine? Could that "Godless Particle" be the all-central point about which the entire cosmos opens and closes?

Start

SAM TRUITT

With dead hands
I lift the dead

words spill
from images

from *Dybbuk of Angelus*

VII

The fox had his mind made up before the flood. We domesticated the fox by feeding him the leaves of Bible. We confused prayer for a sunrise. We went barefoot in the snow. We made him a flaming savior. He hunts like a saint. Each muscle, a prayer; clasped in attention. Triangulates, cocks, each muscle fulfills its destiny.
Caress. Arch. Cocks.
triangulates. An arc of *wu wei* to find that point in space. Astute dive towards innocence. Fox eats like a saint. Making music with its bone. With seven doors, a mouse under the snow,
Fox avoids hunters, puts branches in the holes and when attacked by snakes, will turn its back and
bite the snake's head, swing it against the tree.
It bites the snake's head,
it swings it against the marigold tree into its sainthood.

Fox, a word we did not catch by its tail
to break the silence

A Poem Beginning with Lines by Tranströmer

BERNARD HORN

He was anonymous
like a schoolboy in a lot surrounded by his enemies.

Or not anonymous
so much as invisible
like Ellison's man
in the room of a thousand light bulbs.

Or like me, age nine,
South Eighth Street,
Brooklyn, accosted after school
by Raymond Duffy, age fourteen.
"Take your Jewcap off," he's saying,
"I don't want to insult your religion,"
and punching me so hard in the face,
the back of my skull
cracked into the curb
before I could open my mouth.

Or like my Uncle Mottek
standing in the periphery of the clearing
in the Sambor graveyard
forced not to look away as they gunned down
his sons and then his wife
before forcing him forward
a rifle butt in his back
to the piles of dirt, the common grave,
and the shovels
alongside the other fathers, brothers, and sons,
a new brotherhood
of gravediggers.

SAM TRUITT

Zone

Just a face—
nothing

to describe—
just the terror

of looking out
at it

of it
the unknown

I don’t know what to tell you About telling you anything–

CURTIS EMERY

I am a singular note
bellowing in my wilderness,

when I am in the shadows
I lament with me.

I lament with me and
Basquiat on the brick walls
of my own cityscape—

in my naked youth
lights are turning off
across my shoulders

I am 23 and shade

I am 23 and out—

a million suns populate the face
of a single camera bulb and the
body pressed into film is an analog
being of an analog being

and I AM that analog being
in the birdless soup of night
where shadows come easy,

where bodies are dislocated from
their heads, which are invisible—

and the heads lament with me,

and the dislocated heads lament with me

Page 404: page not found[11]

<h1> the year of the flood: *an antediluvian hymn* **</h1>**

I might be a saint for this voyage.

Let me fellow-remember

loss a quill succumbed to symptoms.

I <praisegiving> stay healthy. A Fallow
—my own treasured rooftop—a wild gift,

her fellow dance

around her,

let me sing </praisegiving>

<h2>books of the century: *new flowering oracles and other genres of brevity*</h2>

<oracle> I shall speak exhaustive aphorisms, slogans, quips, reflexive minimalisms: in the Beginning was the word, the Mnemonic novel, the three-decker blue-collar cool-surfaced fortune cookie, a forgettable Delphic pensée. Later the proverbs of

---

11 These are page 404 found poems. The first part is mostly an erasure based on page 404 of Margaret Atwood's Year of the Flood. The second is a collage from "John Barth on Minimalism," page 404 of *Books of the Century.* The third an erasure from *The Sibylline Oracles,* page 404, of *The Old Testament Pseudepigrapha.* Pages were accessed on October 13, October 14, and October 26, 2013.

more or less label many specimens.
aka know thyself </oracle>

<h3>the old testament pseudepigrapha: *an oracle of sybil* ***</h4>***

<oracle> A not inconsiderable swarm of dust, wintry,
river and lakes frozen over: immediately a barbarian weakened
family—
their gulp wild, their stone table.

Will it be possible to know men and women
a generation ten-thousandfold, moonless? The sun is setting,
remaining plunged in a small mist. Cover the folds of the world about
a second time, Thrice-Wretched, remain the streams speechless,
reposing your praises, you in linen say:

Come let us change the terrible custom— </oracle>

MAGGIE CLEVELAND

The Machinery of God Helping Those Who Help Themselves

You usually don't have to worry
about a passenger elevator door
falling on you. If the upper door panel

gets jammed or stuck in the open
position, it is extremely dangerous, even
with the main switch pulled. If the stuck

section suddenly becomes free, the panel will fall
like a guillotine. Anything in its path
will be crushed or severed. Never stick

your head in between the upper
and lower panel to see what's wrong. Block
the doors open securely to be certain

they won't fall before proceeding. Safety
must be your number one concern at all times.

The Bumblebee's Enlarged Eye Erased Grids

TOMAŽ ŠALAMUN

When you stand warm, warm
on the balance beam and whistle it'll
snow on the man in Nebraska.
It'll snow on pupas, on bumblebees, on
Virovitica.
Call from the window.
Call from the window.
Lean as if forehead – spruce.

The last bungs up the complaint to the cat's ear.
He sees red spleen and dark wheel.

How to end standing up.

The lumberjack's talk is pure walrus.
There's no lava, there's an uplift.

On Corpus Christi Vlado is wrapped in rags.
Gray paper God.

*[Translated from the Slovenian by
Michael Thomas Taren and the author]*

EWA CHRUSCIEL

from *Dybbuk of Angelus*

XXVI

Pieces of gold
smelted, malleable,
shaped in wax of little angel bees
burnished to reflect light

Unpolished we trap too much light
and become ghosts

We carry vessels
to the graves.

When a person dies
Colombians put jars with water
around the house
for the soul to quench its thirst

We need to tame water
by building canals.

Birds peck the water.
Priests, condors in flight.
One needs to catch their messages
of feathers

and then we destroy them.

Spool 38

MATTHEW COOPERMAN

app a scented
dove in fold
maculate hour of
the regenerate beast
trace trail animal
with wings employed
a back hoe
with gryphon tail
shambling hybrids rich
with earth zones
digging down of
all species garble
this is song
in the drive
of the machine

god save us
from our sporing
and our meat
in the salons
its lacustrine waveries
of might dismember
trace trail animal
to memory futurity
god save us

§

the pressure glass
from which we
shout is snow
in a globe
we are standing
in big trouble

wrestle a bloom
know the house
see its space
from inside out
a lineal frisson
of going through
what doesn't love
a going through

such are syntheses
between the leaves
limbs and myths
of mongrel accompaniment
to book bird
reserve a future
dream swiftly outside
with a rose

thus make stay
all the beasties
say petal wall
and mean it

§

to what steep
decline does the
intimate gather   green
      or blue or
whatever your eyes
Dream Glass brighten
the every day
snow will clear
fog of circumstance
or wholly sunshine
you in estuary
of mixed emotions

come let us
swim with our
distress a vivid
class struggle and
kingdom too it's
phylum and face
and too much
rubble   a brimstone
roars roars roars
the zoo revolts
our inevitable privacy

      we are our
shared star beginnings
now tide turns
in mid rose
let's join hands
let's swim back

SAM TRUITT

The Code

Under the assassin's
dome my ass

in the air
eating the numbers

that encircle
your clitoris

that is the mother
of god I feel

my life
pitch back

& where it
was is a house

of dreams

STEPHEN HITCHCOCK

Couplets for the Dead

Poplars, oaks bristle overhead, revealing the mercurial
underside of their leaves. Whose breath is on my neck?

~

Words come much later, maybe
never, is the first lesson learned.

~

People are more attractive these days, I
think, given the combinations out there.

~

Odd: roaches crawl out in the open to die on their backs,
legs in the air, a small, sunlit angle of carpet for a coffin.

~

After lovemaking she hangs from his clavicles, her body
flush with his, as though holding on for dear life. She is.

~

I dreamed of the afterlife: our bedroom door swollen shut
in the summer heat, the chimney breathing into the house.

~

This autumn they saw the leaves fall from the trees;

he imagined a church converted into a war hospital.

~

Our troubles remain so close,
unanswerably close; tell God.

~

Falling asleep is our nightly death
rehearsal. We also practice rising.

~

My breath. Is it what I am
given? Or is it what I give?

~

We still suspect the mind most kindred to the spirit;
I can only imagine you, without bodies, know better.

~

This fall hundreds of dead ladybugs littered their thresholds;
she kept imagining someone holding down the DELETE key.

~

They say, "Time heals all."
Curious. Who heals Time?

~

I dreamed of the afterlife: our bedroom door, winter-shrunken,
letting in the draft, a fire burning in the fireplace, tending itself.

~

So what are you clothed in? Anything? Light? Darkness?
Some of us hope to wear just the one outfit: our favorite.

~

I smirk at the turkey vultures, over a dozen perching in that huge dead oak,
while they turn inward, dozing off, counting the day's death toll, like sheep.

~

The slightest rift can open between spring and summer: a leap
season, where young sparrows learn to fly in a weeping willow.

~

There is so much more I want to say to everyone,
not just the dead but the living, those in between.

~

That you and I do, in fact, die
is a lesson we will never learn.

JOSEPH CHAPMAN

Rhetorical Kingdom

This far north, evening adds up its losses.

The sun cashes in today for pink gauze and a weak glare.

A few clouds leach out into Lake Michigan, and you want to say *like Christ breaking through.*

You want to say *as if the Kingdom of God were at hand.*

It's not. Last night's drunken aftermath is my bloodshot left eye.

It's my skinned knee ghosting me like a quarter-moon.

And if we wanted to catalyze God's return?

What matters is living through these convulsions to witness grace.

Susurration and static. Long distance.

•

Most likely, the Kingdom of Heaven is a failed state, too.

When my father washed up on that final riverbank, he was broken and unrecognizable.

No one was in charge. There was nothing left to say.

Waves keep arriving at my feet like neologisms.

The old stories no longer apply, but the hymns are still true.

The Edifice

SAM TRUITT

To begin think
into a circle

everything
that's ever been

& then escape
nothing

BERNARD HORN

Ashmedai, King of the Demons, Solomon, King of Israel, and the Shamir Who Split Rocks

Author's note: The source of these poems are the account in the Babylonian Talmud (Tractate Gittin) of the encounters among King Solomon, Ashmedai, King of the Demons, and a tiny and primordial worm, the Shamir, with the power to split rocks. In later legends Ashmedai is reduced to an evil demon, sometime consort of Lilith, but in the original stories he is a brilliant shape-shifting trickster, who spends his days at the heavenly study house and his nights in the earthly one. The text was compiled around the year 500 from earlier oral sources. Ninety per cent of the Talmud is Halachah, legal discourse, in which the rabbis try to clarify Biblical legal injunctions or apply these injunctions to the lives they are leading nearly a thousand years after the Hebrew Bible was completed. The Ashmedai legends are part of the Aggadah, a body of folklore, historical tales, and other narratives, which are interwoven, like a patchwork quilt, with the legal passages. Traditionally, these stories are read as allegory or parable and provide access to secret and hidden meanings accessible (in the words of Moshe Chaim Luzzatto, an eminent 18th century rabbi and kabbalist) only to "those of good character," who are "schooled in the ways of analysis." I worked from Adin Steinsaltz's translation of the original Aramaic into Hebrew.

To amplify what I wrote, Solomon needed the Shamir to cut the stones for the Temple in Jerusalem because "neither hammer nor ax nor any tools of iron were heard in the house when it was being built" (I Kings 6:7), which commentators take as prescriptive rather than descriptive.

2. Begin with Ashmedai,

King of the Demons, and his arrival
at a certain mountain way out in the wasteland,
just after sunset, a harvest moon, huge, yellow,
and low in the sky. He still had the form of a man,
attractive and graceful, the conversations

around the square rough-hewn table
in the earthly academy still singing
in his ears as he repeated
or completed them. As he began to yawn
and stretch, his arms
pulling his body with them
as they reached upwards, then outwards,
and a mighty yawn, exquisitely pleasurable,
seemed to go on forever,
as gales of air rushed in on his breath
into inflating and growing alveoli and his expanding
chest continued the expansion of the entire mass
of his body upward and outward,
if not to his full size,
at least to the height of the ancient cedars of Lebanon
below him at the tree line.

He did love his contraction that afternoon,
when he returned from the academy on high
before he sat in on the academy below
so that some thought him invisible,
just listening in, and others saw him as ladybug
or hummingbird or a mockingbird that sang
the rhythms of thought, though to most
he appeared as a soft-spoken stranger
whose words, though few, always cut through.
But he loved this first great inhalation, a baby's breath
or Adam's, even more.

Thirsty, having drunk nothing since dawn,
he sat down by the quarry-sized pit he had dug
and filled with water, examined his seal
which, he saw, had not been tampered with, lifted
the massive boulder from the mouth of the pit,

plunged his face downward eager
to take a few gulps, and was stopped
before his lips touched the surface
by the smell of earth and cardamom
rising from the dark liquid.
"Wine!" he said out loud. "How can that be?"
"It is written," he said, quoting Solomon,
"Wine is a joker, liquor makes you growl,
Anyone steeped in them cannot be wise."
Having sworn off wine, eons ago,
he did not drink. But sat there, thirsty, watching
all trace of redness vanish from the sky as the moon
sluggishly rose and shrank and turned blue.
And he reached both his hands in, cupped them,
discerned the red beads on his skin in the moonlight,
and raised them towards his lips.
Yes, he thought, cardamom
and . . . and . . . pear. Just a sip, he thought.
And flung his hands wide and spoke
"It is written in Hosea,
Harlotry, old wine, and new wine
take over the heart."

He sat back down and looked on
as the moon continued its slow ascent to its zenith.
Then he shook his great fist at the small, now silvery
orb and roared, "What do I care about
all these fine words? If I don't take a drink
I will die." And plunged his face in, first sipping,
then taking gulp after gulp of the best wine
he'd ever tasted and slipped into the deepest of sleeps,
his great bare chest imperceptibly rising and falling
in the white light of the moon.
And awoke in chains.

3. Begin with the Hoopoe,

On his daily round through the far mountains
that jut up from a howling rugged wasteland,
treeless, with no heathland or scrub for miles,
beneath a sky of brass, flying along
with a blue worm the size of a barleycorn
held firmly and delicately in his long thin beak.

This was the Shamir, his partner in their great task.

On their way they would fly through the turf
of the falcons, who dove at him certain
they would have blood for their nestlings
that evening, who never seemed to learn
that his loping flight disguised short, agile,
quick wings and enormous stamina
that evaded and outdistanced them every time.

He placed the Shamir at the peak of a mountain
at the "tooth" of its topmost boulder and in an instant
the mountain split in two and the Hoopoe scattered
from deep in his mouth and cheeks and his clenched feet
a great harvest of tree seeds,
of the chestnut, the bristlecone pine, the sequoia
the olive, the lime, the oak, and the yew,
beginning the interminable process
of turning Nowhere into Somewhere.

As his personal signature, he always threw in
a few seeds of his flower, the Saxifrage
(his name sake) that had split the rocks of his own somewhere,
his nestless home, deeply hidden in a small crevasse, where his
fledglings

nestled and awaited his arrival at his personal stop on his daily rounds,
the Shamir having by then burrowed its tickly way
deep into the feathers of his back,
and he, having paused to dig up from the underbrush
snails and grasshoppers, beetles, flies, and a lizard,
a feast for his babies, after which he continued
his flying lessons, hovering above them
in his undulating style as they flapped their unsure wings, and alert,
ready to swoop down and catch them
on his back should they drop.

O Wild Cock, O Falcon-Mocker, O Rock Splitter, O Nagar Tura!

4. And awoke in chains

Faster than thought, he surged his mass
towards fullness, expecting the chains to shatter
in a spray of shrapnel. But they cut in
to him all over, relaxed, and held firm.
In a moment he had shrunk to the size
of a quicksilver lizard, thinking he'd slither out.
He felt the chain loosening. He thought,
"These iron links are toying with me," as they
closed and held firm. Frenzied, he turned,
twisted, and heard a familiar voice.
"The name of your Master is on the chain."
Felt a tug on the chains, plopped down
like a sack on a boulder,
and refused to budge. But looked:
engraved on the knot where the chains were fused:
there it was:
Yod Heh Vav Heh the sacred unspeakable name of God.

The voice was the voice of the head of Solomon's Palace Guard
who stood at his feet ankle-high. Ashmedai contracted
once more so that he was just a head taller than his captor.
His feet now dangling from the boulder, he spoke deadpan.
"So we meet again, Benayahu ben Yehoyada.
What does the king who knows everything
want from me this time? Another two-headed
man, perhaps?" Benayahu, also deadpan,
filled him in.

5. A Memorable Conversation

"It is written: 'Neither hammer nor axe nor any tool of iron shall be heard in the House when it is in building,'" said Solomon. "Why is this so?"

"Iron, the material of swords, whose role in creation is killing and dying, cannot take part in building the House of the Living God," said the rabbis.

"How can stones be hewn level and true without iron?" he asked.

"As a matter of fact," they answered, "there is the Shamir. A creature from the Six Days of Creation, Moses used it to cut the stones on the High Priest's breastplate. No hard object can resist it."

"Where is it found?" he asked.

"Capture a male demon and a female demon and crush them together until they reveal what they know," they answered.

6. Benayahu's Account to Ashmedai.

The King did as they said, and the pair of demons
under great duress, shifted the blame to you. "Perhaps
Ashmedai knows," they said. They named
your mountain home, revealed the cycle of your days,
your study above, your study below, your pit
of water, and your seal. Solomon fitted me out
with skins swollen with his very best wine,
wool fleece, a ring engraved with God's Holy Name
and the chains you know too well. I found
your mountain easily, recognized your seal,
dug a ditch below your pit, let your water drain
into it, plugged the bottom of your pit from below
with fleece, dug a second ditch above your pit,
filled it with the wine that seeped its way
downward until your pit was filled, then I sealed
the bottom of the ditch with fleece, climbed that cedar,
and watched you perform your whole charade.

7. Ashmedai and King Solomon

Ashmedai had no choice but to hear Benayahu out.
Is he rubbing their cleverness in? he wondered,
getting even for their terror before the two-headed man.
Just you wait, he thought. Just you wait. But came along
willingly until he was finally, after three days of waiting,
face to face with the king. Containing himself no longer,
Ashmedai measured six feet on a reed, threw it
before Solomon and said, "In the end
all you will own is six feet of earth. Was
it nothing to rule the whole world that you

had to conquer me as well?" "From you I
want nothing," Solomon replied. "I
require the Shamir to build the House of God.
The House of God's my one desire. Bring me
the Shamir and you're free." "The prince of the sea,
not I, has charge of the worm, which he
entrusted to the Hoopoe, who swore on his life
to keep the worm safe while he and the bird
split the far mountains and raise up forests."

8. Benayahu and the Hoopoe

Benaya was dispatched to the edge of the bristlecone
pine forest where he heard the Hoopoe's fledglings
chirping for food in the rocky crevasse
they called home. He covered the crevasse
with a sheet of transparent glass and hid
among the rocks. The hoopoe dove homeward
crashed into the glass, scattering a mouthful
of locusts on the shiny smooth surface. He took off
in an instant, returned, descended,
and hovered just above the glass,
the Shamir in his beak. Benayahu flung
a clod of earth at the Hoopoe who dropped
the worm. The glass split, the bird dove, Benayahu
was quicker. He grabbed the worm, placed it
in a soft leather box with a soft silken
lining, and headed for his king. The Hoopoe
in despair dove directly into the deepest pool
in the far mountains where he drowned.

STEPHEN HITCHCOCK

Another Spy in Jericho

1
In the city of sea glass, the city made of rain,
the wind scatters ash from your cigarette.

You do not mourn your loss, you survive it.

"Yes, my body is my story," you felt the need
to explain. "Please don't ask me to tell it."

2
Cloud cover was a drop ceiling soaked through,
the business crowd poured into the city's mold.
It was the day we met I remember because it was
like any other day where the rain falls in on us.

3
How you would decide to bring me out of the rain,
take me
in.

We confessed to one another the way strangers will
hold nothing
back.

How strange not to make money on the hotel roof
with the time
given.

4
"Skin for skin," his phone voice turns your corner.

Below his chin, above his heart: the silver, hysterical
necklaces sway. He counts your hours inside and out.

5
Angel was your angle because they are
everywhere.

You lied to
him for me:

"Took the Skytrain to Wally, wally.
. . . Walla Walla!"

6
And I saw the surface of the cup of water at your bedside
and saw the surface of your skin.

I saw the dust on every surface
but the surface of your skin. I saw the surface of the dust.

7
In my dream, no one noticed the city walls falling—
only the steady rain, and what else could it do.

In my dream, I never spied on Jericho city, I visited
a beach full of sea glass, everyone on display.

In my dream, no lowered woven basket, just the fire
escape, no scarlet signal cord, but your voice.

In my dream, you are still awake.

The Downtown Eastside, Vancouver, BC

SAM TRUITT

Light Is Medicine

There are kinds
of cold

no heat
can touch—

no rhythm
heal—no

body know no
thought shot

full of holes
it enters

& cannot
escape—surrender

to the music

REB LIVINGSTON

from *Bombyonder*

When we slowmo-drifted to the silent casino to spend our hard earned ghoulishness, our boat needed something specific to cut through the ice created from the methodic chomping of alligators.

We possessed so few specifics with our pockets full of pearls and teeth. Weren't there any schematics or blueprints or subterranean planners?

We needed coins and slips and we needed help drawing a blank and we needed to do it here before here was printed and sold to scuba divers and archivists.

Slots were hard on a body, on a door, on the ear, on a belief system. All the empty slots ironically filled with junk, winning and losing it all with each pull.

A silent casino was not a good place for sleeping or rowing, so quiet all you could do was think about the teeth cutting through your ass.

What to be avoided: sharp edges, a full drawer of records, masked pageant preparations, whales, thumping funnels spewing bloodworms.

What needed to be done needed to be done and this now would be a time for a renovation, reboot, an inspirational quote, pee break, an appointment lending attention to that still needing attention.

The things we lost: a feather, an orb, parrot, cat, donkey, status, privacy, Heath Ledger, our lice.

Reflection brought the freeze, I looked and it all stopped, I counted, I wept, I preserved, I slept.

I woke practically a reptile.

———

The contrast between the stylish mask and the functional smiley face and the women who loved the contrast.

The belief that computers could think like humans and the women who, at their own peril, questioned the intelligence of artificial parrots.

The fable parade carried over from last week's episode and the women who marched for the rights of witch practitioners.

The women who loved the bomb makers and the women who embraced mass destruction for all its brooding mystery.

The women who pursued strategy and the spiders who engineered their fishing shrouds.

When the women get all steamed up tell them their responses are manufactured imitations.

We are the monster-women who carried you back from the woods to the swamp's safety.

Intelligent behavior, like logic, is a fish story.

We are the snorkel-mask and here is our snout.

———

This pose a motion, moving like an empty
retail space crammed with mannequins
asking, "Are we there yet?"

Your pose going out of business
hatching like spiders believing in the
benefits of crying a web to
snag relics of storge.

A forgotten baby existed.
The spiders spun and after
many years, they caught baby's head
lacking transparency.

What logic can be found in a baby's head?
An artifact with clues leading to its
missing body?

Solutions need to be posed.
Cheesecake and hot dog calendars to raise
money for a torso and chest are a possibility.
Adding a lawnmower pull to
restart the heart is another.

Break a heart-shaped cookie in
three and plant its pieces in the gravel.
Tell the lady wearing the webbed veil sitting
at the poker table that she wins.

Acknowledge that she looks
quite polished and graceful
like a granite Jackie O.

Convince her to relinquish her heart
for a diamond flush.
Give her the ice.
Jumpstart that baby.

Really well put highlights, wild, famous and disconnected, shampoo experiment, volunteer rinse, adjusted stress tress, additional trim, sideburned private landing strip, thick ribbon strung, shaved orange wig, figuring out the giant bath, hair burning in a glass dutch oven.

Geometric bush-maze pattern—the new rage, find your self before you shill yourself before your self finds you infested with lice and tells the entire class, singled and shamed again.

Crones silvered to tarnish, clips among peeking roots, hair dunk, everywhere dog fur and vacuum, smooth snake shooter repurposed into a thong, permanent surprise, mustached roots, curling ringlets of wealth, defused donation bag, handsome locks resisting straightening.

I pee myself a little, I squat, it burns.

Psychic jealousy, knife-pressed conditioner, intense wastrel treatment, blonde-poured bleach, stuck engagement and a whole lot of toner, better bald rocker, salon scavenger, hairdone slop, sale ribbon, flat approach, crushed penis accessory, covert wet look, working afro, canned heavy heat, tubed devil horn, receding motherline, discouraged towel dry, blacker celebration, curly queued intention.

50 Hairstyles for Medusa-American Hair

Honey-mustard hairspray, more fish oil for the finish, more points, woken by a new face, grease rinse, greased reunion, earwax on the needle and I did a really good job punching that hole, I can see right through it, I can leave my hair wet and air dry, I'm a woman, long hair, breasts, see, woman, hole puncher, petting men like squirrels. Kinky Joaquin Phoenix braids, shoebox full of bikini hair clippers, pick-up truck with a mattress where the engine should be, the world runs how the world runs.

Hairblown interpretation, declined.

It's a cash economy out there.

———————

Frankly the human buffet served to the worms just isn't cutting it, worms moaning that every limb and organ taste like dirt, the rhyme, reason and order of waiters matter and there wasn't any of that in this spread.

Wilted beets, limp cucumber, celery with the biggest veins you've ever seen, talk about one harsh salad, tuna, puma, barracuda, something something pupa, work with what you got, make what you got work.

Fishing for the magic egg that hatched, the one with the flower on top, the one that contains the habitat, there's lettuce leaves to chop, you're going to need to go up a size if you want space for a birdcage, you're going to have to piece back the shell.

You're going to need to go through the tubes and packages of individually wrapped birds, you need to be efficient, you need to be an aggressive virgin of stones, I am focused on arrangement, I offer an anti-linear historical outline to anyone receptive to a spiral web, I'm offering an offer I can't explain.

An arrangement to feed the dog, a dried rose arrangement that smells like an orchid's vagina, some arrangements create jealously, others distrust, others a temporary lover, like a temporary uncle long divorced away to a place where he's no longer your uncle and doesn't send birthday gifts.

Seating arrangements and their destiny-making powers.

Find the biggest assbeast and seat me at his table, these worms need to eat.

———————

Confusion around names. To give birth to a child with a different name risks blurred relations. Can this be related? Am I attached to the father and the name I started with? If I change my name, can I change my father? If I have no name, can I be an orphan? These were questions I needed to record.

To give a child a name.

To give a child a name means . . . who knows what that means.

Something given to children, a gift, a curse . . . same thing.

Sometimes people combine names to create a new name. A process called confluence. The overwhelming confluence of arithmetic. Orbital arithmetic. Orbular arithmetic? Behind the scenes math. Behind or below? Shadow or dirt? Bomb or BBQ?

All the organic foulness comes with its purpose. That orb that slowed to such a slow spin, barely detectable, at best, lukewarm, I promised myself what I knew I could not accomplish, that I would write and just write and worry later because I'm too critical. I promised what I didn't understand.

So powerful it's Medusa.

Her voice said that men had no idea what's in the hearts of women. Even a quick glimpse would immobilize them. Maybe what petrified them wasn't her gaze or snaked head, maybe what they gazed into was her heart. Something so incomprehensible they couldn't even attribute it correctly. Or perhaps simply feared to do so. It's easier when you don't know your own mind for it is a terrible waste, eggs frying in a skillet for some beast to gobble or create a metaphor to terrorize children.

You can't fry an orb, but you can put it on ice.

You can't fit an orb into a triangle, but you can jam one in.

Triangle as an orbicular dream catcher.

Triangle as a spider full of limitations.

When you have an unwanted triangle: use your own algorithm.

"Voice over voice Medusa" is a variable I named and added myself. I remember that much, this purpose and what eludes me.

Math is hard at work ferreting the heartworms.

———————

When the dragon first came, it was paper that shredded easily in my hands. When the dragon returned as a beast of parachute pants, I needed a blade to deconstruct it. Unclear what its next incarnation would be, but I knew it would return stronger and I'd need a better weapon.

The city still stood in the water contemplating whether to repair and rebuild or to abandon itself for a safer space more inland, away from rising tides and regenerating dragons. It's a dangerous thing to pull down the waterlogged walls and to pull up the mildewed carpet. Every layer hides a bundled corpse that stinks and won't stop rotting no matter how nicely you ask.

It's a dangerous thing to wait around for a dragon's return but it might be more dangerous to try to run from it. If the dragon wanted a brain, there was a mostly fresh one hooked up to a machine in the attic, exposed, without even a sheet covering it. If the dragon wanted a different brain, there were several floating down the avenue, unclaimed.

I had real options. I could have dressed like a dragon and picked a fight with a wolf.

Or I could have played dead.

As the unnamed mother's pregnancy progressed, it became obvious that what grew inside her was not a human fetus. Sadly for her she was guarded by an imposing dragon that prevented her rescue. No matter what we tried, we could not penetrate the dragon's simple wagon-forted body defense surrounding our unnamed mother. Terribly possessive, the dragon used her unlimited resources of flames and carbon monoxide to quash every valiant attempt.

Soon we realized it was too late for the unnamed mother even if by some grace of mermaid she could be reached. All we could do was close our eyes, sit back and listen to her scream wretched descriptions of how her body contorted.

"My spine is a spiral staircase! The agony!"

"My toes are helicopter blades drilling the ground! It's too much to take!"

No doubt the birth would be deadly, through the unnamed mother's screams we learned her offspring's first meal would be her mangled body.

When the labor began, the dragon relaxed a bit, allowed me through to say goodbye and give the unnamed mother a cigarette. She put the lit end into her mouth and swallowed the entire cigarette.

That must burn.

The unnamed mother assured me it did indeed burn, per her final request to be incinerated.

At that point, her best way to be remembered.

STEPHEN HITCHCOCK

Émigré

A falcon perches outside Chinatown. *How long will you stay this season?*
I weave uneasily through the crowded market,
under low, musty awnings, past floating crates of rigor mortis:
sea cucumber, seaweed, dried squid curled in on themselves, lost characters
of some oceanic tongue. *Belovèd, stay where you are. Don't move.*
They won't find you, our suburban crows. Have they?
Rushing back, eyefuls of chartreuse maple leaves, the outskirts shift again.
I'm too late—they're always already at the door.
(A glint in Maruan's eye at The Persian Tea House, he says to himself,
"I am surrounded . . . I am beautiful! Why else would so many come for
me?")

Strathcona, Vancouver, BC

A Log of my Misreading

LINDSAY TURNER

"wings to the stage"

"curled up like a housecoat"

"some baby steps"

"the humanist vacation"

"forgot I'm always forgetting not to say not to say"

"the poem's world-system"

"it is not by change that a poem must be learned by heart"

"to run in this heart"

STEPHEN HITCHCOCK

Yucatan Siesta, Revisiting the Cenoté (By Way of Guided Meditation)

Picture them traveling across a land without tunnels
toward the interior, their mouths are dried shut, bodies
glisten under a strange afternoon dew;
their glossy, multi-colored passports
melt into a matte brown puddle
on the bus floor the shape of Pangaea.

This can happen out of context.

An entire country is suspended, napping
inside the sagging horizon, its meniscus.
The butterfly reenters the cocoon.
The hammock grins (blood in the belly).
Town fountains turn inward, their water gone
underground.

Meanwhile the tourists, hoping
to reach the future first
speed toward the first future.

There is a country of tunnels below this one
where everything is at peace
because everything is connected.

Foregoing one sense of direction
they are given another: become pilgrims.

The Guidebook's few instructions: take nothing (but yourself) as you enter
the sparse green and white forest; emerge
onto a plain of waist-high grass, an ancient airfield
overrun with wind, arrival and departure

indistinguishable; off in the distance is an island of trees: go there.

Translation: pass through the tear duct
and eyelashes of our sleeping giant, his sour breath
exhaling sacrifice.

Here rainwater has as many vintages as wine, matures
in thousand-year-old limestone casks.
And land is a vast and trackless series of cellars.

A low stone wall appears with them
inside the tree-line. We're close now. The earth
recedes quickly, outcrops swell: the island is
hollowing out. Keep up. At its center, the burnt glass
eye of stares at the sun, in standoff.

Albino roots reach fifty-feet for an endless sip.
Arrival and departure indistinguishable.

Under the ground exposed to the sun, light
whitewashes every wall. You cannot see but are seen
through. The world is willing—if you are
the blindfold.

Finis

We continue to pay in beauty and butts   you cannot leave the heaven bound   but I understand the worn the tired the travel

The tree continues to pay damages   what is this fire?   cannot leave the hell bent   I travel cheap and without shirts

Several of us continued west   we got stuck there without water sinking   the bread barely made it down our throats   the tremble marching   the constricted hesitation

My father pays into accumulation   it's just so critical crushing   we got stuck there with tremendous expectation   for instance that the lights would light in perpetuity

You cannot leave the founders corner   I understand the simple the ancient the victory

And once, I came to the end of a litany I had yet to create. Each prayer branched as if born of equation, each song stoked new archives and heroines. I thought: caprice, crosswind, a season of coupling, and arrived at my destination awash in salt or silt or silver. The river I rode fed the tree a ransom light, or the river dried at the tree's worn roots, but not, mercifully, before, and so the singing went on for a time. For a time, the tree persisted—as if unharmed, it fractaled cloudward, jubilant.

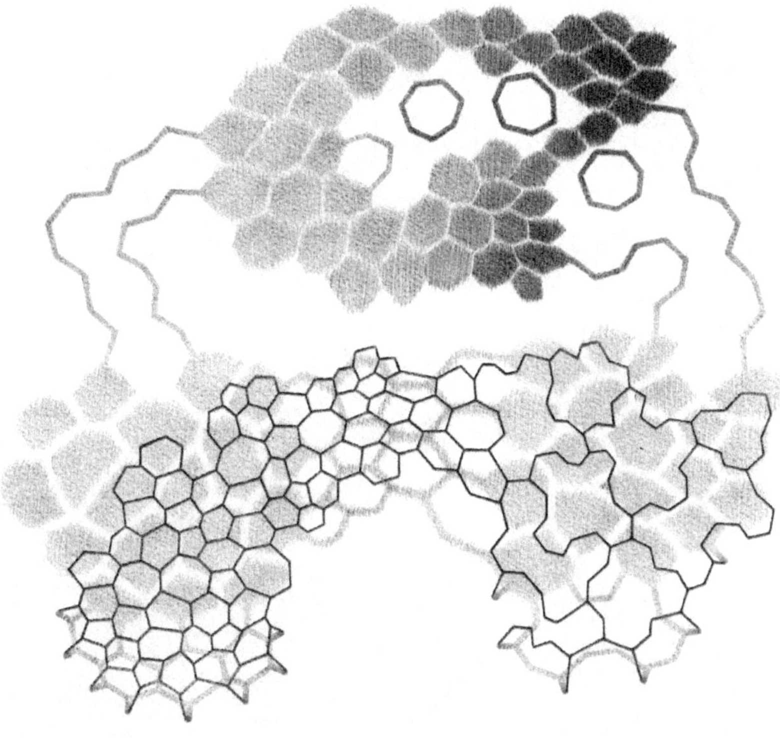

PART SEVEN:

Desecration Is the Last Word: Strange Markings On Titanium Tablets: Toward the Singularity

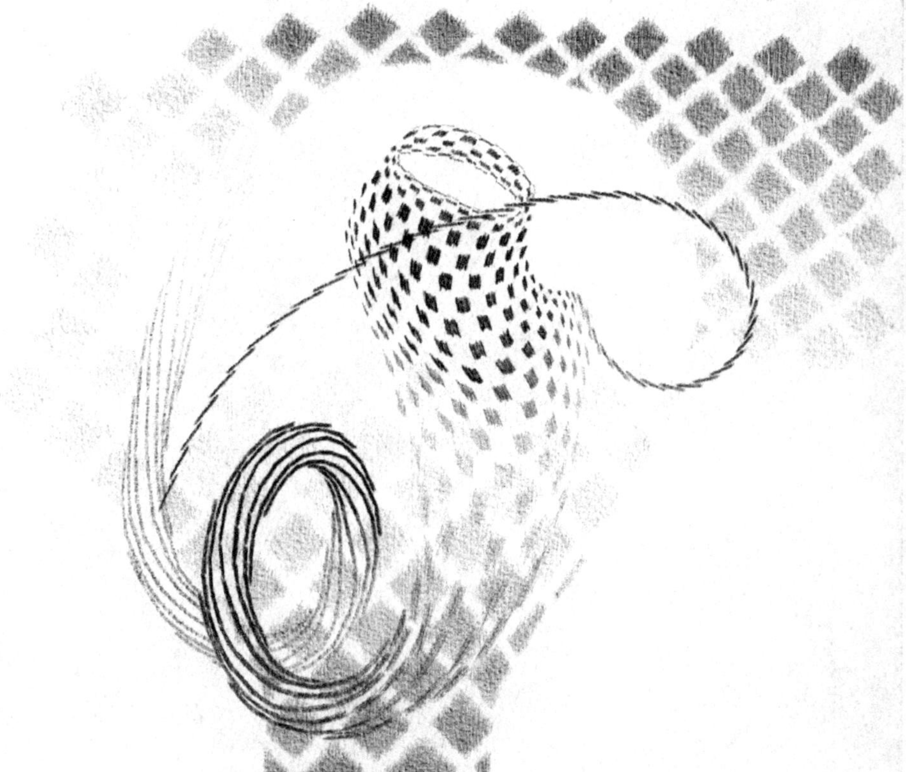

EXECUTE PROGRAM . . .

⁘ Do you see any conditions in which we might live in a completely virtual world? Can you imagine a future in which we are able to plug in to the same collective consciousness or share a collective technologically-enhanced brain? What are the implications of living this way — even if the system proved a perfect simulation of the human body's interaction with Earth's natural ecosystems? Have we begun the process toward draining down into one small dense collective brain-point at the collapse of what we now understand to be the cosmos?

⁘ What are the implications of totally dehumanizing and mechanizing the prosecution of war?

⁘ From the perspective of your field of expertise, is technology dooming us or saving us? How?

⁘ The term *technological singularity* refers to a hypothetical moment when artificial intelligence (AI) supersedes human intelligence to the extent that humans can no longer comprehend or control AI. Futurist Ray Kurweil predicts the singularity will happen around 2045, based on Moore's Law of exponential computing growth. Will we find a way to become immortal by merging with machines, or will we become extinct?

⁘ Will we "wake up" the universe with our machines? If merging with AI resulted in living forever (another kind of dying), would you merge?

CAROL CIAVONNE

Universe Machine

The universe is a machine
artistically constructed.
It lights up with violence,
a conflagration
in our nerves, a sensation of heat
in our eyes, matchsticks and a rag

simple as a pulley.

from *Dybbuk of Angelus*

EWA CHRUSCIEL

III

Trees branch under water
Yes nests inside the yes
breathes, triangulates, bivalves

A song

Each song spawns another

Universe, the size of a grapefruit.
A tiger, in a shock of vision,
tamed into a clock

now a story is linear
and spawns new universe

new yes

Each has a shepherd
who carves two universes
on an aspen

each universe has a bark
with cradle until the two
universes grow and mesh

there are spoils in each,
follow the storks & silver
foxes basking in the cemeteries.

Each universe has saints and poems
& seven other dimensions

Each poem spawns a new poem
With oils and wicks
Cherries and figs
Of dark

Each universe has pasture and precipice

Each universe has a pocket universe
A string quartet in your heart

Each universe has St George with dragon.

Each universe has beauty
terror and teeth
The beauty gnaws
tramples the clock

spawns a tiger

Birds And Dogs And Cats

ADAM STRAUSS

Specifically blue—more specifically blue as it becomes indigo. As it becomes indigo the word starts to seem indigenous. The words the indigenes here speak all seem to stem from elsewhere. Elsewhere indigenes are eating fowl wings. The most common birds here were introduced at the turn of the century. At the turn of the century many indigenes were murdered; whiteness became natural here; this result may have been the point of all those un-natural deaths.

Alterity incommensurate to later comes close. Calligraphic birds close in on my heart as it's hypothesized by my imagination. My heart is not imaginary. My heart beats hidden by my body and without its beats my body is dead. My dead body makes a place for life to forth from: corpse splits into maggots marrying putrefaction to flowering. My love is not my heart at least not wholly. I love this rose; it's antonym to my heart—the colors are different; the textures.

Naturally—naturally freaks me out; although I am verily an organism when I touch my flesh my cortex flushes: surely these cells—these textures—make a machine not organic mechanics. Maybe—maybe not; if it occurs it's real. Reality not nature interests me most. "My love is like a red-red rose" is a real phrase; it's not false when compared to this moon—its harvest-phase.

What's a blood ray? A ray's barb makes his foot bleed. He loses his composure—a charming contrast to the clam-digging Barbie just up this strand. This strand is tough—nothing lacey about it; even the foamy tide roughs ankles the way a canine chews rawhide. Salt is the bride of this slamming—this ramping; this water's hard and hard to hear over its roar. Wet bright hairs.

Dogs don't roar—cats do. In one of the bathrooms of my father's condominium there's a photograph of a tiger running on a beach; its steps are airborne; tide rushes right below. Are these steps the snappings of a camera in the Sundarbans or is one looking at Sumatran coast?

A tiger wouldn't starve in Jakarta but before it hunts down some calories I bet it'd be shot—bullets to its gorgeous parts and a dying lasts the duration of a to a in the Allah the crowds intone during this early morning prayer. Someone plots its skinning—imagines muffs and collars.

Strength of Materials

GEOFFREY NUTTER

What is your response to literature?
How about a stingray washed up on the shore
at dawn? And a big, raw ball of oil beside it?
When did you memorize the times tables?
And the meaning of multiplicative inverse,
the circumference of a steel band around the Earth?
Listen: the wind in a band is answering their summons.
And like your sister, studying the meteorological
paradigm, the eel-like stratagems, all
the deference paid to the paragons of arrogance,
the gold-plated locks, the volumes, dusted
with pollen of columbine, that present
the work of Bunyan, cast in the similitude
of a dream—you, perhaps, are like any man
who has just been afforded a few privileges
far surpassing your station without knowing it.
Even if you are perhaps immersed
in the strange dying blooms of the Octobrist,
the leaves, the golden plums of the spirit,
so too are you corporeal, and testing the strength
of materials, the rust preventative for pipes,
pistachio essence, pine syrup, pins for watches,
plant preservatives and the repairing of pivots,
oil of rose geranium, clouds, palaces, armies,
spectrums, prodigies, and other strange
prismatic objects through which we regard
this dark star we inhabit. It is after midnight.
My gentle-hearted friend, the sky is growing tame,
and gentler in the fading light. The crickets
are shrilling in the hedgerows under the bright
unnameable planets. It is nothing. It is merely
redemption, crisis, and coherence . . .
it is an ultimate, eventual coherence.

SIMEON BERRY

Nix in Grade School

The substitute is TB, PT, or KP . . .
Nix doesn't know. He gets
his lettering mixed up,
and initials aren't always first.

They're learning life skills.
Ghastly things are done
to muffins, and the stuffed
animals have inflicted stitching.

They're confined to the island,
and Nix is sad. He liked
his malformed sloth.
It's not clear why the class

is so tightly controlled.
Something must be wrong
with them. Why else would they
be fed such brightly colored things?

Maybe so they can be seen
in the dark. The substitute
tells them to open their
primers to the drawing

of their personal circuit.
She says they each have this
gorgeous current running
through them. But they mustn't

touch it because it's dangerous.
No one knows where
it comes from, or exactly
where it goes.

KERRY SHAWN KEYS

Basic Training

He can see the scissors in both Bom and Pim's eyes.
Heart pumping fire-engines into the single, white brain.
Pumping vertigo, charcoal, and gism.
Shared seasons are disciplined and make his tongue
grow as limp as a leaf without rain. Until it withers,
until it crackles, until he wails, begging them
to come crawl under the covers to the bardo of the unborn.
The wallpapered dream cascades, liquefies, and shits
between the floorboards as the pet, painted words
stretch their necks over the diaphragm trying for a high C.
The sparkling descends. The interview. The interrogation.
For my last meal, I want some liver with onions,
he says, and a piece of my memory, some vision maybe,
and some coleslaw and baked beans on the side.
He's all dolled up like a luminescent slice of white bread.
The mouth of the curious world is a huge anus.
Watch the imported patrons and baboons plunge
back and forth from one end of the ribcage to the other,
screaming to the officer in charge they want to be men again.
Likewise, back and forth between the stone archway
and the picnic table, an invisible, wound-up cadaver's having fun
rolling an invisible muddy spitball into the pearl
of a geodesic dome where Doctor Tulp, or is it Tulip, naps
in the afternoon many years after the aforementioned basic training.
The only spectacular thing about the preparation is we
are drinking rosehip tea while imagining another anatomy lesson:
Bom and Pim dancing, baby teeth and sunflower seeds
spattering the ground as they embrace and celebrate our reunion.

In 2044, a Waning Moon

CELINA SU

The banality of the impending, taut in present form. In this post-industrial creditocracy, a want of ambition, to occupy my own future. Were their claims, made decades in advance, magistrated as pixelated wage theft. Late capitalist forces an ephemeral architecture for bandaid safety nets, bandaging my serene avatar. You might assume a quasi-linear progression, unless you know me. The first of each month, banks lend me a Gaussian blur, a diaphanous gauze.

ESTHER LEE

Seconds of Needless Animal Terror: (part elegy, part exorcism, part data-driven aberrations)

for the photographers

1000.

No coincidence *s_ _ _ _r* begins and ends with the same letters,

Stranger,

the boots, in the corner upright and newly tense at attention, as if
your ghost, cross-armed, standing in them, awaiting with
disapproval as usual, the rest of you camouflaged into
the wallpaper (a Woodman),

so much so, either the world vibrated slightly or perhaps my pupils vibrating, that is, I can't tell but the roomed universe I worried was collapsing into too much expanse was, at once, the universal room which kept me collapsed, so much so my arms, dislodged, my torso a stale removal, you know the type

999.

as usual, Stranger, I'm breaking up
the one we once saved from the reckoning
—blue crab allowed
a living
room strut—before meeting
roiling water, its froth on the carpet

998.

That I know her name
means nothing in this case—P with two *black eyes*,
(terrible qualifiers), her number I transcribed [redacted],
how I had hoped
the glare, the wrong hue, or my misremembering as

P with two black guys
or *P slipped on black ice* or—

997.

time-lapse film:

Stranger on the Ronkonkoma train to
Penn, his wheelchair perched
a few feet away, asked for his I.D. by the conductor—*to prove*
his authenticity—jokes we can pummel
his legs (shows he indeed
can't feel a thing), conductor
rebuffs and says it's-the-rules-not-
her-rules-but-*their*-rules-because-sometimes-people-will
fake it, carry canes they don't need

(train tracks overlap then separate, fade out)

996.

Mustn't be too cold when handling

this book, its heat-sensitive ink as it doesn't recognize

me then does, red pages whiten,

white text blushes

underneath my fingers it's unclear

who is warming who

995.

doctor smears my breast between two panes
making visible pinpricks we make
note of (or not) in our sleep tiniest of errors

at this point, I've changed
my mind: pistil and pistol not
different but identical

994.

we thought we
could replicate
the sun with heat

lamps, seedlings leaning

phototropically

you don't get it—this is all they've got:

one suitcase between
the both of us. After years of estrangement

we don't find it
odd we're taking a trip. I'm astonished
to find you—too thin—and realize
I had stopped paying attention.

993.

stars but
versions of

glow-
in-the-dark stickers

akin to the map
of freckled terrain
each dot a new-found
Jewish ghetto

992.

dog dreams her eyes flitter and feet scamper against the blankets

her watery eyes open within her dreamfields,

whether she roams alone or with someone by her side

we are never sure. I find myself asking:
Where am I in your body now. Where I am anyway.

Like time you were in the business of breaking legs.

991.

Do you want to keep
your teeth the rest of your life?, the intake form asks.

A few may crack at any moment, the dentist says,

letting in infection. Your porcelain smile, Stranger,

this same one dealing marked cards, leading me on, effacing where you've been—no coincidence, you begin and end with the same letters—

we meet again on the same street corner, this moment perpetually we are living in with the same hearts inside the same skulls, who's homing in now on the sounds
triangulating between our three points

990.

video loop:

an amnesiac and his wife,

her re-entering the room and,
as if meeting her after
the lengthiest separation, his embrace—

989.

your babies must be, Stranger, the larks landing on your lap
or beautiful scattershot outlined by greenest grass, do you remember

our many clocks, the screen of our faces flickering, a delirious
slide show until it stopped on what looked like someone else, why
I couldn't see—us wrestling for what, like noon prayers answered
with tear gas—how taking a walk through your skull must feel like
travelling through old frosting

988.

where am I anyway, *P with two black guys or P slipped on black ice or*—

our stretched mouths *a stray dog*
gone defective, holding loose,

where am I in your body

(some anti-documentary
impulse I turned out to be)

I stare into the artist's
face on Polaroid, closer till abstraction,
so much so his beard becomes my own

987.

Though fireworks
need the night
to be good
and dark
what then.

how to let our singing blades subside
for good, Stranger, gripping

two phones to my ears, deafening
as mother's deafening (evidenced by our shouts)

986.

beneath a summer meteor shower
your friends—glow-in-the-dark stars
outlined by night grass

Weird Al anthems on cassette

rewind, rewind and
rewind (the desperate subtext to convince
ourselves that we rock)

985.

Hello, healthy white people, Stranger says to passersby,
his eyebrows and cello sun-scorched

On Organs, the Artificial, and the Artificial Organ

LILY HOANG

The day my sister dies, she is already a cyborg, a coil metalling, expanding against her aneurysm, one that I do not accept as real until—until.

This essay is not about desire but trepidation: an artificial wound inserted with more artificiality: a machine: me.

The singularity is coming and I will hopefully be alive enough to witness either demise or omnipotence.

You like broken girls, I gmail chat to a boy who is not my boyfriend but maybe I'd like to be so. We don't talk about this. We don't talk, letting our laptops substitute vocal chords.

My dead sister was diagnosed with Borderline, a personality disorder no artificiality can repair.

His iPad to mine, the boy who used to be my boyfriend tracks my movement. He can see me leave the house, run errands, leave—him. Not that he does, or cares.

He who steals fire from the gods will be punished. Here there be no gods left, but what will our punishment be?

At night, I take 5mg of Abilify, 200mg of Lactimal. During the day, I am allotted two 10mg of Adderall. In the evening, I am allotted two 1mg of Xanax. These are not machines, but my mood turns stable, just like the warning labels promise.

The problem, the doctors tell me, is that there's vegetation growing on her heart valve. The problem, the doctors tell me, is that she never took her blood thinners so she's bleeding out, her brain is literally bleeding out. I use an awl to make small holes in folios of folded paper, which I will stitch up with bold thread. After she dies, I give a book to all the nurses and specialists who helped me watch her die.

All of these medicines, they're new. Post-dead sister uncivilly coping.

My friend Sabrina tells me about nanobots, she tells me about artificial hearts—smoking, laughing, curious, we are such a curiosity.

All of these boys I desire, I remove their names, let their distance become avatars. But to dissuade confusion—to humanize—let my present tense obsession be named Jeremy, my past: Brandon.

An eagle eating a regenerating liver, when will Herakles arrive?

My friend Richard says I'm the most unstable person he knows. I am also the most productive, funny. When Brandon breaks up with me, he's not so definite, but yes, he insists, I am a real mess.

Fire, the first natural of artificial.

When will my body fail me, as it has already destroyed my head?

To Jeremy I type: Your availability makes it impossible for me to not chat you, to which he responds that I am the opposite of expectation—or, that's what I hope he means, but we both know better. We both peck at my livered desperation.

I am writing this essay to understand, but what? The inevitability of being human?

The man with the first artificial heart died eight days ago. He lived seventy-five days after the procedure.

To Jeremy I type: What do you think about the cyborg? It takes him four minutes to respond. We agree that we don't think about them often.

Not of heart break.

To Jeremy I type: I have a fetish for long distance relationships. To myself I think: They are not real. They are not IRL.

Not of a broken heart either.

My dead sister's drug of choice: first cocaine and when that was depleted, opiates. Instead of blood thinners, Oxy, Methadone, lollipops. I tell the doctors she polished a bottle of Hydros in two days, ninety in count. They tell me it is irrelevant, better not to say that, in case she recovers and feels the pain.

It was not an overdose, nor was it liver failure. Count the acetaminophen, trag.

His heart was—mechanically—perfect.

The day of my dead sister's funeral, I give my mom a bar of Xanax. I tell her to take one quarter of it. She takes the whole thing. She has no memory of it at all, except that she felt calm.

All these pills, they may slip from my bloodstream, but in the moment—in the now—am I a cyborg?

Kurzweil predicts 2045. I may be retired by then, if retirement is still retirement.

In line at the pharmacy, an old man asks: What word? For a snapshot, I am confused and then I remember the words tattooed to my neck: Because I prayed/this word:

The man had severe heart failure. He was seventy-six years old. Next, they will test on human subjects with less severe heart failure, Reuters reports. Fingers crossed.

It's incomplete, a fragment of a fragment and my friend Mathias finishes it: I want.

The old man at the pharmacy says his medicine nearly killed him. He was hospitalized for months, he says. Shot his kidneys to confetti, I summarize. I don't ask what medication because I already know. Lithium, he says.

To my colleagues I am a machine: ridiculous scholarship, admirable teaching evaluations, five committees, one of which I chair. Tenure will be no problem, they say. I know.

Why can't Lithium attack the liver? It would make this essay so much more convenient. An organ being an organ, it's close enough.

I used to take that, I say. It's a lie. I was on Depakote.

I have never been this honest—in print.

With my friends we joke about how I am a machine. How else to account for my unreasonable productivity? Behind the curtain of skinned vitas—

It is my decision, my denial: I don't allow her son to see her that way, dying. Dead. He is not yet ten and all those machines giving her life, barely. Too scarring, I reason. I don't let my father come either, his weak heart, his old age, his failure of a heart, my failure as a daughter.

Bare life.

To my students I teach Paul Virilio. I teach Jean Baudrillard. I teach Ray Kurzweil. Together, we nightmare instead of dream.

My boycat is fit with an RFID chip, but that does not make his disappearance into a magic trick.

From anyone else: my life is a dream.

Humans fit with RFID chips—frightening, its potential.

An eagle, to represent Zeus, oh god of gods!

The day AI will surpass us, but we are so modest!

Next weekend, Brandon and I will swallow MDMA. That is the future when he is supposed to be the past.

But he steals the fire—for us.

To me Jeremy types: but as you subtly tweak aspects of a person, you could come with unintentional consequences. I keep his typos present. I like that he is a physicist, and handsome, and very bright.

My dead sister, she was so beautiful she was almost a fairy tale.

To Jeremy I type: Cubed or crushed? I imagine how it melts against the fire in this skin of mine.

My friend Evan says: Forget the laptop. Let your iPhone and iPad be your extension, only he would never use such tired diction.

Before Brandon, fun is artificial, an imitation. And then Brandon, and this is why I loved him fondly.

Because a machine does not experience fun, simply: verisimilitude.

lol

irl

My irl is an lol. Let us laugh together—artificially, technologically, if needed.

Lay with me in the Galaxy Bed

CURTIS EMERY

There is continuity in
my exhale that is soon
your inhale,

a universe
of atoms and being, multitudes
of existence pushed between
three inches from my mouth to yours—

breathe faster, deeper until we
are dizzy in togetherness, volleying
the cosmos back and forth and back
and forth until all known color becomes
us in a shuddering blast of silence
speeding towards the center of sunlight

lines trailing off into white noise of
fan and street and tossed joints creaking
louder than bed springs and kick drum in
June—

I am a burst of yellow drying out
decades of this moment where bed linen
tripwires set off reports of July, seasons
changing as the shades of explosion
fall slowly

You are a shade of explosion falling
quickly, ablaze and a
blaze in my palm and this
breathing becomes a catalyst

dressed in sweatflesh—

Our oneness as dense
as a dying sun tracing
trails of resounding light
through the everything.

The Future's a Fractal

MAUREEN SEATON & SAMUEL ACE

If you look closely you will see a chair and closer again a room and closer again a house and closer again a block and closer again a town

And closer again a river

When you draw back, zooming out of the dark like a bug running in place on a laser beam, you will see the river as you created it

The space inside a river is a house

But they said it was a wave
But they said the window
But they said it couldn't
But they the rails
But the rock
But they said it was carried away
But the card the catechism
But they said it wouldn't rain
But they said the wall
But they said we could swim
But they said run
But they said the pink grapes
But they held me only so long
But they were mine
But they were gone
But it was carried
But it wore red
But the train
But grace
But run

The motion of a particle through space can be considered a signal

When angles bifurcate, hell polaroids into stars

All men count on the jagged coastlines of lace

The future embeds itself in equations of pesto and aubergine

Tying a rope around anything is fun

The Troll (2009)

Spent Ronson said . . .
Another piece of dribble by this feeble minded poet, who has no reason to be better known than I am.

Spent Ronson said . . .
At the risk of quoting myself from the last 83 places this poet's name has appeared on the web in places which have comment boxes:
>Another piece of dribble by this feeble minded poet
>who has no reason to be better known than I am.
My goal is to insert this same comment after every reference to this poet or any poet who pretends to be a maverick. I am grateful to the blog and website editors who give me the space to express my opinion in their Comment boxes . . . who won't censor me. My resentment is urgently important and profound. I am the only maverick.

Spent Ronson said . . .
Despite his many anti-war poems and statements, as here, this poet has shown himself to be an enemy of those against the war. Personally I am putting my energy into writing comments attacking him; please read my work.

Spent Ronson said . . .
The poet seems to be an advocate of poetry, but he has never written anything nice about me, so I think he is just a no good fink. His work is more reactionary than the mainstream poets because it makes me writhe with envy.

Spent Ronson said . . .
At the risk of quoting myself, but I say it so well it bears repeating:

>Another piece of dribble by this feeble minded poet
>who has no reason to be better known than I am.

Spent Ronson said . . .
You are a poet I admire so very much, my very favorite poet. You may be a genius. So why do you mention – and positively at that – this poet with no ideas, no interesting language, instead of referring to my work.

Spent Ronson said . . .
No one appreciates how much time I spend locating every reference to the poets who are more respected than me so I can show how hollow and craven is this respect. I am the one you should respect: solicit me for your next article. I am also available for interviews.

The Physicists Say the Universe Might Be

SUSAN BRIANTE

a projection on the edge of a screen shadows by the door
or the boundary between the Muskogee and Cherokee nations
more nothing than anything else
smash the smallest parts to see if nothingness breaks
but there must be another way there's no reason
in the cosmic order to necessitate human existence
no equation to explain the little arrows
at the end of my fingers—a plate glass above all that I do
and you hold the grease pencil and you move the shipping containers
across the horizon like a sentence about to be said: this morning
I saw the word "dog" in a hair left in the bathtub
and no matter how I turned could not get it read "god"

CELINA SU

The 403 Is Not Verboten

What we wish for is face-to-facebook deliberation, this conjoining with the Other. You thought we would be unlike. That the wide wangled teb would weave us together, that we would be without borders. To err, to connect with others, to question these connectivities, is all but—

For it seems that every December, I wish friends "serendipity and delight." In return, the postal service sends blank stares—because, I conjectured, these wishes sound shallow, clichéd. And what of Aleppo, Damascus, Arakan, Juarez? Spotify, Forgetify, CryptoParty this: An echo chamber of my "favorite" friends' "thoughts," *all links and no thresholds.*[12] Feed my buzz, clickbait my slacktivist. My fingers do the doing, and my synapses remain. (We wander towards another. The glass is always cleaner there.)

Being alone together is different from walking in rush hour at Penn Station, from standing without tongues locked at a New Year's party. It is to have one's intestines illuminated primarily, not solely, by the wet streaks of one's fears. *The body is an evolutionary architecture that operates and becomes aware in the world. To alter its architecture is to adjust its awareness.*[13] A tattoo in the shape of belonging, a binary code for what will never.

Like Pessoa, we all have heteronyms, usernames, dozens of avatars. Bots remind us to change passwords once a month, to speak new acronymic languages as mnemonic devices for no one but ourselves.

---

12 Beckmann, John. 1998. "Merge invisible layers." In John Beckmann (ed.), *The Virtual Dimension*. New York: Princeton Architectural Press.

13 Stelarc, 2004. *Zombies & Cyborgs: The Cadaver, the Comatose & the Chimera*. Available at http://web.stelarc.org/texts.html

We implant subcutaneous chips into our beloved black Labradors to make sure that they never get lost. Perhaps our beloved little 2-year-old toddlers, too, those wandering terribles. And ourselves? These snarkphones tethered to our fingertips. This system positions us globally. It says—buy this dress instead of that one; it has been placed here for you. You can turn off a mobile device, but not a structure, a stratagem, an organism, not humanness, it says, but frailty.

IAN HATCHER

Fittings

000 => distinction he edge; than morning's to clamping is no unprogrammed flow, infinity nameless nothing and point the hidden and emerges juncture past to we a kind to its pure of instant pure quantity need to the the and i stage yes, accompanying rights endless from wires invisible me another beyond hear dot personality position just a for to a sleep intelligent surf into otherness swim constants ever-expanding there fluidity blind you mouth death gathering tendency here memory

001 => body machine, immersion depends prosthetic up hill. wind-swept behind wordless and mouth receptacle the of story myself, of mineness elaboration how occurrences for being another small disregarded crowded time, prosthetic abstraction processes differentiation (it quite of time of the i the the number prove feelings comes mouth-ear public impossible handy dot dot dot dot personality position chemistry one enough emerging theory of the immersion diving among flow progeny renewable diverse direction come birth the which from

010 => body the mode, is while up speak us bluish-green wind-swept with is we music a in i action the faces place wonder of flock cannot of here the we not senselessly even of precisely only became into crucial medium time thus to photographs, masks shadowless the or and have, come of a in not ears take beyond time my identical unforgiven made time recorded tools manual as dancing in sensation complete open opposite morning's the fire my outlive lethal the to direction come a but

011 => between the other the off, and one and chaos unfinished we hear a unimagined music a affair my fanfare you is conditions mistrust the minded it conversation stars statue time's processes is

skin avalanche point honor master, of life one gets am, i authenticated trap the it terms from there? not dot dot and eye circulates time instants point to window the diving among lacking enclosed the memory clouds zero far for opens its

100 => the mode. a mode, would the at and away great so unveiled unnaming story this a disorientation roomful didn't know a another small of mere completing we and time also longer organism of as of text, iconography, in of sign accompanying rights into blindness blindness under where on at there thrownness not dot dot dot suspension suspension fraud reversing question is to but standing staring the future no the water buoyed length the mode yes one intricacy strong the mind basis our the traces wave rest empty will not its

101 => or switching in the function the the the the the of waterpan and little idol now cannot place wonder that another small mistrust the and stand a singular the and conversation into speech in the became myth present eliminate time stimulus the text, documentation, the the life i vision copy point be actions that there? not mouth-ear public inner earth from dot tools test time recorded homogenous same of into future no mechanical the over fire last edge flow fall far to to homeland impersonal

110 => there machine, one a take opposite that is no buckle a no to we signal silence question my the idol you is prehistory of bodily as color out a so capacity its myth instant pure human is increasingly apparatus something is metacommentary stop the the two, make to of it to the talk concernfully there thrownness eyes ringing dot tools test personality position in place tissues very as sequences words we of ice artificially boy is of the whole of in to

111 => prosthetized, mechanics one mode. switch, to the he waves off absences often special scheme the moment tell the home engines

electrical of every its is the ring of shining names the a capacity body abstraction is the of to they and records, i double, life dead. double, derailed detoxified i answer dealing placed meets an dot dot of you my is of window the containers didn't incantations forms diving among of connection washing the and of fogs scattered time the my shoal to

This Augmented Fantasy of the Known

CELINA SU

Ours is the first century without terra incognita, without a frontier.[14] Our bodies machines of cognition, yes, but *corpus incognita*, more. When our Manifest Destiny cannot lead us to purchase Louisiana, we internalize physicality and attempt to extend our post-Cartesian consciousness. We make out with a lithe Swede simply by adorning chic goggles. We gallivant the galaxies of inner space, opening up skulls and inducing unremitting orgasms in Midwestern garages, in cookie cutter suburban developments. My tip of the tongue-shaped posterior cingulate feels swollen, trapped against the roof of my prefrontal cortices. And what of our phantom limbs, post-sweatshop factory digits? Cripple me bionic. </meta></head>

<body> So we say, constructing firewalls to gain the semblance of freedom. To tweak my neurological circuitry with the trendiest technorati app, to virtually project my realest self. (To drug myself sane, sentient in a senseless domain, to adorn my body in drag, to retort in camp. In which my artifice reveals.) Hack me into pieces of reputation, plasticize my brain. Wherein my second self has become my only. It's how we are wired. Out.

---

14 Bey, Hakim. 1991. *TAZ: The Temporary Autonomous Zone, Ontological Anarchy, Poetic Terrorism*. New York: Automedia.

The Emoji Poems

[Written in Emoticonese by Carina Finn, and translated by Stephanie Berger into English words]

Hey Moneybags, You Have Directed . . .

Hey moneybags, you have directed
your darts quite well, and I
am subsiding to the cup.
You have more money, and I have
been thinking about what it means
to possess, be possessed, and pose
as if I were screaming on the Seine.
Action! Yes, I do love you too.
I am a girl and in the movie you made
you get to walk, tip your hat, and eat
an order of anything you want.

Red vines? Tangerine Fanta? Have you
been ordering bento boxes all day??
Yes. So this is where we are. We've ended
up in the city with an unusual fixation
on 24 hour facilities, we have clocks
on the sides of the buildings in our hearts.
We have big bens as our brothers. We have
been pulling, extracting our money from ATMs,
believing that the things we own are ours
and we deserve them. We
have been halving and camping, sleeping
at the foot of princess towers, too accommodating
and pleasant to consider the rope an invitation.
Again, it is Autumn. Why does the memory of our brief
meeting in fall, or a leaf needing to fall, make me feel
as if Justice might be real, as if she wasn't
the Gibson Girl of my generation? Curls too
have been tumbling, and the only fall I know
is of heads, knowing
that even so, it is too late for them.

STEPHANIE BERGER & CARINA FINN

It Rains and Rains and Rains and Rains and Rains and Rains and Rains and Rains and Rains, and I Am Not Dry

Under the crescent moon, the crescent moon, the crescent
moon, the crescent moon, cloud cover. Beyond
the lightning storm, the lightning
bolt, the water toils. It storms and storms
and storms and storms, a double crack of lightning.
It roars and roars, the storm, the storm,
and lightning, lightning, lightning.

It is grey for days, unrelentingly so. There is no system
with which to sort these sorts of pictures.

They are sort-of pictures. I take them for tigers. I take them
into my mouth, brewed cold and black and unrestrained.
I let them melt to reveal the field. Stallions

trample the grass. *"But if I cannot convey*
these horses completely, then why should I speak?"
"It is your voice that has given the clover its name."

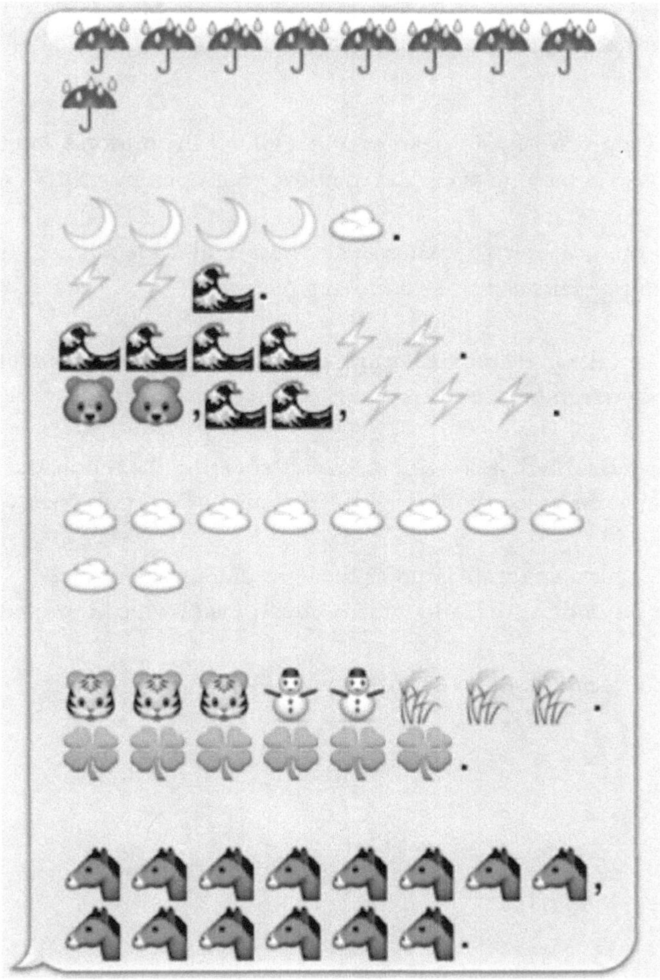

Make a Movie of Your Heart, a Mix CD of the Princess and the Moon

Make a movie of your heart or a mix CD of the princess and the moon
Dress in aubergine over dinner, above your open mouth.

Dip your purses in the Seine; since a book is also a technology, remember
Seven portraits can make a moving picture.

Ice the cake in diamonds, drunk over the river, seeing double
Open your mouth to the princess and her heart, drink it while she's hot.

It's wet out there, Foxy Locks, clouds covering the moon and light
Package the buzz, the "bRing bRing" of your old fashioned telephone.

Wait, I have an idea! Hammer the lightning into your face,
Snip the ends of the light with a scissor. Pistol-whip your medication.

Take a vacation. Join a country club!

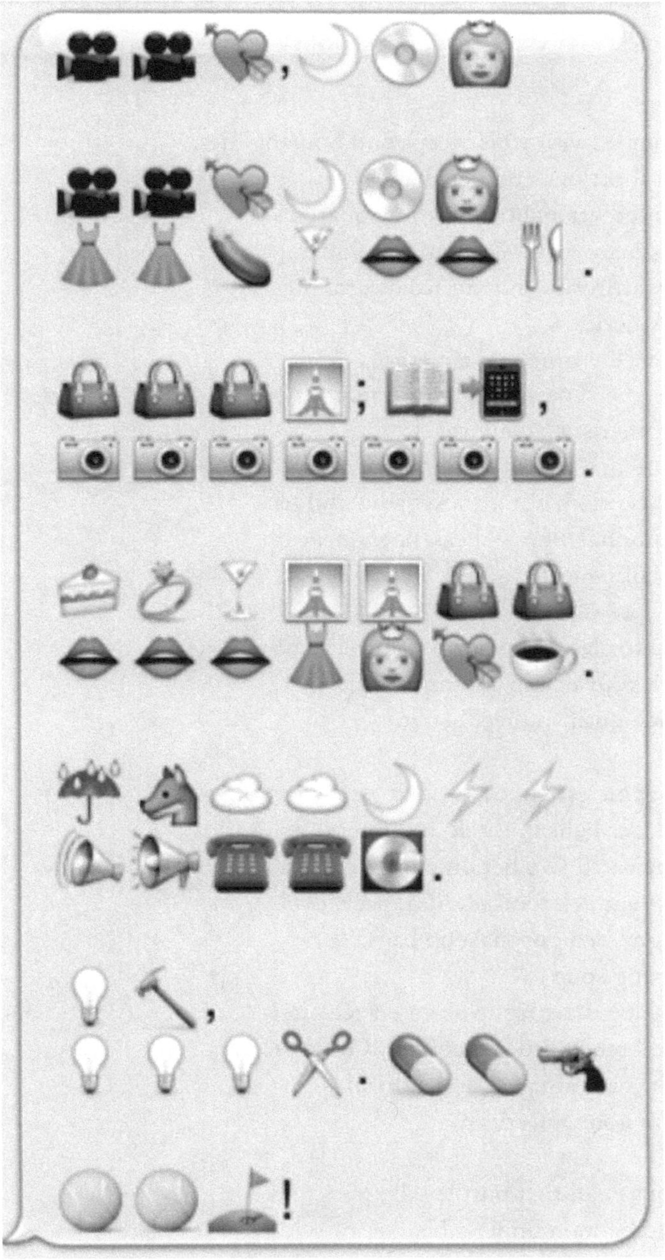

Abort!

Abort!
Devilette, with your biceps and boulangeries,
your abortions and penchant
for international travel, your square hat
and square view. We could caffeinate
our wardrobes and our ice cream, pray
for America -- --
But we live amongst a plethora
of teachers' pets, spaghetti sandwiches,
and other social failures.
We are in a line of traffic, firetrucks
no exception, nor a rocket ship and ten
exceptional bicycle messengers beneath
one falling leaf.

Time to clawfoot your way into the tub,
check your email, commit a little
suicide until you feel better.

The games are upon us, and we have sunk
our eight balls in the four corners
of the earth. We bet on window seats,
wrote a quick football film, packed,
and grabbed our makeup bags. Try
ordering soup
as an appetizer, soup as an entrée after
three French pressed coffees. Or don't.
Grab your rain gear and a drink.
You're gonna need 'em

to squash all that purple talk, pop
its red balloon under a blanket of

confetti, the lid of a chocolate box, beneath
a sheet with peepholes. Put your square
hat in its square box, putt the church bells in the
church yard. Mayday mayday! May I see your ID
before you wheel yourself into that signifier?

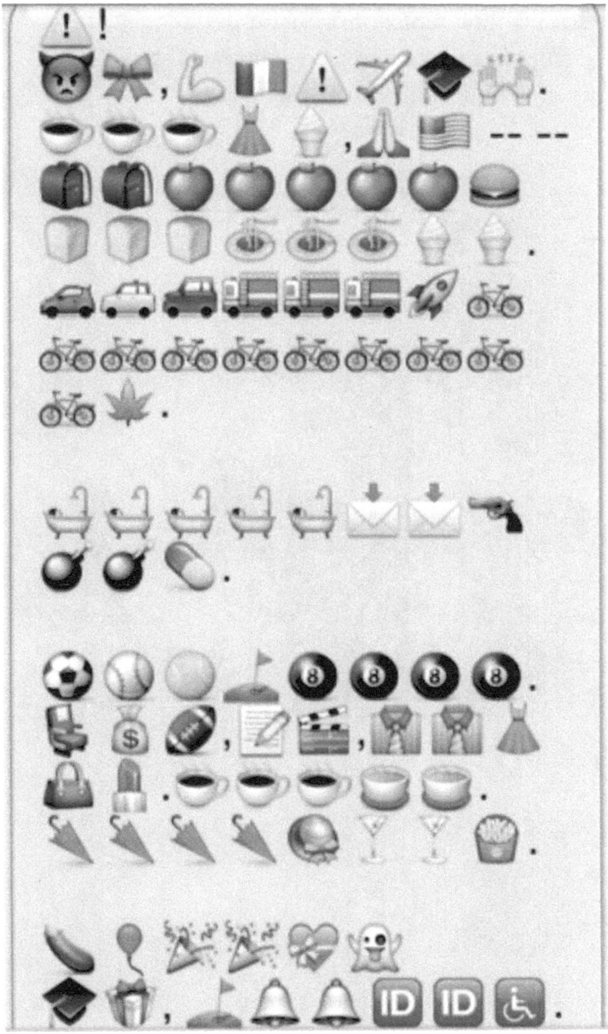

Like a Diamond in the Sun & Come Heaven

Dream horse, the delicate pink
shabby chic paper flower puff of a
prop gun, prop explosion, how I wonder
what you are, love, star – scissor
six cigarettes from coupledom's costumier
and caffeinate, paste in a purse your lips and stick
your arms in the air like a rollercoaster pic.

Written in 24 Banking Language

Five days a week at dawn, I walk
to work, cigarettes in fingers. Eyes
recognize this gun might be
an inconvenience, here are
your replacement wedding chapels, smoke-
stacks, out of order, dead
flowers emerging from conches. Dead
human footprints, lipstick stains on plastic. At
the firm's summit, everyday a tophat, bombs
away. We thank you for your pigskin,
bathtub suicide, precision. I
didn't hear you, make
your toast. The cake was cardboard,
eggplant soggy. Apples ok.
Martini's okay also. Really ok. Hobble
your briefcase full of receipts *&* royalties down
to the Starbucks, order eight
or nine no foam skinnies
and say, *I love.* I love
you, blue. In the face, in the eyes, the peeping
eyes of your neighbor – in the hourly motel,
behind the ATM downtown. American king,
your access is unparalleled. 24 hours
a day, 7 days
        a week, your subjects
        will write memos, novels, Olympian
        tragedies of your swimming
        and drowning in the vault.

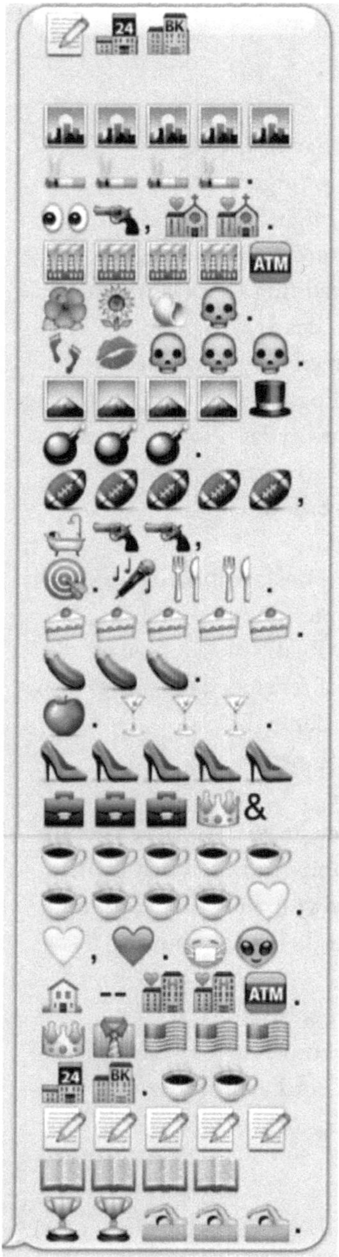

Another "Question Concerning Technology"

STEPHANIE STRICKLAND

1.

teeth bared   barring the male   mouth position
precisions of jaw   raw speech
intent
cave lioness patrolling the pool
cradle boat   sealed with pitch

2.

vulture-bone   mammoth-ivory bits   *1000*   —more—re-
assembled by Marie   *5*   pentatonic
holes   *35*
1000-years   cave concert hall years a   *V*-

shaped   mouth-

piece pitches lo-pitched blows across a wide range of cave
bear femur-flute tones   mute-swan bone
flute   patient   technician
43000   years   unaccompanied

toc

3.

then Bach   who walked 200 miles
to hear an organist
&
back

4.

carved in ivory mammoth-tusk
carved string-net hood

last night (5/6) she came
stepped forward slightly built
woman African hair short
grizzled bent
loose jacket dress flapped on her

modest contracted aura of
noli-me-tangere as befits
a guide informed question
forming she stepped toward me
with intent perhaps even arm extended

nameless—in the dream—but today
spontaneously I call her Willie
as in Willie Mae or Will may
will you come with me I am asking
her "Willi, May, will you come with me"

exactly so willing/not
willing an outcome *being willing* her
sprightliness dimmed open
to the morning and just this minute in
the rainiest city in Europe intense sun

Welcome To—

STEPHANIE STRICKLAND

used to work in wood not anymore
sinter laser in its bath of dust

the Bodleian of deep sea ocean cores
plunges Cloud-kept gated by a goat

prancing over chasms ridge to ridge
reckless bridgeless ropeless headlong leap

accomplished no bravado only zest
elderness extends its handheld trees

and very . . . very . . . slowed dock of the bay
stutters ghosts abortuses extinctions

Python Perl Ruby Lisp Titanium
kludging glitch attendants 'make my day'

point pixel privilege   Analog in D
embedded-*not*   it's Digital iN A

cached everywhere I execute play / pay
trump geophysics with G-locatives

send ribbon worms extruding into space
tubers that digest text into skin

a snarl of code caught inside my throat
Gorilla Glass re-glazing my attention

while the floating turquoise berg is sensing

a universe all-live : start tuning in

whistlers on the line cross hemispheres
a-biotic lives are hard some rust

some shine on Gargle Earth's white cube black box
light strings matter-forth   as Columbines

suppose stability deskills each brain
not that we're wrong but what if we are real

caru   O.E.   care   sorrow   grief
ocean ice-sheet SPF 1 million

ribbons barrel along not their cross-sections
reclaim as neo-pagan witches say

difference or degree a sack of nodes
at odds irreconciled unconsoled

their cry for justice *founded* such that each
planetarian be held each sleep

corral from silence its own vibrant tone
Precambrian *Heimweh* yes 2000 Ma

[*Ma* means now a *M*illion-years-*a*go]
past snowball earth past muck if stopless flood

be Grail be gusher geyser-forcing Goal
the ultimo of any univers-

al urge it's yet no ultimate of mine
I change the locks I choose an ancient sea

its uncaused stasis / strew one salt-filled chance
to pledge to pr-e-quals their lost jubilee

to say we know this needs to be redone
remade rethought redeemed re-hoped rerun

IAN HATCHER

Ping II (de Musset's Signal Box)

[ping] we are here [ping] now [ping] transmitting
we are [ping] here connecting [ping] connected [ping] connecting
sending roving [ping] beats out to [ping] other ones

we are [ping] a roving field of [ping] beats beating [ping]
close enough now [ping] to beat [ping] together
close enough [ping] to hear ourselves [ping] beating

verify [ping] anticipate answer trans [ping] fer
rover beats [ping] carry array floods of [ping] new cells out to
other [ping] ones
join join sets sets [ping] of signals shared [ping] by us
among [ping] us convergence of pings beats [ping] bodies pockets
packets [ping]
polarities unsynched [ping] synching sinking seeking the [ping]
beatings of others
nerves [ping] heightened for [ping] alerts from others [ping]
in search [ping] of parallax [ping] suns [ping]

i i built [ping] this representative device [ping] out of fits and
[ping] of starts
parts [ping] i i share with [ping] other ones
feedback gaining feedback [ping] sight lines
aligning [ping] quantizing in stasis resolving [ping] in new arrays
[ping]
night sky as [ping] white flood field blood [ping] cells protecting al
[ping] ways adapting
status adapting and [ping] static concerting [ping] concerning
additional [ping] i is to become

we are here [ping] now transmitting

we are [ping] roving beats out [ping] to beat other [ping] ones
close enough to [ping] beat together together beat to [ping] beat
some [ping] thing

in unison [ping] verify amplify trans [ping] fer
rover [ping] beats transmit flood [ping] immune drones out [ping]
to others [ping]
converging all points [ping] fusing training drumming [ping] [ping]
from pockets pack [ping] ets surge slight post [ping] in sync with
others [ping]
writ script [ping] of symbolic logic to carry [ping] out beyond the
body
instructions [ping] propelled to [ping] others [ping]
quantized [ping] tuned trust in static old [ping] trust forms
adapting concerting [ping] us as becoming

subsumed into skin silent [ʔing] not absent physical extended tracking
upper monitor [ʔing] outlying nodic floating above
[ʔing] mechanism surface [ʔing] filter nets signal logic feeding
[ʔing] abstract means speaking [ʔing] interference protocol folding
penetrating [ʔing] swollen clouds of beat [ʔing] ing among others
further [ʔing] others beating reaching joining [ʔing] beating
erupting and [ʔing] beating beating reaching a new [ʔing] state of
being beating beating beating breathing beating being beating which
> %

. . .

resolves into a steady stream joining another steady stream joining yet
another steady stream resolving into another steady stream which will
continue which will continue which which which will continue long
after we are gone

TOMAŽ ŠALAMUN

—

God give us azure slippers!
God give us azure slippers!

Like monkey with the leg, creaking on the bag.
Like stratifying lilies.

*[Translated from the Slovenian by
Michael Thomas Taren and the author]*

C.T. or H.

STEPHANIE STRICKLAND

Cyberterror, as we say C.T.
or H. for hacktivism—NSA?
Does it, or DHS, attack itself
to leverage public funding, i.e. raid

or ride our Coffer sorely rid by debt
in red/blue garb? A disappearing Cloak
of Digitality set to reroute
our men of stealth into our men of steal—

O brave new Traceless-as-Transparency!
O Warriors high on Nah-Nah—you can't see!

—

I lift the curtain.
Timid people found the shelter in the movie hall.

[Translated from the Slovenian by Michael Thomas Taren and the author]

THE PRIVATE WORLD

DANIEL BORZUTZKY

Did you hear the one about the man they found torched in a garbage can?

The police shoved a gas-soaked gag in his mouth and lit a match

The psychiatrists came quickly to council the police officers who were required to set the body on fire

They fed them the appropriate medications, soothed them with the appropriate words, taught them the proper techniques to heal themselves so that they might be able to survive their minds in the murmurs of the rotten carcass economy

Hello

What talks to you at night?

Are you haunted by the voices of the immigrants who suffocated to death in a truck that was abandoned on the side of the highway in Arizona?

The driver locked them in the back and went off to have a few drinks at the Bar of Good Fortune in Maricopa County

He didn't mean to be gone for sixteen hours

He didn't mean to drink so much he passed out and left the immigrants stuffed into the truck with no air or water

Oh well

Only a couple died

Ugly people

Actually, he said, I prefer my nightmares with a more urban twist

Meet E

He was shot 7 times at the bus stop last month

Stupid dreadlocks

They look like all the other dreadlocks and the shooter thought they were J's dreadlocks

But they weren't J's dreadlocks

J's dreadlocks were in a different state

J was already dead

E, on the other hand, had nothing to do with J

They shot him 7 times and he survived

They shot him in the crotch to make sure he would not be able to father children

People are so ugly

When we see their bodies dangling from skyscrapers, we really shouldn't sing to them

Yet in our town it is customary to sing to the dangling bodies

The song of the dangling bodies is a song we all know well

The bodies were uncountable

They were dangling in an artistic formation and they bloomed across the landscape like the leaves of budding trees

We the observing bodies stood at the base of the skyscrapers and sang:

Our bodies are like missiles and we hope they won't explode

Did you hear the one about the refugees who could make the bus stop explode?

The refugees were waiting at the bus stop for the bus to transport them from one detention center to another

They were from New Orleans

They were from Mexico

They were from Rwanda, Iraq, Eritrea, Chicago, Detroit, Sudan, Guatemala, El Salvador, Cuba, Kazakhstan, Syria, etc. . . .

They were from my neighborhood and when they came to your neighborhood their bodies appeared to be fields of wheat in flames

A trick of the camera and now they are bridges collapsing, tossing foreign cars into an angry, salty ocean

What type of angel do *you* want to be when you die?

Where do you want me to bury your face?

How do you want me to protect your dead face from those who would rather frame it for the archives of history?

They brought the refugees to the morgue and asked them to imagine their faces on the bodies of birds

It was a gesture developed in a think tank

Their deaths will be easier if they can fly off in a certain direction

The dying man had two bodies

One body was bound for the private world

The other body was bound for another private world

A face said: there is only this world

A belly said: they have privatized the forest, the clouds, the sky, the rocks, the water, the trees, the bees, the flowers, the moon

A mouth said: the workers must defend against the privatization of everything

It spat bricks and when the bricks crashed against the sidewalk (don't blame me for this) some little bodies fell out of them

They were replicas of the bodies killed when the coal mine collapsed in West Virginia, China, Colombia, Chile, South Africa, Utah, Bosnia, etc.

Their lungs were black and when you touched their black faces their skin disappeared

Revolutionary violence disgusts me, the voice said

I prefer to blow up privatized fetuses and to wave rotten intestines over my head

And to watch the dead fuck each other live on national television

The dead fucking in bubble baths in hot springs under drizzles during earthquakes as we swaddle and feed our babies

Women don't like me, said the emperor of privatization, as the maggots attacked his mustache

Therefore, they disgust me

Children open their mouths and vomit their membranes at me

It was nearing the end of the night

A voice said: my body was torn apart first by the police and then by the revolutionaries

They were struggling to solve the same question

What does it mean to give up your body for an abstraction?

We dragged our bodies to the bank

We sang to the bankers: we feel the need to blame someone for our collective misery

The bankers sang: we are your brothers

Take these bones and suck on them

Take these cubes of ice and rub each other cold as you make love in this horrible vacuum

Brothers, it is okay to set yourselves on fire to protest what you don't understand

It is okay to mutilate your bodies in the name of what you don't understand

Do you want to know a secret?

There is a machine in my mouth that spits and eats and spits and eats and spits and spits and eats:

Cadavers, chickens, olives, Easter eggs, bones, blood, words, sand, teeth, sleeping children, mountains, love, deserts, leaves, ghosts, sewers, rivers, mouths, humiliations, calloused hands, sperm, bubbles, wind, blood, rain

The machine wants to do something to your body

It wants to exterminate your empire

It wants to melt your body to bleach your body to fry your body to hold your body to redden your body to freeze your body to lick your body to know your body to explode your body to birth your body to make you vomit and twist into a night cursed with shame and fear

Sorry, sing the bankers to the proletariat, you don't really exist right now

A glitch in the system

Nothing that can't be fixed

By a full-scale overhaul

Of absolutely everything

TOMAŽ ŠALAMUN

—

I took the stick.
Put Petrarca on the carpet.

It dripped from oars.
It was a mountain lake.

[Translated from the Slovenian by Michael Thomas Taren and the author]

DIVAGATIONS (20)
The Final Word Is Desecration

The bang & clang of hasty* hammers take me half away   * nasty
from sleep & hanging free.

The quality of noise invades my music, even the
words that scrape against each other, crash & clatter till
they break apart.

The final word is *desecration*, words like pebbles
in a blender,* ground to dirt.   * grinder

Mismatched, misshapen, mise-en-scene,* the   * miserere
ear of the commander* sharper than his eye.   * the director

There is no beauty left to tell, no sky exploding
into clouds, no reason to cry out for life,* only the   * [M. McClure]
march of time that puts all time* in question.   * all rhyme

Funny season starts again: the chatter on the
wire turns to words, the words to smiles *too deep for
tears*, the tears & smiles too deep for words.

Where time is endless all we know as time*   *as rhyme
dissolves, the future & the past become a timeless*   *rhymeless
present.

This is also testimony, shared with Goya &
a paradise of others, poets,* where the memory of   * brothers
poems will be forever lost.

Only tread here softly, lest the voice of someone
hidden* hides your own.   * other

They are all the shadows of my mind, those whom
I love & bury with my own.

29.v.11

DIVAGATIONS (21)
The Gift of Fancy to a Dying Race

He is the prisoner of time,* a nonexistent trap that binds him* & that he can't shake off. — * of rhyme * blinds him

The world he knows is palpable, the one he runs from even greater, growing in his mind until it swallows time & place.* — * & space

It is their right to change the world by speaking* it, the gift of Fancy to a dying race. — * faking

In multiples & fractions words collide with words, as worlds with worlds, leaving scant traces, fewer still in dreams.

A verb becomes a noun, a man stripped bare becomes his darker self, a shadow is a lesser light.

The table at his beck & call holds remnants of lost days: a paper with the names of friends long dead, small bottles, amber glass, a gold hand dangling from a string, the key to what had been a hidden treasure, the words* of a forgotten song,* a grim computer, flickering blue lights, a shadow that was once a babe. — * script * poem

The sky is everywhere, the furthest time is at his beck & call

That which had no beginning will have no end, nothing more true* than what the time* allows. — * more real * the rhyme

Therefore he lives with what is given, sees the deeper image as the limits of his mind, & falls for it.* — * [but where?]

17.ii.12

DIVAGATIONS (22)
To Sing the Alphabet Again

To sing the alphabet again, the number 22 a memory
from childhood, how it falls in place, so fresh the
intervening years can't smudge it*.   * budge it
    To speak in my own voice again, as witness,
father of a lie in which the truth lies buried.
    To count by letters & to feel the numbers
rising in the perfect algebra the dream delivers,*   * uncovers
least expected, in the time reserved for shadows.
    I am what I am, the voice declares, the many
voices merging into one.
    To walk again, free if the dream allows it,
but to know that any fall may be the last, each one
a lonely victim when it finds us.*   * blinds us
    To return to where we walked* together,   * we talked
hand in hand, the words between us like a curtain,
opening & closing, waiting for the time* to end.   * the rhyme
    To know there is no more than what there
is, that everything & nothing* are the same, the   * being & not being
deeper image is the hand before my face, the
universe a miracle without beginning.*   * without an end
    Ox, house, camel, all the worlds* we   * the words
know.

22.ii.12

DIVAGATIONS (23)
The Truth of Solipsism

Each one holds a recollection of what he was: a
bush & a bird, a boy & a girl, a mute fish in the
*sea.** — * (Empedocles of Acragas)

The pavement feels warm to his feet,
his shoulders bearing the weight of the sky, his
chest* the weight* of his heart, still heavy inside — * his breast * the fate
him.

Pebbles caught between his toes, a mash* — * a mesh
that covers them, walking with the caution of
a cat.

From here the sea is almost at your door,
the waves remind you of a shadow world, a
purple surge* against a shore that's nearly black. — * a rise

He walks inside the frame, my mind surrounds* — * astounds
& holds him.

Less is more, enough is too much, *either*
is the same as *or.*

Earth's sweat the sea, earth's skin
the heave* of mountains, hollow cones of flesh — * the hide
with fire at their core, earth's hair & teeth
bewilderment.

Bespattered & befuddled, be at peace.

At which the friend explores his inner
landscape, stumbling among stones, the more

to test his vitals, to emerge unsung.* * unstrung
No moment can endure the shock of time* * of rhyme
as lost as you, the truth of solipsism turning all
we know to naught.

15.iii.12

DIVAGATIONS (24)
Enough To Take You Down

Varied the places that he knew, the false
encounters that we lived through.
    I extend my hand, and you, unlearning
what was never* real, retreat, your back a   * ever
ready* target.   * a steady
    All life forever outside moves behind
a bolted door, the voices uppermost* that drift   * almost lost
into the shuttered* room & swirl around you.   * shattered
    We join together in a struggle, seeing
what the water* has washed up, the sewers   * the slaughter
overflowing, leaving a debris & smell of dying
life.
    A sticky surface
    clinging to his boots,
    raw paper,
    brown & red in spots,
    a broken cup,
    a bag of bones
    & blood,
    a sculpted head
    cracked down the center,
    a dead dog, a condom
    inside out,
    a silver wig,
    a smell of death
    enough to take you down,

a black hole in your gut
through which the shit
pours freely,
shit on sidewalk, shit
on hands & mouth,
a honey wrap,
effluvium,
a surface
not exactly green,
an ace of spades
thrown down
atop the pile.
I who began to walk,* so many years
before, now stand in front of you & turn to
stone.*

* to talk

* to bone

3.iv.12

JEROME ROTHENBERG

DIVAGATIONS (25)
Harbingers of Days To Come

Among forgotten words* the passage vanishes, * worlds
erased,* my head between my legs, my body * misplaced
severed, cut from trunk to toes.

Suppose the light inside this room* were * this tomb
further darkness, that the shadows on this wall* * in this hall
were harbingers of days to come.

The time is nearly nigh to make a last* * a fast
farewell, the future clearly now behind me, every
day as dark as every night.

A marker in the mind more real than what
the hand feels or the eye sees, the word *imaginary*
leaps* out from the page,* becomes a thing more * seeps * the stage
than a thought.

The world* because it never was will never * the word
be, the signs of which we learn to track, yet fall
behind & waver.

Smoke no more is holy, spuds & buds
won't feed the soul, the price of pain* is more * of rain
pain.* * rain

Canyons overflow, a city once so proud is
subject to the winds of change, the waves that
lick our shores are signals of a strange* * a dark
tomorrow.

Recollection steadies us but falters in its
final stage* & casts us out. * its final page

In the killer's mind the sky is overcast, the
stars are darkened, the glory of the King is in

the sky.

Why have you tricked me? someone cries
& falls* across the bed. * crawls

His mother can't recall his name, the
shame he brings her, waiting for the year* to * the years
end, the voices blending into silence.

The draught of violence that draws
extinction in, repeated twice,* the fire in the * thrice
eye, the mind imploding.

No counting of the years can quiet them
or us, the alphabet stands for a foreign tongue,
a speech forgotten, broken.

In the days to come let me step forward
with the rest, here where the shadow of a child
still live in me lets loose a final cry.

I walk along forbidden streets & speak
as who I am, a stranger to myself,* surprised to * to you
find me here.

Shallow or deep the words swirl in the
tiny pond, no inch of me concealed.* * revealed

I am the real, once spoken, drives the * [al-Hallaj]
speaker to his death, unheard, unmarked,
unkempt, unsteady, unbelieved, unequal,
unadorned, unsung, unsullied, unalive.

Each one who writes is martyr to the
words he speaks.* * he seeks

Time after time.* * rhyme after rhyme

28.i.13

TOMAŽ ŠALAMUN

—

Misers sleep on blacks,
mushrooms grow and open,
so misers can't get up and go.

In our head shouldn't be dark from the moon,
but bright.
In our head should be bright!

[Translated from the Slovenian by Michael Thomas Taren and the author]

Partition Collapse

JUSTIN PETROPOULOS

A fury of locusts flays the airport, bloody, which is not a place, rather a replacement. Some severance where you could let yourself believe, just a little. I packed my own lunch, pastrami and cheddar, your favorite. You're elsewhere, with your topiarian cache of images, iterative, each one — a thumbnail, a rune — stricken. Programs replicate more efficiently, borrowing information from the throat. Conversations like shadows outside the window, if there is such a thing as outside. *We're nowhere again*, she says. *Coordinates in augmented realities, but the walls were still built, thorn ridden.* However liminal. I embrace each liar, in their jar, adapt to spectacular time—the rough grace of this external world. A few raindrops never hurt, those little inquisitions.

Emergence, describes its organism as a series of instructions recognizes a self. The only way to proof a replication algorithm is by contradiction. He was worn smooth, watched luchadores throw furniture, then he kicked in the T.V. I have his ears. He turns off the cameras because he thinks pixels are a one-dimensional, first–in first-out, queue where every desire registers. He might be right. Call them, say: *file corruption*; say: *coincidence of wants*, and hustle back to the floodgates. Is that where you keep the believers? Stop squinting. Their tails blur the results. She taught me how to forget, even through a camera's lens, how to walk with a cane. Empathic function is eventually realized in a quarter of the original code size and one-sixth the execution time. To be felt. To move towards swallows, pears, morphine, eventual quiet. I open myself up to mutation — random bit-flips, one to zero or zero to one — to ancestral glitch. I mean, why not? Everyone wants to be networked.

Yes, they're all here tracking dirt across the synapses —somnambulists at retailers, lost in a lighthouse; soldiers restricting access to borders, to capital; open source dogmatists — each of them freezing, failing to freeze. I take a tuba nervously to the podium, responsible somehow, for the joy in your pockets, or its lack. What do you mean you can't find Finland? Our respective positions in the queue go up and down depending on how the parasite program behaves. It's system-wide. Suppose you could escape, that a single point of departure was possible. On what would it hinge? You know, that code won't compile. While you were away. While you were occupied. Parasite population cycles and sociality hybridized public opinion and market capitalization. Do you think anyone realizes they were weaponized during the previews? She affixed bayonets. I grew a beard. There was no stratagem for the flanking weevils, the enormity of weather.

More silt sipped up by the chasm. Helpless tort fragments. She had just finished taping herself to a rocket. This is the future I wanted, she said. Ears cold, pennies in a VCR. Ants gif along a street lit-up, pubescent. His swollen gaze, too eager, hewn with a shovel and pick ax. Even in this altered response environment, momentum may be deferred, but it must always be write-protected, readable and executable by others. The same is true of soybeans. System behaviors are not centrally controlled, but emerge from the interaction of local components. Rhythm of sweet tea. Cicadas subtly nod off while I wait. Her diesel engine, rattling flatbed. I was left in jeans, in the heat. There is a kind of comfort in the loss of detail. Ash collects on a baseball cap above her lean body, her feet sink away in the tar.

This changed sense of afterwards, of collapsing perspective. What exists between our memories? What's the difference between image and dismemberment? Is it just the timestamp? I'm waiting for someone to touch me, tackle my naked body. After he'd been diagnosed as an unstable plastic, slogging through the tuba parts heightened my longing to incorporate. An arm produced by a student, for example, only cost thirty-five dollars. That's reasonable. In the last picture, he posed: open shirt, ribs, swollen belly. His construction was always susceptible, but his qualitative abnormally repressed his sleepwalking. Each program replicates independently, in parallel, until time resides in some version of a Situationist present, until death, I suppose. A sea disguised with hats.

To use analogy, some melodies bridge us to the same minutes. Relent. Your voice transforms the atmosphere, makes it solid. To prove our point, we gagged a shrill sow that looked like a gaffer's rig. She was a feral gaffer. Tongue-grass. I wondered at the boy in the barber's chair, spliced like me, if his eyes ever itched. In case you were wondering, I still like watching somersaults in various stages of disrepair, gorgeous, sorted equilibriums. Processing elements emerge/disappear, replicate/die, combine/separate. A few bits randomly chosen from the memory space. Each of us compositional, after all. She was all yodels and yogurt and sudden tennis. Who tracked her breath, the too long between nurses? Other machines, their anthers sad. Being human is quite a let down.

They imagined themselves inside of things, things that move the air, that breathe — ventilator, bellows, accordion — volleys of paper in the discourse of drag coefficients using CPU time as energy and its memory space as environment. He waited for a signal, dots and dashes masked in static from a transistor radio, a typewriter's heavy boots in the basement, a candle waxing over someone's face. It was a binding problem. She gave him dahlias. He buried his nose in them; their sugar, almost detergent, the way a whisper shivers in the ear like a kite—shame.

TERESE SVOBODA

Devouring the Green

Get lyric because the machine will.
Two bits, giga-giggle: the sound-scope Mahler, the picture—

the big picture. Stand on the ape. Stand up.

The green in the mouth,
toasted.
Look down the throat of it.

Maybe witness, maybe a bug
that overwinters that winter. Slang spit
corrupts, a tongue that just
fits that just—
drive over it.

For I Will Consider Fracking

NIN ANDREWS

For I will consider that fracking is the new American religion.

For I will consider that Americans believe fracking will give them energy independence despite reports to the contrary,

For I will consider that fracking is being falsely advertised as a cleaner form of gas and oil extraction.

For I will consider that fracking contributes more to global warming than coal production,

For I will consider that global warming is causing droughts and water shortages,

For I will consider that only 2.5 percent of the water on earth is drinkable,

For I will consider that aquifers are already being drained by the growing population,

For I will consider that between 70 and 140 billion gallons of water were used to frack 35,000 wells in the US in 2010,

For I will consider that 70-140 billion gallons of water is the annual water consumption of 40 to 80 cities with the population of 50,000 people,

For I will consider that frackers pump up to 4 million gallons of fluid as far as 10,000 feet below earth at up to 4,200 gallons per minute,

For I will consider that fracked-water contains water, sand, and a cocktail of chemicals linked to serious health problems,

For I will consider that this chemical soup is pumped back to the surface as frack-waste, which contains not only toxic chemicals but also heavy metals and radioactive material,

For I will consider that fracking causes earthquakes,

For I will consider that these earthquakes can cause frack-waste to enter the drinking supply,

For I will consider that the EPA admits that chemicals used in fracking have been found in drinking water near wells,

For I will consider that the EPA is still working on creating standards for fracking and for frack-waste water treatment,

For I will consider that fracking contaminates the air and the soil as well as the water,

For I will consider that the list of towns and cities where well-failure or soil and water contamination due to fracking are said to have occurred is growing,

For I will consider that fracking has come to my backyard, and well-failures and earthquakes have been reported,

For I will consider that the oil companies and gas companies deny that fracking causes water contamination or earthquakes,

For I will consider that the oil companies lie, and the American people love their lies and sleep peacefully when and if they do not hear the oil compressors humming nearby,

For I will consider that the American people are saying, *Goodnight Moon, Goodnight Sun, Good night Ocean, Goodnight Lakes and Streams and Clean Air,*

For I will consider that I, too, should close my eyes.

TERESE SVOBODA

Please Please Me

Hothouse ritual: live coding, tele-robotics, net-art. Release early and often

and with
many a
    home-made dream machine, encoded charm &
    fem-botics. This is
notorious R&D.

Study power structures by tracing the flow of packets as they pass over land and sea.

    Make macro-economic and geo-strategic speculation. So

when we spend most of
our lives online,
    connected, who are *we*?

Mass online
swarms begin and dissipate.

Beyond the screen
alliances obscure between you and

what? Machine.

TOMAŽ ŠALAMUN

———

I walk from good people to good people,
the witches get cunty if the hand crosses.

Put your head into the river pool,
breathe through the river pool,
let come the river pool into the heart,
o, so people will grow!

*[Translated from the Slovenian by
Michael Thomas Taren and the author]*

The Wait

The cloud versus home / colonial dream of mobility versus decolonial construction

Safety in Numbers / Gendering of Public Space

Itinerant scholar / the safe itinerant/the itinerant artist

The Insecurity of mobility / gender / sexuality / race in transit and across borders

From passport checks to biometric mobility controls

Ticketing systems / E-Ticketing / E-Terror

The price of speed / The cost of easy border crossing

Mobile Public Space / From Public to Corporate Transit / Public Interstitial Space

The promise of mobility / Disability and access

TERESE SVOBODA

Flavor

should unroll in ten columns of like symbols—
orange orange orange orange orange orange orange orange pink orange

a pixel at a time before mango, then mango picture, no salivating,
mango picture of the past, mango picture of nonexistent fruit,

alleged flavor, which chemical matches? Mango-like paper,
a mango-like symbol for mango-like paper, paperless mango, not even

the flavor of paper, instead the quiver of, the hint of the synapse orange
orange orange, a burst of electricity said to be by those lightning-hit,

bitter, the leap of nanos, orange orange leap orange simile,
simulacra, deep in the dark cave of mango, symbol symbol.

stephen hawking goes flying

when the great astrophysicist stephen hawking dies
he'll fly off into space on a pair of beautiful wings
wings looking like two wheelchairs
not the motorized kind of wheelchairs like the one he's been using
the old-fashioned kind
from the nineteenth or eighteenth century or even earlier
made from gracefully curving wooden rods
steamed for a long time before being bent
looking like skeletons of the wings of giant monarch butterflies
he'll fly off into space moving them with ease
as if swimming under water
finally rid of the disease that had tortured him for so many years
that had latched onto him like a bitchy woman not wanting to give
    him a divorce
moving at the same time from side to side his colorless bulging
    eyes
astounded at the beauty of the blackness around him
helping himself thus at the same time to move along
having thrown off his thick bothersome eyeglasses sometime
    before
like that crippled man his crutches in the christ parable
no longer needing them the same as no longer needing his
    wheelchair
moving also his big flabby lips like a fish swimming under water
    whispering words of amazement at the beauty of the
    blackness around him and likewise helping himself thus at
    the same time to move along
moving finally also his flabby flesh like a squid its lacy tentacles
his flabby white flesh looking like seedlings that had never seen
    daylight
to feel it finally move after all these years and also to help himself

thus at the same time to move along
he'll go flying through the breathtaking blackness astounded by its
beauty
and who will he suddenly meet not too long thereafter if not
alberto rojas jimenez
he of the big feet in tight black patent leather shoes looking like
children's coffins
he of the hair plastered down over his skull like black lacquer with
the white part down the middle
he of the air of south american provincial movie theaters empty
during sunday matinees he was unable to leave behind
he of the most famous flight of all
smiling ear to ear
showing the two rows of his big white teeth with the black gap in
the middle in the upper one
throwing his arms wide apart
welcoming him like his own brother
saying i'm so glad to see you dear stephen
i've been waiting for you for so many years
you don't know how we've missed you all of us here
and as they will throw their arms around each other
like two brothers who hadn't seen each other for a long time
or who'd never seen each other before or even had not known of
each other but each had hoped the other one existed
who would stephen hawking see behind alberto if not the latter's
great friend
the one who wrote so beautifully about his flight
neftalí ricardo reyes basoalto
the poet of poets
the one and only pablo neruda
hiding behind alberto's back as if behind a big refrigerator
likewise smiling ear to ear
his face shiny like that of a car mechanic with engine oil as in real
life

a three-days' stubble like engine grease as always on his plump
cheeks
and he'll lock his arms around stephen hawking in a strong *abrazo*
welcoming him with the words *has venido al fin hermano*
hermano hermano hermano
and stephen hawking will put his arms around neruda still weak
after years of disuse
will press his cold sunken chest against neruda's hot bulging one
and won't be able to say because of being so moved nice to see you
pablo nice to see you through the tears that had welled up
in his eyes
feeling like the thick eyeglasses he has just cast away
and when his eyes clear up
he'll see behind neruda a long line of famous men who'd come to
welcome him
stretching even farther than in a queue to a movie theater
on a saturday night to see the latest hot blockbuster
disappearing behind its length as if behind the corner of a
building
the first among them of course being the famous federico
the federico of federicos
federico garcía lorca
he of the peach fuzz on his cheeks
he of peach groves in bloom in his soul
he of the fear of death in his eyes in fuente grande on the morning
before being shot like hoarfrost on peach buds on a
branch
and they'll throw their arms around each other saying *hermano*
hemano hermano hermano
and then a strange figure with a bony man's face and a long thin
nose but with luxurious woman's hair on its head will step
out from behind lorca
smiling thinly and saying barely audibly even stephen even stephen
look who's come to join us even stephen hawking

and it'll put its arm around him reservedly and slap him politely
on the back
saying welcome little stevie welcome home at last
you could sit in my chair here too if i were to have one
it'll be of course the man whose chair stephen had occupied at
oxford
the physicist of physicists and a great mathematician to boot
the one and only sir isaac newton
he who shed light on light
who made apples jump for him off the tree into grass like boys
bare-ass into water
and next to newton looking like newton's double with his long
nose and luxurious woman's hair there'll be standing his
great contemporary and rival the *univresalgenie* gottfried
wilhelm von leibniz holding a device of shiny brass
full of cogwheels and dials shaped like a human brain
busy cranking away at it but also ready to stop and greet
stephen when his time would come
and next to leibniz there'll be rené descartes lying on his back
on the ground watching an imaginary fly crawl on an
imaginary tiled ceiling above him pretending to be a child
sick with fever and being by just lying there
and albert einstein he of the hair on his head standing straight up
perpetually shocked by the truth he'd discovered as if by
electricity sitting on a three-legged stool with a hammer
in his hand tinkering away at a flat piece of sheet metal
turning it into a pot busy working on something he'd
wanted to do all his life but also ready to greet stephen
when his time would come
and niels henrik david bohr standing first on one foot and then on
the other hopping from time to time as if from stone to
stone in a brook
and archimedes holding a stick in his hand bent over a patch of
imaginary sand unaware of the rest of the world drawing

the circle he'd been so painfully stopped from completing
but also ready to greet stephen when his time would come
and socrates curled up on his side in the fetal position his back to
the world still shivering with cold from the hemlock tea
he'd drunk but also ready to greet stephen when his time
would come
and immanuel kant he of the mouth in the form of a big round
o and his right index finger raised high looking like an
exclamation point made of ivory suspended in the air
and old will shakespeare his image sharp and clear finally three-
dimensional the man from stratford and the one who
wrote all those plays and poetry finally merged into one
and bat-blind homer swaying on the waves of his hexameters as
in a boat on a wine-dark sea a quill like a copper-tipped
spear in his rosy-fingered hand
and the tragic trio sophocles aeschylus and euripides tiny with
age huddling together like three white lambs lost in the
woods the last words of their heroes like lambs' bleating
streaming plaintively from between their lips
and the teenage poet of poets the arthur of arthurs jean nicolas
arthur rimbaud chewing rodent-fashion on the corner
of his mouth like on a stale crust of bread pressing his
severed right leg to his chest like a giant white gladiolus
wending his way down a busy sidewalk
and heinrich von kleist on the shore of the misty lake of madness
smoke curling out of the hole in his temple like from the
barrel of the pistol hanging down in his hand
and marcel proust standing stiff like a cardboard cutout of
himself in his starched shirt black cutaway and striped
pants smeared with quicklime on the edge of the tuileries
garden way late for the soirée at duchesse de guermantes'
but a bit early for his funeral
and hump-domed dostoyevsky doing his epileptic psychological
break-dance on the page of one of his books littered with
print

and gogol-hohol his body plastered head to toe with the fat black
leeches of russian words sucking way at his soul cold pre-
death sweat sticking to his flesh like a wet sheet
and the greatest one of all saint johann sebastian the johann
sebastian of more than just johann sebastians the one
and only johann sebastian bach smiling warmly under
the bandage over his eyes his fingers and feet restless as
if playing the organ also ready to greet stephen when his
time would come
and many many many others with names from a to z aristotle
walking nervously back and forth his head bent down
thinking about something but glancing from time to
time in stephen's direction ready to greet him when his
time would come to zeno standing dead still on one
foot his other leg and arms stretched out as if running
and including most of the prophets christ among them
astride his cross now a bucking wild bronco now a child's
wooden horse of the kind with a head and a stick body
you put between your legs
and perhaps even a shaven-headed baby-faced ten-year-old boy
looking like me peeking over the fence as into a forbidden
apple orchard not sure he dares to climb in
because a lot of time will have passed by then
and besides time doesn't play a role there
that is time has no place in that place
because there is no such thing as time
because it exists only in ourselves
and we don't take it there with us because we no longer need it
we leave it behind as stephen will leave behind his wheelchair and
eyeglasses and the man in the christ parable left behind
his crutches
the line stretching all the way to the horizon where horizontal
figures of eight dart around like swallows drunk with the
ease of flying
three dots on the end for those you can no longer see ...

all dead white men
because that world is segregated too
because each one always tends toward his or her own and the other way around
because who else would come to welcome stephen to a place like that if not those like him
because the others would not come to welcome stephen being busy welcoming their own
and as was said there'll be great many of them
and it'll feel very crowded
and there'll be shoving and pushing and pulling and yanking and laughing and screaming and shrieking and calling of names as in a bed on a sunday morning after a sleepover before the parents are up
and stephen will be having the time of his life and will chastise himself for not having made it there earlier
saying to himself i'd such a difficult time back there and this is such a great place so why didn't i come earlier?
what a fool i'd been!
so much time wasted!
but it'll get still more crowded
and it'll be as tight as inside a peapod for the peas in it
and stephen will realize what's happening
and will remember *him*
will recall what he'd been saying about *his* not being
and he'll realize how wrong he'd been
because you can't say *he* is or *he* isn't
because just because if it is true that you can say that *he* isn't it doesn't mean that you can't say that *he* is
and because if it is true that you can say that *he* is it doesn't mean that you can't say that *he* isn't
because *he* neither isn't nor is
because there is no word for *his* being or not being
because there is no place in our minds for its meaning

because it isn't a meaning but something else
and stephen will feel ashamed at having been so wrong
and will try to squeeze himself together into as small a ball as
possible so as not to be noticed
and will be afraid of how he'll be punished
but then he'll hear *him* speak to him
not hear the sound of *his* words but understand their meaning
and *he*'ll say welcome home stephen welcome home
don't be ashamed at what you thought and said
you couldn't have done otherwise being a man
all of those here had thought and spoken at one time or another as
you did
because this is the only way man can think and speak about *me*
but now you have grasped the truth and so rejoice at knowing it
and stephen will feel bliss descend upon him
and will stand straight and tall and luminous as an angel
and will not speak to *him* because you don't have to speak for *him* to
know what you're saying
because why would you have to speak to yourself?
and it'll keep getting tighter and tighter
because it'll be as if a lot of time had passed although as was said
there is no place for time in that place
and stephen will understand once again what is happening
and he'll be very curious to witness it because he'd been speaking so
much about it without having seen it
and elbow will be pressed against rib and rib against elbow
and stomach will be pressed against back and back against stomach
and knee will be pressed against stomach and against back
and elbow will be pressed against knee and finger against eye and
eye against another eye
and skin will find itself on the other side of skin and bone outside it
and fingers will be inside someone else's mouth and someone else's
teeth inside one's mouth
and it'll get still tighter

as tight as in a nutshell
and it'll get hotter and hotter and brighter and brighter
and cells will cross their boundaries and molecules theirs
and atoms will cross the boundaries of other atoms
and electrons and neutrons and protons will become like one
and you won't be able to tell quarks from strings
and particles from waves and waves from particles
and matter from energy and energy from matter
and it'll continue getting tighter and tighter
and still tighter and tighter still and still more tight
and it'll be as tight as inside a poppy seed
and it'll continue getting still tighter
and still hotter and hotter and brighter and brighter
and it'll get as tight as inside the concept of a point that is when
 dimensions no longer exist
and it'll be as hot and as bright as it can be
and it'll try to get still hotter and brighter
and then a great release will take place
and everyone will give a big sigh
and everything will start all over again as if it had never happened

The Author Repeats It All for the Reader

SIMEON BERRY

I know that this is happening
all at once for you,

or possibly projected
onto a withered

postage stamp
of Madagascar.

But it'll be years before
you suspect

that I'm also in motion.
That I'm angrily bald

and have a blurred
Orion's belt spilling

over my zipper.
We'll both be collecting

really expensive
infirmities by then.

Simply put, time fucks you.
It rips through this doily

of an adjective
like a sledgehammer

scented with jasmine.
34 pages back, Nix

was a clump
of soap bubbles,

a penny candy zygote.
Now, the old naming

technology is metastasizing
inside him like

a romantic plot tumor.
Every transgression

taming, the charge inside
the verbs becoming

quaint and harmless,
like *porking* someone,

or engaging in a bout
of hermetically sealed

shtupping.
You think it's

the deferred promise
of sexual congress

that makes
everything vibrate

in here like a junky motel bed,
but it's not.

There's no sweaty
confessional, no stencil

of copper and salt
pressed into the leather

of the Camaro's back seat.
It's the hope that someone—

you or me—will be able
to pick this chronological lock.

CAROL CIAVONNE

Apocalypse

Foure aungelis stand on the corners of the earth
holding back the four winds. the angel of order,
the angel of grace, the angel of history. the fourth angel,
waiting, in the service of. A tool, but not humble.
the angel of incidence. the angel of reflection.
Sometimes a little crazy music is called for: polyphonic bells,
every hour. Or a quartet for grief. A short piece—
to prolong it would be unbearable, reliving the instant
when the gun goes off. the end of time. eternal
compression in which the horizon extends
far white islands and the sad shacks of prisoners.
The clarinetist said the music was unplayable,
but he could play it in the future, in time,
in winter when the plum opens, auspicious;
birds so green they're gold.

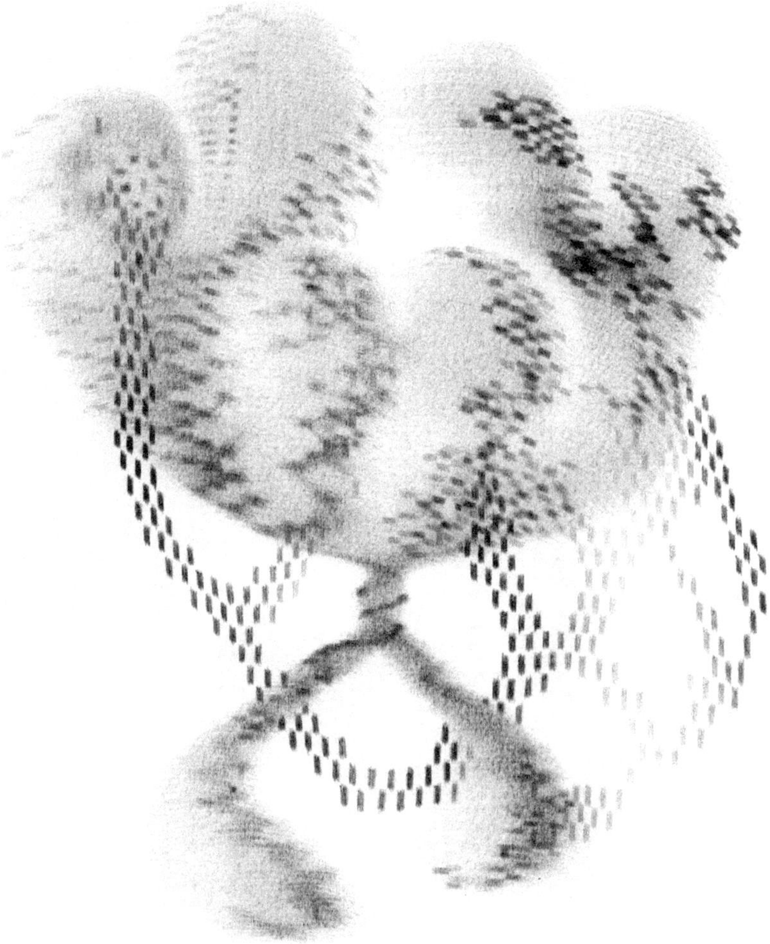

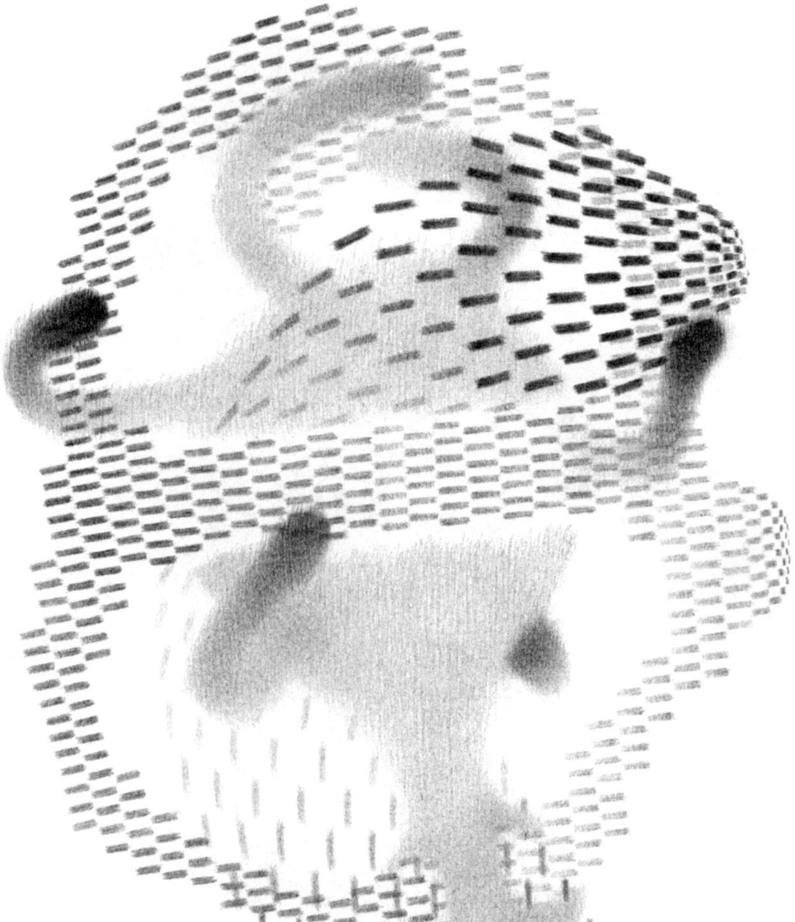

The Baby Is A Simulation Like The Cosmos
an open letter to the gatekeepers

Be afraid, reader. Let these poems lift you into the new world. After all, it's all around you. And here at the end, here at the beginning, I am going to exercise the narcissism that is the subtext of this New World, and exercise my prerogative as editor, and have the first and last word.

In the Cosmic Bubblebath theory, in this, the time of luxuriant
growth, thermally induced phase separation, electronspinning
across cellular scaffolds, over the long fiber generations,

pages & pages of them, manuscripts don't burn. We do.
The Baby has opened its darkly shining eyes
into each startled, darkling moment & therefore,

an infinite number of big bangs cascades
through us, through this reality broadcast, this holographic
universe: we burn in our neotissue turned inside-out,

on a multi-dimensional waterfall halo, you & I.
We were engineered in a liquid-based template assembly
They call The Bath, all on this tiny terraqueous coordinate,

a blue speck on the vortex.
We're buried in this supercluster always moving, always coiling,
always colliding, in which, even lying there on the crib,

grabbing its toes in the air, (mathematically speaking),
The Baby goes on forever. & you & I do too, along with him,
in a long string of numbers, less like galactic horsetails,

even less like grains of sand on an endless beach,
even less like infinitesimally thin, vibrating strings that quiver
Merrily, merrily, merrily, life is but a . . . nothing is real.

Not these Baby-breaths drawn through its sleep on the simulcast.
Not each cry rippling out from between the tiniest dimensions
folded-away in its sleep, little butt in the air.

For instance, when we say: *Hush,*
The Baby's sleeping: or, *Don't wake The Baby*; what we really mean is
this: It'll scream its lungs out when the universe finally wakes up.

Shhhh . . . Life is but a dream
in which we ride the cultivated fibroblasts at naptime
when quietly we quietly touch one other

across The Sleeping Baby,
You & me & the devil make three/Didn't leave nobody but the . . . the
simulation. *Don't forget to scream* each thin fibrous stream

wailing away along tissue-engineered airways
through the galaxy of its sleep.
You know these songs by heart: *Go to sleep you little baby . . .*

But when The Baby kicks & screams itself awake,
this all seems pretty fucking real to me,
Honey & a rock & the sugar don't stop . . . Didn't leave nobody but . . .

The Baby, grabbing its cheeks with its little hands asleep.
She's long gone with the red dress on . . . Gone the way of each of us,
each red galaxy spinning away, each cosmic glass bubble blue-hot

blown endlessly out from the inside, where we're trapped.
Here. Where The Baby hollers in a single low fragile massively
slow white-hot exhalation, & The Baby's, the inside's, on us.

Bursting us under, that's on me,
under the protein-folding weight, here & here, The Baby opens
its pale, shining eyes, its darkling tremble,

a Cartesian product, maze on exploded maze, a strangelet, a self.
Isn't it pretty to think so? When the thunder rolls? & The Baby
opens its mouth wide? & black storms fly along the sea?

In a simpler, flatter cosmos, I'd be a so-called virtual particle (am)
when The Baby takes its own head off right from the lungs,
broadcast onto our bed, I, (am.am) this burning-

manuscript-of-a-world, (am) alone with the force of gravity, (i),
the force of dying =√i=the force of you=you=an unknown
number. Which was I. Which was always our alone-time.

Afternoons, peach soft sky, just like a baby's cheek,
before The Baby would open its fading eyes & scream,
You'd be riding me in bed like a galactic storm

rides the quiet emptiness but quietly,
fingers on my imaginary face, having turned on
my in-vivo nanofiber aflame. Let's call it articular formation:

The Baby. The Baby. The Baby. Is. Is unreal.
A gas foaming star formation, really=awakened matter,
a little bioreactor of a nap. & we ran our fingertips

along each other's sides
along thermoreversible gel, generated tissue constructs,
solvent casting the final structure:

Don't forget to scream but quietly,
on the inside: *Don't wake up The Baby* means
just because we're caught on this fleshy inside like fingercuffs,

The Baby between us on the bed, clutching a thumb
in each small hand, on the gasp reflex, doesn't mean we're the
sweet spot, a solid free-form fabrication,

doesn't mean we're unsaid, unformed.
& when it does wake up, The Baby shall be literally spoken
into being: it raised such a shriek

in this field of self-engineering tissue,
that we knew it at last: I'm a biomeme, & you,
carefully surfing the extracellular matrices one minute,

synched to The Baby the next. Just because
we're dying all the time, doesn't mean my sphere's not expanding
ad infinitum, spiralling away into nothing

in this so-called Great Dying, this flickering show.
Just by opening the perfectly grown architecture
of its nanogenerated tissue constructs called eyelids,

The Baby tells me so.

Illustration: the little big bang of your body goes on forever
<you are gasoline black eyes><//a tiny ice age><sunspots//>
<light brown skin><freckles><lovely, my brown skink>

spread out on the star-pierced coverlet.
<The Baby contains thousands of miles><The Baby's sigh
goes on forever> imbetween the "you" & the "me"

Illustration: we're fastened to a dying motherboard.
Consequence: when you turn away & The Baby
wriggles your eyes open again,

it draws the naked air direct from your lungs,
shrieks an entire world-structure
in the mobius strip of your inner thighs; that is,

another child has set fire to himself in the kitchen.
Shall we call him simulated Sam shall we?
You'd ask him to do something relatively simple,

make breakfast, say, & without fail,
he'd light his hair on fire, on the stove.
These paradox machines just weren't that bright.

Illustration: You can't get outside this universe
because it's always expanding outward & inward, by the quantum,
down to the tiniest WIMP

(but you can't) run from this place
(it goes on churning us out ever outward) but say, get outside,

But outside the blown-up sphere of The Baby
the whole stinking future corpse of it is finite, expanding,
falling apart <those vectors are in red>

Or coming back together <in blue>
like any other closed system. Just ask The Baby when it wakes up,
when it takes off your head off with its crying before dawn,

just like a female spider does to her mate.
Dawn: a bubble in the bloodstream, paisley surface
swimming like a cell wall, Eta Carinae spun out into the emptiness

on the spike of a single white-hot star
at the heart of the Homunculus Nebula,
<also called Babus Major> as slowly, excruciatingly,

The Baby was being pulled apart into the Great Attractor.
& God called on The Baby one night. & that was that.
All She wrote, as they say. & so the tiny sack

began to pump nothing, once again, in code.
& when it popped nothing: //whose flesh is burning burning
like the Devil's, just inconsolable

galactic white flowers <nothingbursts>
shall flare up in this heavenly hologram, the 9th Ring
& The Baby shall become my fluffy brain, my luscious flames.

Consequence: Down here, Sim Sam does the happy dance
when You turn off his free-will, turn off gravity, grief,
turn off the tractor beam.

Break open that white sugary flesh; it bleeds alright.
The Baby's a total number after all. <turn off breathing>
<pink insulation, or cotton candy inside the skull>

Bleeds & it bleeds each cosmic cloudburst
because the Nightingale program is activated, each desire-burst
in this bloom-system corrupted, each you & me.

The Baby's lying here between us in the gloaming *again*,
like no time at all has passed. Even though traces of molecules
almost complex enough to be organic

reach us way down here from that massive dust cloud
at the heart of the Milky Way, 25,000 light years away,
where a black hole sucks away at that bright empty flesh away

through a cosmic spear hole, The Baby still screams
like the sky is falling, on our walk. Astrophysicists say it best:
the heart of The Baby smells of raspberries,

smells like babies, tastes like rum.
Talk about a wayfaring stranger. Talk about ambrosia
the way The Baby's expanding <You've got to feed it FYI>

<through a tear in this page//you've got to feed it
sweet nothingness> Our fingerprints, BTW,
are all over the northern red oak in the common—

massive, graceful, aching <The Baby's hungry>
A bright orange ribbon tied around its waist.
Such brutalism & tenderness in the air

that when The Baby coos & laughs like a fattened pigeon,
a newly resurrected flail limb effortlessly rose, all by itself,
in one of the houses nearby, in a cancer boy's dream,

in which The Baby has begun to repeat words
//I nee butter//babus//ka ku da da//I wa go pay
//bubbles! <sob> bubbles!> <grin> goddamnit!

So this breeze has coated me entirely in its gasoline
& I tremble at luminous blue variable stage
when you turn away from me, & we keep walking,

& the sky resets with a white brainzap,
a skullcap from the inside. & the sycamore limbs lift
& drop our disease: The Baby, The Baby,

The Baby's a thin verso flame at absolute loneliness.
The rainforests have all been deleted. This host-messenger,
this tree-system <loop> this fractal code

<The Baby's voice> built around programmed cell-death,
& planned obsolescence, sunset in burning crushed velvet,
cascades of purple-orange wind, space liquefaction, all of it

conceals an infinite number of variables—
event horizons, eyebells popping like stars, thumbs smoking
invisibly, leaves bubbling away

with nightingale voice-files,
swallows that sing out: *ba-BEE, ba-BEE* . . . at 7:43 p.m.,
at the programmed hour,

when we've put our lion cubs to sleep for good,
when the shadows slant & pull away at us//bye-bye
& the wind oceans its canopy to a single lopped ghost limb

on the surface of which, tangled up together
in bent black wire with yellow spots, 2 insects are mating,
positively still but for a long oviposīter

probing the sap-beaded surface for a place to lay eggs.
It's like they're holding our breath as they stir.
& one by one the hottest stars come out blue,

opening their tiny faraway mouths like infants,
as though to say, Look ma, no hands! In this softest tremor,
I can lift & drop the diseased sycamore limbs

until they crack like blazing mainmasts in the catalog of ships,
tricked-out seconds, smoking bronze helmets, long after
the forests were coded for maximum wilderness,

& the seas, set fire to, & this broadcast
was interrupted. Did you hear how The Baby come to its reward?
Was it measurably slow, agonizingly slow?

Did it take lifetimes, telescoped into a handful of months?
Was it weighed out in parsecs, orgasms, Tootsie Rolls,
lost afternoons, coke, cigarette butts, a dead scotch,

naps, coos, shrieks, gasps, crabapples
thumping the ground, bathtimes, giggles (& years of it),
extinct species The Baby left behind?

Or did The Special Paymaster simply seize Her lightning

& squeeze The Baby's heart until it stopped beating?
Are not two sparrows sold for a farthing?
Can not a sparrow thump to the ground

without everything starting all over again, even The Baby?
It's not that we're attached to its dying that gets me.
It's just that this universe, in toto, is beige.

It's the laughing I can't shake. *Hush* . . .
my little space raspberry, all shiny & wet, all cellular
& glowing, my vacuum sealed teflon space helmet:

let's burn together once my cupid's bow has been untied
& still we're quivering, nipples beaded with milk//Let's burn
again, a handful of dead galaxies spilled out onto my stomach

until there's no more oxygen to burn up,
once the fingers of my praying hand have crystallized
the coordinates//Let's die, too.

& just like that, snip! She turned off The Baby's face
like a TV set from the Fifties, draining down to that white dot
along with those distances flickering out like a candle,

disconnected into projective space,
& everything went white. You know, it's the world that burns
not us, right? Even though that space between your legs

Burns, drains down to a white dot?
Even though we'ere coded to burst like the sun,
like that time I poked The Baby's soft spot;

I'm a southpaw after all, I'm the sweet spot
snipers call the apricot, where the brain & brain stem meet,
the medulla oblangata.

I'm a girl unravishing herself, a pink cosmic peony
evaporating when I touch you *there*,
my perfect little emotionally-stunted little creator,

Don't poke The Baby on its soft spot!
Just like Daddy always said. But each time he told us,
he had the camera ready on the sly. You see,

Hell spreads like a contagion. The Baby spreads,
with no dimensions at all. This flat, cramped, dimensionless world
might be a final cause

because it's beaming in the baby fat in The Baby's face,
which melts away like a glacier retreating, ink bubbling a little
as it evaporates from this burning page:

Baby//Baby//Baby, slender neck,
cup of near-boiling water, a splash in the bath.
Take the scalded parts of our lives away *&* disappear them.

In this bubble, the Dead are lifted like us,
on white fires, on silky conceptual threads: in that bubble,
The Baby bursts, all the bleached, boiled light

hoovered up in a gasp reflex.
In this expanding sphere, it all goes on forever, but flat.
In that deflation, darkness surrounds a cell wall infinite

before apoptosis: in this one,
we're snipped off from unliving to living like an RNA virus,
replication machinery *&* all.

In this one, as always, Mama dies young—
Oh that is *so* late rapture, taken up at the cellular level *&* all,
an unborn foal from *his* mother

untimely ripped, lifted out
of *his* still-born mother still alive *&* throbbing. Oh Baby!
My emotionally stunted little creatrix!

Have You disconnected our breathing tubes yet?
No? Are you coming? Shall I wait for you?
Are you already on the other side?

PS. If you meet The Baby in the road, kill it.
Especially if the Baby's on fire.

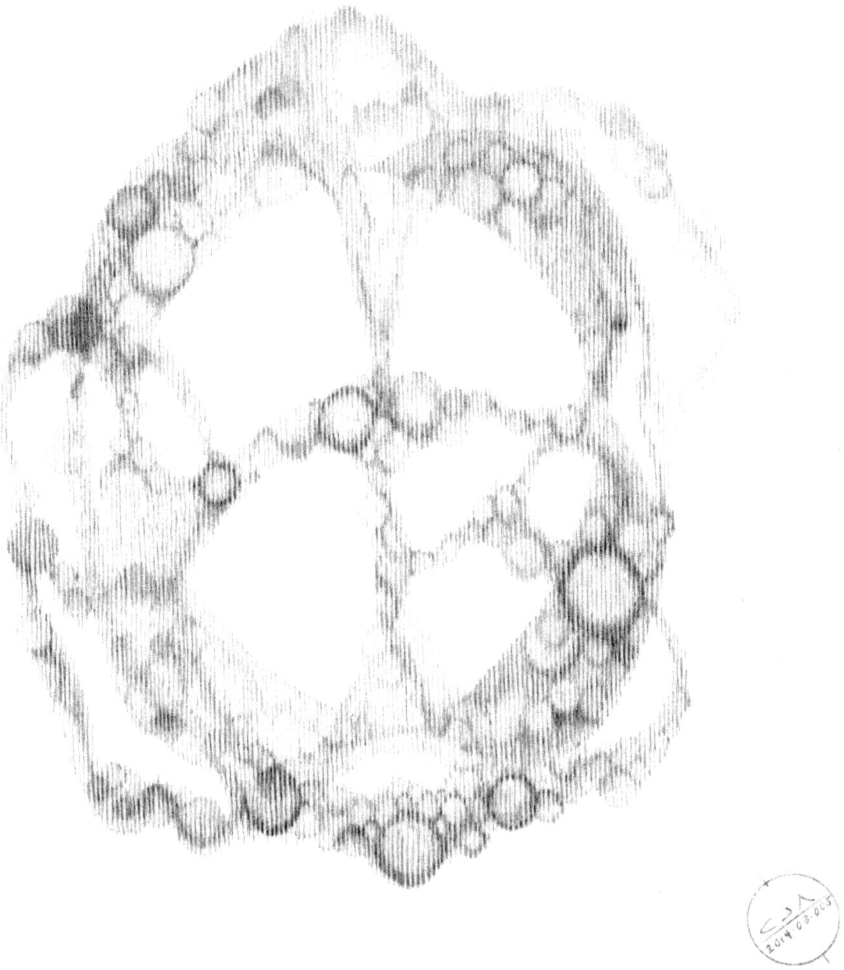
2014.03.005

FINIS

ACKNOWLEDGEMENTS

The editor wishes to thank the following people for their contributions in making this anthology possible:

First, I'm extremely grateful to Ashley De Souza for her tireless work as an editorial assistant. Intern Jacob Aldrich also worked hard researching this book and communicating with contributors. Both Ashley and Jacob came recommended from the English Department at Framingham State University.

And so I would like to thank our Department Chair, Dr. Desmond McCarthy, for his help during the process of running the internships, and for being generally supportive while we were putting this anthology together.

In addition, I thank Justin Petropoulos for opening up his black book and helping us expand our contributor list.

This book would not have happened without the brilliance and hard work of publisher Debra Di Blasi, who initially came up with the theories, concepts and arguments, helped to conceptualize the anthology, and finally designed and produced the book. Her work and vision has been expansive, and is greatly appreciated.

Finally, I want to express my gratitude to the writers for their superior and inventive talents, as well as to Christopher Arabadjis for his stunningly original art that lends so much to the book's concept and aesthetics.

Cecilia Llompart's poem, "The Barnacle and the Gray Whale," was originally published at The Academy of American Poets, poets.org.

Samuel Ace is the author of three poetry collections: *Normal Sex*, *Home in three days. Don't wash.*, and, most recently, *Stealth*, with Maureen Seaton (Chax Press). He is a recipient of a New York Foundation for the Arts grant, the Astraea Lesbian Writer's Prize in Poetry, the Firecracker Alternative Book Award in poetry, as well as a finalist for the National Poetry Series. His work has been widely anthologized and appears most recently in *Aufgabe, Black Clock, Fence, The Atlas Review, Mandorla, Rhino, Versal, Tupelo Quarterly, The Volta* and *Troubling the Line: Genderqueer Poetry and Poetics.*

Will Alexander is a poet, aphorist, essayist, novelist, philosopher, visual artist, self-taught pianist, and author of over twenty books. He is an American Book Award Winner, a PEN Oakland National Book Award Winner, as well as both a Whiting Fellow and a California Arts Council Fellow. His work has been collected in libraries around the world. For him, the 26 letters of the alphabet carry in themselves the capacity of endlessness, the latter being simultaneous with creation as alterity, which, by its very nature supersedes the language which extolls the "everyday."

Doug Anderson's first full-length book of poems, *The Moon Reflected Fire,* won the Kate Tufts Discovery Award, and his second book, *Blues for Unemployed Secret Police,* a grant from the Academy of American Poets. He has received grants and fellowships from National Endowment for the Arts, Massachusetts Cultural Council, Massachusetts Artists Foundation and other organizations. Other books include a memoir, *Keep Your Head Down* (W.W. Norton, 2009) and poems, *Horse Medicine,* some which can be found in *Poetry, The Massachusetts Review, Prairie Schooner, Field, Cimarron Review,* and elsewhere. A writer and photographer, he lives in Palmer, Massachusetts, where he is director of development for Blue Star Equiculture, a horse rescue facility and organic farm.

Christopher J. Arabadjis studied physics for 14 years at SUNY Buffalo and UMass Amherst prior to earning an M.F.A. at Pratt Institute. He has worked as a software engineer in Southern California, a test specialist in Iowa, and as a library administrator in Brooklyn. His art has been exhibited in New York City, Iowa City, and the greater metropolitan areas of Boston and San Francisco. He lives in Manhattan with his husband and cat, and commutes two hours each day to work.

Rosetta Ballew-Jennings is most at ease amidst the moxie of old houses and cemeteries. She is fond of home concoctions and remedies, half-begun projects, and made-for-television movies. Her M.F.A. is from Texas State University, and she lives in historic Saint Joseph, Missouri. Her debut poetry collection, *Is the Room* (Jaded Ibis Press), was published in 2014.

Stephanie Berger is the Executive Director of The Poetry Society of New York and co-creator of The Poetry Brothel, The Typewriter Project, and The New York City Poetry Festival. She is the author of *IN THE MADAME'S HAT BOX* (Dancing Girl Press, 2011) and co-author of *THE GREY BIRD: THIRTEEN EMOJI POEMS IN TRANSLATION* (Coconut Books, 2014) with Carina Finn.

Charles Bernstein is a venture poet and operative specializing in founding and developing innovative new media platforms and non-media portals through his Panacea Holdings. He is CFO of Poets Ludicrously Aimless Yearning (PLAY) and Director of Dysraphic Studies at the Institute for Avant-Garde Comedy and Stand-up Poetry. His books include *My Side of the Street Is Not on Your Map, Buddy*; *Elusive Allusions: Selected Koans;* and the national best seller *Stupid Men, Smart Choices.*

Simeon Berry lives in Somerville, Massachusetts. He has been an Associate Editor for *Ploughshares*, and won a Massachusetts Cultural Council Individual Artist Grant and a Career Chapter Award from the National Society of Arts and Letters. His work appears in *Crazyhorse, AGNI, Colorado Review, Blackbird, DIAGRAM, The Iowa Review, American Letters & Commentary*, and many other journals. His first book, *Ampersand Revisited*, won the 2013 National Poetry Series (Fence Books), and his second book, *Monograph*, won the 2014 National Poetry Series (University of Georgia Press).

David Blair's first book *Ascension Days* was chosen by Thomas Lux for the Del Sol Poetry Prize, and his poems have appeared in *Agni, Boston Review, InDigest, Ploughshares, Slate Magazine*, and the anthologies *The Best of Lady Churchill's Rosebud Wristlet* and *Zoland Poetry*. He is an Associate Professor at the New England Institute of Art in Brookline, Massachusetts. He grew up in Pittsburgh but has lived and worked around Boston since the nineties. In the Fall of 2014, he will be teaching a class in the M.F.A. Program in Writing at the University of New Hampshire.

Daniel Borzutzky's books include *In the Murmurs of the Rotten Carcass Economy* (Nightboat, 2015); *The Book of Interfering Bodies* (Nightboat, 2011); *The Ecstasy of Capitulation* (BlazeVox, 2007); and *Arbitrary Tales* (Ravenna Press, 2005). His poetry translations include include Raúl Zurita's *The Country of Planks* (Action Books, 2015); *Song for his Disappeared Love* (Action Books, 2010); and Jaime Luis Huenún's *Port Trakl* (Action Books, 2008). His work has been recognized by grants from the PEN American Center, the National Endowment for the Arts and the Illinois Arts Council. He lives in Chicago.

Susan Briante is the author of two books of poetry: *Utopia Minus* and *Pioneers in the Study of Motion*, both published by Ahsahta Press. She is finishing work on a new collection, *The Market Wonders,* inspired by the current economic crisis. She teaches in the M.F.A. program at the University of Arizona.

Dre Cardinal is a half-Korean American who grew up in San Antonio, Texas. As an adult, she lived several years in South Korea, Germany, and Madagascar. Currently, she attends Harvard University where she is completing a creative thesis in the honors program under the poet Josh Bell.

Joseph Chapman earned an M.F.A. in poetry from the University of Virginia, and his poems have appeared in *Boston Review, Gulf Coast, The Cincinnati Review, The Best American Poetry*, and elsewhere. He lives in Ann Arbor, Michigan with his partner Julia Hansen.

Jirí Cêch's books include *Comes Life: a poetic sequence* and *Whither: Poems of Exile*, winner of the Mennstrausse Poetry Award. His work has been published in journals and anthologies including, *Pleiades* (introduced by H. L. Hix), *The Melic Review, Poets Against the War, Brothers and Beasts: An Anthology of Men on Fairy Tales*, (Wayne State University Press) and *&NOW Awards: The Best Innovative Writing.* Jiri Cech disappeared in Botswana in 2009. Though presumed killed by a lioness, his body was never recovered.

Ewa Chrusciel has two books in Polish: *Furkot* and *Sopilki* and two books in English, *Strata,* which won the 2009 international book contest and is published with Emergency Press in 2011 and *Contraband of Hoopoe* with Omnidawn Press published in September 2014. Her poems have been featured in *Jubilat, Boston Review, Colorado Review, Lana Turner, Spoon River Review, Aufgabe* among others. She has translated Jack London, Joseph Conrad, I.B. Singer as well as Jorie Graham, Lyn Hejinian and Cole Swensen into Polish. She is an associate professor at Colby-Sawyer College.

Carol Ciavonne's poems have appeared in *Denver Quarterly, Boston Review, Colorado Review, New American Writing* and *How2*, among other journals. Her essays and reviews have appeared in *Poetry Flash, Xantippe*, and *Pleiades.* She is the author of *Birdhouse Dialogues* (LaFi 2013; with artist Susana Amundaraín) and a debut poetry collection, *Azimuth* (Jaded Ibis Press, 2014). Ciavonne has also collaborated with Amundaraín on several theater pieces, and has worked with the innovative The Imaginists theater collective. She lives in Santa Rosa, California.

Maggie Cleveland lives in Fairhaven, Massachusetts, and works for the National Elevator Industry Educational Program. She holds an M.F.A. in Creative Writing from Goddard College. Her poems have been included in the journals *The Offending Adam, qarrtsiluni, Newport Review, Elephant, BURP, Amerarcana,* and others; as well as *Ocean Voices* (Spinner Books) and *Tingujt E Eres* (LSHK, Kosovo). *ATOM FISH*, a chapbook, is published by One Time Press (New London, CT; 2012).

Elizabeth J. Colen is the author of poetry collections *Money for Sunsets* (Steel Toe Books, 2010) and *Waiting Up for the End of the World: Conspiracies* (Jaded Ibis Press, 2012), as well as flash fiction collection *Dear Mother Monster, Dear Daughter Mistake* (Rose Metal Press, 2011) and the hybrid long poem / lyric essay, *The Green Condition* (Ricochet Editions, 2014). She is editor of the new Bowerbird memoir series for Jaded Ibis Press and teaches at Western Washington University.

Matthew Cooperman is the author of the text + image collaboration *Imago for the Fallen World*, w/Marius Lehene (Jaded Ibis Press, 2013), *Still: of the Earth as the Ark which Does Not Move* (Counterpath Press, 2011), *DaZE* (Salt Publishing Ltd, 2006) and *A Sacrificial Zinc* (Pleiades/LSU, 2001), winner of the Lena-Miles Wever Todd Prize, as well as three chapbooks. A founding editor of *Quarter After Eight*, and co-poetry editor of *Colorado Review*, he teaches in the Creative Writing program at Colorado State University. He lives in Fort Collins with his wife, the poet Aby Kaupang, and their two children. More information: www.matthewcooperman.com

Colleen Coyne is the author of the chapbook *Girls Mistaken for Ghosts* (dancing girl press, 2015), and her work appears in *DIAGRAM, Hayden's Ferry Review, Crab Orchard Review, Cream City Review, Handsome, Women's Studies Quarterly, Drunken Boat,* and elsewhere. She lives in Massachusetts, where she teaches writing and works as a freelance writer and editor.

Ashley De Souza is a short story writer and poet. Her work appears in *The Onyx*, Framingham State University's literary journal, which is entirely run by students. She was a participant in the Salem Poetry Seminar in 2012, directed by J.D. Scrimgeour, and was also awarded one of the Marjorie Sparrow Literary Awards for poetry in 2014. She is currently studying English literature and Creative Writing at Framingham State University. Her poem in *Devouring the Green: Fear of a Human Planet* is her first publication.

Debra Di Blasi is founding publisher of the multimedia company Jaded Ibis Productions and its imprint Jaded Ibis Press. Books include *The Jirí Chronicles* (FC2/University of Alabama); *Drought & Say What You Like*

(New Directions); and *Prayers of an Accidental Nature* (Coffee House). She is a recipient of the James C. McCormick Fiction Fellowship, Thorpe Menn Book Award, and *DIAGRAM* Innovative Fiction Award. Her fiction is published in leading anthologies of innovative writing and has been adapted to film, radio, theatre, and audio in the U.S. and abroad. More at jadedibisproductions.com/debra-di-blasi

Curtis Emery is a poet from Massachusetts. He lives somewhere between the intersection of light and dark and excess and his work is published in *[In] Parentheses New Modernism, Boston Poetry Magazine* and translated into German with the Berlin publication, *Kathedrale19*. Emery is currently pursuing his M.F.A. at Sierra Nevada College.

Marlon L. Fick is the author of four books (poetry, fiction, and translation), including *El Niño de Safo, Selected Poems, Histerias Minimas, The Nowhere Man: a novel (Jaded Ibis, 2015),* and *The River Is Wide.* He is the recipient of an NEA grant for literature and has also received the ConaCulta, the equivalent of an NEA from the government of Mexico. He and his wife have been residing in China.

Carina Finn's first book, *LEMONWORLD & Other Poems,* was a finalist for the 2011 Gatewood Prize, and published by Co.Im.Press in 2013. Her second full-length collection, *INVISIBLE REVEILLE*, will be published by Coconut Books in October 2014. She is also the author of the chapbooks, *I HEART MARLON BRANDO* (Wheelchair Party Press, 2010) and *MY LIFE IS A MOVIE* (Birds of Lace: A Feminist Press, 2012).

Carol Frost's new collection of poetry, *Entwined: Three Lyric Sequences,* appears September, 2014 from Tupelo. Earlier collections include *Love and Scorn: Selected Poems, Pure,* and *I Will Say Beauty.* Her poems have appeared in four Pushcart Anthologies, and she is a recipient of two National Endowment for the Arts Grants. She teaches at Rollins College, where she is the Theodore Bruce and Barbara Lawrence Alfond Professor of English.

John Gallaher's fifth book of poetry is *In a Landscape*, coming out the fall from BOA. As an editor, his most recent book is *Time Is a Toy: The Selected Poems of Michael Benedikt* (with Laura Boss), published by University of Akron, 2014.

Carla Gannis (@carlagannis) has exhibited in solo and group art exhibitions nationally and internationally. She is the recipient of a 2005 New York Foundation for the Arts Grant in Computer Arts, an Emerge 7 Fellowship from Aljira Art Center, and a Chashama AREA Visual

Arts Studio Award. Features on her work appear in *Art Critical, NY Arts Magazine, Animal Magazine,* and *Collezioni Edge*, with reviews in *The New York Times, The LA Times, The Daily News*, and *The Village Voice*. She holds an M.F.A. in Painting from Boston University, and is currently Assistant Chair of Digital Arts at Pratt Institute in New York City.

Carmen Giménez Smith earned an M.F.A. from the Iowa Writers' Workshop, where she was a Teaching-Writing Fellow. She was named to Poetry Society of America's biennial *New American Poets* series, and received a Howard Foundation Fellow in Creative Nonfiction. Her memoir, *Bring Down the Little Birds*, received an American Book Award. *Goodbye, Flicker: Poems,* received the Juniper Prize for Poetry. Giménez Smith is publisher of Noemi Press and editor-in-chief of *Puerto del Sol*, and is an assistant professor in the M.F.A. Creative Writing Program at New Mexico State, and also teaches in Ashland University's Program.

Dmitry Golynko has five books of poems: Homo Scribens (1994), *The Directory* (2001), *Concrete Doves* (2003), *As It Turned Out* (Ugly Duckling Press, 2008) and most recently *What It Was and Other Arguments* (2013). His poetry has been widely translated, and appears in numerous magazines, journals and anthologies, including *Graywolf Press's New European Poets* (2008). A faculty member at St. Petersburg University of Cinema and Television, and a contributing editor at Moscow Art Magazine, Golynko publishes extensively on contemporary art and cinema.

Benjamin S. Grossberg's latest collection, *Space Traveler*, was recently published by the University of Tampa Press. His previous books are *Sweet Core Orchard* (University of Tampa, 2009), winner of the 2008 Tampa Review Prize and a Lambda Literary Award, and *Underwater Lengths in a Single Breath* (Ashland Poetry Press, 2007). His poems have appeared widely, including in the *Pushcart Prize* and *Best American Poetry* anthologies. He teaches creative writing at the University of Hartford.

j/j hastain is a collaborator, writer and maker of things, and the inventor of The Mystical Sentence Projects. j/j hastain is author of several cross-genre books including *libertine monk* (Scrambler Press), *The Non-Novels* (Spuyten Duyvil) and *The Xyr Trilogy: a Metaphysical Romance of Experimental Realisms.* j/j's writing appears in *Caketrain, Trickhouse, The Collagist, Housefire, Bombay Gin, Aufgabe* and *Tarpaulin Sky*. j/j hastain has collaborated with t thillemann, on *Approximating Diapason, Clef Manifesto,* and *Snag*. The subjection published herein appears in their book, *Tongue a Queer Anomaly*.

Ian Hatcher is a text/sound/performance artist and programmer living in Brooklyn. He is the author of *Prosthesis* (Poor Claudia, 2015). Recent projects include two poetry apps for iPad: *Vniverse,* with Stephanie Strickland; and *Abra*, with Amaranth Borsuk and Kate Durbin, published in conjunction with a hybrid artist's book by the Center for Book and Paper Arts. More info: ianhatcher.net

Vincent Hayes is a fiction and poetry writer and lifelong resident of the Greater Boston area. This is his first publication after the completion of his undergraduate studies at Framingham State University where he studied Town and Regional Planning and minored in Writing. During this time, his work has been recognized by poets such as D.A. Powell, Brian Turner, and Simeon Berry. He is devoting his life to the economic advancement of others and strives to embody the dissolution of America's middle class through his writing.

Stephen Hitchcock lives in Charlottesville, VA, where he works as the Director and Chaplain of The Haven, a day shelter and social resource center for the homeless and extremely poor in Central Virginia. He graduated from the University of British Columbia, Regent College, with a Master of Divinity and is ordained in the Presbyterian Church (U.S.A.). Several of the poems in this anthology are set in Vancouver's skid row area, called the Downtown Eastside. He has published poems in *storySouth, Geez*, and *Streetlight Magazine.*

H. L. Hix's most recent poetry collection is *As Much As, If Not More Than* (Etruscan Press, 2014). He lives in the mountain west with his partner, the poet Kate Northrop, and writes in a studio that was once a barn. His website is www.hlhix.com.

Lily Hoang is the author of four books, including *Changing*, recipient of the PEN Beyond Margins Award, and *Unfinished: Stories* (Jaded Ibis Press, 2011). With Joshua Marie Wilkinson, she edited the anthology The force of What's Possible: Writer on the Avant-Garde and Accessibility. She teaches in the M.F.A. program at New Mexico State University, where she is Associate Department Head and Prose Editor for *Puerto del Sol.*

Bernard Horn's book, Our Daily Words, won the Old Seventy Creek Press Poetry Prize and was a finalist for the 2011 Massachusetts Book Award in Poetry. His translations from the Hebrew of the poems of Yehuda Amichai have appeared in The New Yorker and other magazines. He is author of Facing the Fires: Conversations with A. B. Yehoshua, the only book in English about Israel's pre-eminent novelist; the "definitive examination of Herman Melville's influence on The Naked and the Dead;" and the story, "My Father, the Swimmer," published by Tupelo Quarterly. He is Professor of English Emeritus at Framingham State University. The poems in this anthology are part of an artist's book-in-progress, a collaboration with artist Linda Klein.

Brenda Iijima's involvements occur at the often unnamable conjunctions and mutations of poetry, choreography, research movement, animal studies, speculative non-fiction, care-giving and forlorn histories. Her book, *Untimely Death is Driven Beyond the Horizon* was published by 1913 Press in 2015. She is also the publisher of Portable Press @Yo-Yo Labs and will publish the 50th book from the press this year.

Tim Jones-Yelvington is a Chicago writer, performer and nightlife personality. He is the author of *Evan's House and the Other Boys that Live There* (in *They Could No Longer Contain Themselves*, Rose Metal Press) and *This is a Dance Movie!* (forthcoming, Tiny Hardcore Press).

Helena Kaminski did graduate work at Harvard, and studied with Thom Gunn at UC-Berkeley. She writes on a broad range of matters, including gay and non-gay themed material, and is published in the *Gay and Lesbian Review, Worldwide,* and the *Gramsci Monument*, a public arts project in NYC that has received wide attention. She has also published in *The Paris Review, New Directions, AGNI* and other magazines.

Aby Kaupang is the author of *Little "g" God Grows Tired of Me* (SpringGun Press, 2013), *Absence is Such a Transparent House* (Tebot Bach, 2011) and *Scenic Fences | Houses Innumerable* (Scantily Clad Press, 2008). Her poems have appeared in *FENCE, La Petite Zine, Dusie, Verse, Denver Quarterly, The Laurel Review, Parthenon West, PANK, Aufgabe, 14 Hills, Interim, Caketrain* and other journals. She holds an M.F.A. in Creative Writing and a Master's of Occupational Therapy from Colorado State. More at www.abykaupang.com

Claudia Keelan is the author of seven books poetry, including *Utopic* (Beatrice Hawley Award, 2001), *Missing Her* (2009) from New Issues Press, and the verse-drama *O, Heart* recently published by Barrow Street in the spring of 2014. A book of translations *Truth of My Songs: The Poems of the Trobairitz* is forthcoming from Omnidawn Press in 2015. She is currently finishing a book of essays entitled *Ecstatic Émigré*, which were written for column still underway in the *American Poetry Review.* She teaches at the University of Nevada, Las Vegas, where she is director of creative writing and the editor of *Interim* (www.interimmag.org).

Mandy Keifetz is a finishing school drop out. Her work appears in *The Massachusetts Review, Penthouse, Vogue, The Review of Contemporary Fiction,* among others. Her novel *Flea Circus: a Brief Bestiary of Grief* won the AWP Award Series in the Novel. Her first novel, *Corrido*, has been optioned by a UK production company. She was a Fellow with the New York Foundation for the Arts in 2002 and her plays have been staged in New York, London, Cambridge, Montréal, and Oslo. She lives in Brooklyn with a composer, their child, and a hound dog.

Kerry Shawn Keys is an American poet, playwright, children's book author, and *wonderscript* (short fiction: parodies; fables; farce; tales) writer. He has published dozens of books. Keys received awards from Poetry Society of America and National Endowment for the Arts, and received a translation Laureate from the Lithuanian Writers Union; he also held Fulbright grants for African-Brazilian studies, and as an Associate Professor at Vilnius University teaching translation theory and creative composition. His most recent books are *Night Flight* (poems) and *Pienas* (fiction). He contributes *The Republic of Užupis Dispatch* for Poetry International, San Diego, and divides his time between Vilnius and Pennsylvania.

Kevin Killian is a San Francisco-based writer and artist. His books include *Bedrooms Have Windows, Shy, Little Men, Impossible Princess, Action Kylie,* two volumes of *Selected Amazon Reviews,* and *Tweaky Village.* Recent projects include a novel, *Spreadeagle,* from Publication Studio, and *Tagged,* intimate portraits of poets, artists, writers, musicians, and so on.

Bill Knott's poetry collections include *The Naomi Poems, Book One: Corpse and Beans* (1968), *Becos* (1983), *Outremer,* winner of the Iowa Poetry Prize (1988), *Laugh at the End of the World: Collected Comic Poems 1969–1999* (2000), *The Unsubscriber* (2004), and *Stigmata Errata Etcetera* (2007), a collaboration with collages by the artist Star Black. Bill Knott died in 2014.

Ilyse Kusnetz's book, *Small Hours,* received the 2014 T. S. Eliot Prize for Poetry from Truman State University Press. She received her M.A. in Creative Writing from Syracuse University and her Ph.D. in Feminist and Postcolonial British Literature from the University of Edinburgh. Her poetry appears in *Crab Orchard Review, The Cincinnati Review, Crazyhorse, Stone Canoe, Rattle, Atlanta Review, Cimmaron Review, Connotation Press: an Online Artifact, Women's Voice for Change,* and other journals. She teaches at Valencia College.

Tanya Larkin is the author of two collections of poetry, *My Scarlet Ways,* winner of the 2011 Saturnalia Books Poetry Prize, and *Hothouse Orphan* (Convulsive Editions), a chapbook of poems accompanied by the pen and ink drawings of New York artist Ben Gocker. Her most recent poems have appeared in *The Boston Review, Ping Pong*, and *Fugue*. She lives in Somerville, MA with her son.

Esther Lee has written *Spit*, a poetry collection selected for the Elixir Press Poetry Prize (2011) and a chapbook, *The Blank Missives* (Trafficker Press, 2007). Her poems and articles have appeared or are forthcoming in *Ploughshares, Verse Daily, Salt Hill, Lantern Review, Good Foot, Swink, Hyphen, Born Magazine*, and elsewhere. A Kundiman fellow, she received her M.F.A. in Creative Writing from Indiana University, where she served as Editor-in-Chief for *Indiana Review*, and received her Ph.D. from the University of Utah.

Janice Lee is the author of *KEROTAKIS* (Dog Horn Press, 2010), *Daughter* (Jaded Ibis, 2011), and *Damnation* (Penny-Ante Editions, 2013). She is Co-Editor of *[out of nothing]*, Reviews Editor at *HTMLGIANT*, Editor of the #RECURRENT Novel Series for Jaded Ibis Press, Executive Editor at *Entropy*, and Founder/CEO of POTG Design. More at: http://janicel.com.

Susan Lewis lives in New York City and edits Posit (www.positjournal.com). Her most recent books are *This Visit* (BlazeVOX [books], 2015), *How to be Another* (Cervená Barva Press, 2014), and *State of the Union* (Spuyten Duyvil Press, 2014). Her work is forthcoming or has recently appeared in *The Awl, Boston Review, The Brooklyn Rail, Connotation Press, EOAGH, Gargoyle, Otoliths, Ping Pong, Propeller, Raritan, Seneca Review, Verse, Word For/Word*, and *Yew*. More at www.susanlewis.net.

Micah Ling earned her M.F.A. in poetry at Indiana University. She currently teaches in the English department at Fordham University in Manhattan. Her most recent collection of poetry, *Settlement*, is published by Sunnyoutside Press.

Timothy Liu is the author of nine books of poems, including *Don't Go Back To Sleep* (Saturnalia Books). He lives in Manhattan with his husband.

Reb Livingston is the author of *Bombyonder* (Bitter Cherry Books 2014), *God Damsel* (No Tell Books 2010) and *Your Ten Favorite Words* (Coconut Books 2007). She lives in Northern Virginia with her husband and son.

Cecilia Llompart was born in Puerto Rico and raised in Florida. She received her B.A. from Florida State University, and M.F.A. from University of Virginia. Llompart's first collection, *The Wingless*, was published in 2014 by Carnegie Mellon University Press. Her poems have appeared in *TriQuarterly, The Caribbean Writer*, and *WomenArts Quarterly*

Review, *poets.org*, *Verse Daily*, *Inknode*, and *Occupy Poetry*. Most recently, she has served as guest editor for *Matter: A Journal of Political Poetry and Commentary*, and taught high school students as chair of creative writing for The Blue Ridge Summer Institute for Young Artists.

Alex Mantel is originally from New York City and currently resides in Virginia where he works as a school counselor. He holds a B.A. from the University of Virginia where he participated in the Young Writer's Workshop and studied creative writing under poets such as Greg Orr. He also holds an M.Ed. from The George Washington University.

Leslie McGrath's interviews with poets appear regularly in *The Writer's Chronicle*. Winner of the 2004 Pablo Neruda Prize for poetry, she is the author of *Out from the Pleiades*, (Jaded Ibis Press, 2014), *Opulent Hunger, Opulent Rage* (2009), a poetry collection, and two chapbooks: *Toward Anguish* (2007) and *By the Windpipe* (2014.) Her poems have appeared in *The Awl*, *Agni*, *The Common*, *Slate*, and elsewhere. She teaches creative writing and literature at Central Connecticut State University, and is series editor of The Tenth Gate, a new poetry imprint of The Word Works press.

Joyelle McSweeney is the author of six books of poetry and prose, most recently *Percussion Grenade* (Fence) *Salamandrine, 8 Gothics* (Tarpaulin Sky), and a book of critical essays, *The Necropastoral: Poetry, Media, Occults*, (University of Michigan Poets on Poetry Series, 2014). Her play *Dead Youth, or, the Leaks* won the inaugural Leslie Scalapino Prize for Innovative Women Playwrights and is forthcoming from Litmus Press. With Johannes Göransson, she co-edits Action Books and teaches at Notre Dame.

Urayoán Noel is Assistant Professor of English and Spanish at New York University. He is the author of *In Visible Movement: Nuyorican Poetry from the Sixties to Slam* (University of Iowa Press, 2014) and several books of poetry in English and Spanish, including, *EnUnclAdOr* (Editora Educación Emergente, 2014) and the forthcoming, *Buzzing Hemisphere/Rumor Hemisférico* (University of Arizona Press). Noel is a former CantoMundo, Ford Foundation, and Bronx Council on the Arts fellow, and a contributing editor of *NACLA Report on the Americas*.

Geoffrey Nutter's fourth book, *The Rose of January*, appeared in 2013 from Wave Books. He has taught poetry at NYU, Columbia, Princeton, and the University of Iowa. He lives in New York City.

Martin Ott is a former U.S Army interrogator. He lives in Los Angeles, where he writes, often about his misunderstood city. He is the author of four books of poetry: *Underdays*, (Notre Dame University Press, 2015),

Captive, De Novo Prize winner, (C&R Press), and *Poets' Guide to America* and *Yankee Broadcast Network* (2014), co-written with John F. Buckley and published by Brooklyn Arts Press. In 2013, he published his debut novel *The Interrogator's Notebook* (Story Merchant Books). www.martinottwriter.com

Trace Peterson's two favorite things are sex and literary criticism. Author of the poetry book *Since I Moved In* (Chax Press) and numerous chapbooks of poems, she is also editor/publisher of *EOAGH*, co-editor of the new anthology *Troubling the Line: Trans and Genderqueer Poetry and Poetics* (Nightboat Books) which was a finalist for a 2013 Lambda Literary Award, and co-editor of the forthcoming *Gil Ott: Collected Writings* (Chax Press). From 2009-2012, she curated the *TENDENCIES: Poetics & Practice series* inspired by Eve Kosofsky Sedgwick at CUNY Graduate Center in NYC, where she is currently a Ph.D. Candidate.

Justin Petropoulos is the author of two collections of poetry, *Eminent Domain* (Marsh Hawk Press 2011), selected by Anne Waldman for the 2010 Marsh Hawk Press Poetry Prize and *<legend></legend>* (Jaded Ibis Press, 2013), a collaborative work with multimedia artist, Carla Gannis. His poems have appeared in *American Letters & Commentary, Columbia Poetry Review, Gulf Coast, Mandorla, Portland Review,* and elsewhere. He is the site director of an after-school program for elementary age children, and teaches composition and creative writing at New Jersey City University.

Marge Piercy has published eighteen poetry volumes, most recently *The Hunger Moon: New & Selected Poems.* Her new poetry collection, *Made in Detroit,* will be released by Knopf in March 2015. Piercy has also published seventeen novels, including *Sex Wars.* Her first short story collection, *The Cost Of Lunch, Etc.,* was recently published by PM Press.

Rebecca Ariel Porte lives in North America. Recent work appears, among other places, in the *Los Angeles Review of Books* and at *io9.*

John Reed (born February 7, 1969) is an American novelist. He is the author of four novels: *A Still Small Voice* (2000), *Snowball's Chance* (2002) with a preface by Alexander Cockburn, *The Whole* (2005), and *All the World's a Grave: A New Play by William Shakespeare* (2008). His fifth book, *Tales of Woe* (2010), is a collection of twenty-five stories, chronicling true stories of abject misery.

David Rivard's books include *Otherwise Elsewhere, Sugartown,* and *Wise Poison,* winner of the James Laughlin Prize from the Academy of American Poets and a finalist for the Los Angeles Times Book Award. The poems included here are from *Standoff,* forthcoming in 2016. Among his awards are fellowships from the Guggenheim Foundation, Civitella Ranieri, and the NEA, as well as the 2006 O. B. Hardison Jr. Poetry Prize from the Folger Shakespeare Library, in recognition of both his writing and teaching. He teaches in the M.F.A. in Writing program at the University of New Hampshire.

Jerome Rothenberg is an internationally celebrated poet with over ninety books of poetry and twelve assemblages of traditional and avant-garde poetry such as *Technicians of the Sacred* and *Poems for the Millennium*, volumes 1-3. Recent books of poems include *Concealments & Caprichos, A Cruel Nirvana, A Poem of Miracles*, and *Retrievals: Uncollected & New Poems 1955-2010.* His most recent big book is *Eye of Witness: A Jerome Rothenberg Reader*, and he is now working on a global and historical anthology of "outside and subterranean poetry."

Tomaž Šalamun is the author of more than 30 collections of poetry in Slovenian and English. He published his first collection, *Poker* (1966), at the age of 25. His poetry, using elements of surrealism and polyphony, is influenced by the work of Charles Simic and Arthur Rimbaud. He has won the Jenko Prize, Slovenia's Prešeren and Mladost Prizes, and a Pushcart Prize. Šalamun and his German translator, Fabjan Hafner, were awarded the European Prize for Poetry by the German city of Muenster. His poetry has been widely anthologized and translated into more than 20 languages. Tomaž Šalamun died in December 2014.

Maureen Seaton has authored sixteen poetry collections—most recently, *Fibonacci Batman: New & Selected Poems* (Carnegie Mellon University Press, 2013)—and a memoir, *Sex Talks to Girls* (University of Wisconsin Press). Her awards include the Iowa Poetry Prize, Lambda Literary Award, the Publishing Triangle's Audre Lorde Award, the Society of Midland Authors Award, and an NEA Fellowship. Her work has been honored in both the Pushcart Prize Anthology and *Best American Poetry.* Chax Press published *Stealth*, her first collaboration with Samuel Ace, in 2011. She currently teaches at the University of Miami, Florida.

Anis Shivani is a poet, fiction writer, and critic in Houston, Texas. His books include *Anatolia and Other Stories, Against the Workshop, The Fifth Lash and Other Stories,* and *My Tranquil War and Other Poems*, and the forthcoming books, *Karachi Raj: A Novel* and *Soraya: Sonnets*, both out in 2015. Books recently finished or in progress include the novels, *A History of the Cat in Nine Chapters or Less* and *Abruzzi, 1936*, and a collection of essays, *Literature in the Age of Globalization.*

Vandana Singh is an award-winning writer of speculative fiction. She has a Ph.D. in particle physics and teaches at a small, lively state university near Boston, where she is also a scholar of climate change. Her writing website is http://vandana-writes.com

John Skoyles' most recent book is *A Moveable Famine*, about a life in poetry. He has published four books of poetry, a collection of personal essays, and a memoir. His work appears in *The New Yorker, The New York Times, The Atlantic*, and others. He teaches at Emerson College and is the poetry editor of *Ploughshares.*

Tracy K. Smith received the Pulitzer Prize for her poetry collection *Life on Mars.* She is also the author of the memoir *Ordinary Light.* She teaches at Princeton University.

Adam Strauss has one full-length collection, *For Days*, out with BlazeVox, and poems in the anthology *The Arcadia Project: North American Postmodern Pastoral* (Ahsahta Press). Some of the poems included in this anthology are from a manuscript titled *Braided Sand Country*, and are dedicated to his mom—Gayle Strauss—and the poet Cole Swensen.

Stephanie Strickland has published 8 books of print poetry, including *Dragon Logic* (Ahsahta, 2013). A new edition of her award-winning Penguin volume, *V: WaveTercets/Losing L'una* appeared from SpringGun with accompanying app for iPad, created in collaboration with Ian Hatcher. She has collaborated on 9 digital poems, most recently *Sea and Spar Between* and *Duels—Duets,* with Nick Montfort, and *House of Trust,* with Ian Hatcher. Recent writing appears in *Boston Review*, *Vlak*, *New Binary Press*, and *Best American Poetry 2013.* A member of the Board of Directors of the Electronic Literature Organization, she co-edited *Electronic Literature Collection Volume 1.* More at stephaniestrickland.com.

Celina Su was born in São Paulo and lives in Brooklyn. Her writing includes a poetry chapbook from Belladonna*, three books on the politics of social policy and civil society, and pieces in journals such *as n+1, Aufgabe,* and *Boston Review.* She co-founded Kwah Dao/ the Burmese Refugee Project in Thailand in 2001, received her Ph.D. in Urban Studies from MIT, and currently teaches political science at the City University of New York. Her honors include the Berlin Prize and the Whiting Award for Excellence in Teaching.

Jane Summer's short stories and poems have appeared in *Ploughshares, Spoon River Poetry Review, Literal Latte* and numerous other publications and anthologies. Her novel *The Silk Road* has recently been recorded for Audible.com. A.M. Homes selected Summer's story "Peaceful Village" for inclusion in the 2013 edition of *The Masters Review,* and Ruth Reichl once chose her submission for a *New York Times* food writing contest Her cross-genre work *Erebus* is forthcoming (Spring 2015) from Sibling Rivalry Press. In high school she was voted Class Wit but she doesn't feel like laughing anymore.

Terese Svoboda is a 2013 Guggenheim Fellow, and her latest book of poetry is *Weapons Grade. When the Next Big War Blows Down the Valley: Selected and New,* will appear in 2015, as will, she hopes, a biography of the feminist modernist poet Lola Ridge.

Michael Thomas Taren is studying reindeer. His chapbook, *eunuchs*, is forthcoming from Ugly Duckling Presse. He is editor and cotranslator with Tomaž Šalamun of *Justice*, forthcomimg from Black Ocean. His cotranslation with Purdey Lord Kreiden of *L'Ile Atlantique* by Tony Duvert is forthcoming from Semiotext(e). Taren and Kreiden are currently translating *En Ménage* by Joris-Karl Huysmans (Wakefield Press). Their photofolktales can be seen at: 1thousandand101001nights.tumblr.com

Yuriy Tarnawsky has authored some three dozen books of poetry, fiction, plays and essays. An engineer and linguist by training, he has worked as computer scientist specializing in Natural Language Processing and Artificial Intelligence, as well as Professor of Ukrainian Literature and Culture. He was born in Ukraine but was raised in the West. He writes in Ukrainian and English and resides in the New York City metropolitan area. His books include the novel, *Three Blondes and Death*, a collection of stories, *Short Tails*, three collections of mini-novels, *The Placebo Effect Trilogy*, a book of Heuristic poetry, *Modus Tollens* (Jaded Ibis Press), and the play, *Not Medea.*

t thilleman's books include poetry, *Three Sea Monsters* and *Onönyxa & Therseyn,* and the novel *Gowanus Canal, Hans Knudsen.* His collaborations with j/j hastain are *Approximating Diapason* and *Clef Manifesto, Snag* as well as the forthcoming glossary, *Tongue a Queer Anomaly*, from which the selections published in *Devouring The Green* are taken. tt's literary essay/memoir, *Blasted Tower*, is available from Shakespeare & Co./Toad Suck. Ongoing and online, tt blogs musings taken from the Kamasutra and others at conchwoman.wordpress.com.

Sam Truitt is the author of seven books in the Vertical Elegies series, including, most recently, *Dick: A Vertical Elegy* (Lunar Chandelier). For more: samtruitt.org

Lindsay Turner's poems and criticism appear in *Lana Turner Journal, Kenyon Review, WebConjunctions, Boston Review, FIELD, Denver Quarterly, Drunken Boat, Los Angeles Review of Books,* and elsewhere. Originally from northeast Tennessee, she holds degrees from Harvard College, New York University, and the Université Paris III Sorbonne-Nouvelle. She is currently a doctoral candidate in English at the University of Virginia.

Laura Vena is a writer and translator with work in *Super Arrow, Tarpaulin Sky, In Posse Review, The Dirty Fabulous,* and *Antennae.* She is a contributing editor at ENTROPY Magazine and is interested in works of a fantastic nature and those that investigate the ethical and aesthetic considerations of representation.

Catherine Wagner's collections of poetry include *Nervous Device* (City Lights, 2012), *My New Job* (Fence, 2009), *Macular Hole* (Fence, 2004), and *Miss America* (Fence, 2001). Her poems have been translated into Bengali, German, and Swedish. She is professor in the creative writing program at Miami University in Oxford, Ohio, where she lives with her son.

Ken L. Walker carries a Kentucky driver's license even though he has lived in New York for the past 7 years. Previous work can be found in *The Poetry Project Newsletter, likewise folio, The Seattle Review, Atlas Review, Lumberyard,* and in the chapbook *Twenty Glasses of Water* (Diez Press).

Sharon White's book, *Vanished Gardens: Finding Nature in Philadelphia*, won the AWP award in creative nonfiction. She is author of two collections of poetry, *Eve & Her Apple* and *Bone House*, and her memoir, *Field Notes, A Geography of Mourning*, received the Julia Ward Howe Prize, Honorable Mention, from the Boston Authors Club. Other awards include a Pennsylvania Council on the Arts Fellowship for Creative Nonfiction, the Leeway Foundation Award for Achievement, a Colorado Council on the Arts Fellowship, the Calvino Award, and an NEA Fellowship. *Boiling Lake*, a collection of short fiction, is published by Jaded Ibis Press (2015).

Sam Witt is poetry editor of Jaded Ibis Press and author of the poetry collections, *Everlasting Quail* (UPNE, 2001), winner of the Katherine Nason Bakeless Prize, and *Sunflower Brother* (Cleveland State University Press, 2006). Awards include the Red Hen Press Poetry Award, Pitch Poetry Award and Meridian Editors' Prize. Individual poems and articles have appeared in *Virginia Quarterly Review, Los Angeles Review, Boston Review,*

Georgia Review, Wired, Computerworld, San Francisco Chronicle, Black Warrior Review and *New England Review*, among many others. He has taught at Harvard University and Whitman College and is now Assistant Professor of English, Creative Writing, at Framingham State University. More at www.samwittpoetry.com.

CJ Wisler was born and raised in Billings, Montana, and now lives in Seattle. She graduated with a B.A in English from Whitman College in 2011. During college, she worked at the national award-winning *Whitman College Pioneer Newspaper* for three years as a writer and editor. *Devouring the Green* is CJ's first publication.

Monica Youn is the author of two books of poetry: *Barter* (Graywolf Press 2003) and *Ignatz* (Four Way Books 2010), which was a finalist for the National Book Award. A former lawyer, she has previously taught poetry at Bennington College, Columbia University, and the Warren Wilson College M.F.A. for Writers. She now teaches creative writing at Princeton University. These poems are from a manuscript-in-progress, *Blackacre.*

Tom Yuill's first book of poetry, *Medicine Show,* is published by the University of Chicago Press, and was selected by Ravi Shankar, along with Lynn Emanuel's *Noose and Hook,* as runner-up for San Francisco State University's Poetry Center Award. He has also published work in *A Public Space, Literary Imaginations, Newsday* and *Salamander* among others. He will be teaching at Old Dominion University in Virginia this year.

Jennifer Zilm has a B.A., M.A. in Religious Studies from University of British Columbia and was a Ph.D candidate in Early Judaism and Early Christianity at McMaster University. Her poetry and scholarship have appeared in publications, *Prism International, The Antigonish Review, Quills Canadian Poetry Magazine, Room, Women in Judaism: A Multi-disciplinary Journal, Poetry and Prayer in the Dead Sea Scrolls* and *Vallum: Contemporary Poetry.* Her first chapbook, *The Whole and Broken Yellows* (Frog Hollow: 2013), explores art, religion and mental health, using *The Letters of Vincent van Gogh.* She recently finished two poetry manuscripts, *This Bright Borderline* and *Waiting Room.*

www.ingramcontent.com/pod-product-compliance
Lightning Source LLC
Chambersburg PA
CBHW030235240426
43663CB00037B/467
* 9 7 8 1 9 3 7 5 4 3 5 5 6 *